THE MYTH OF A
PROGRESSIVE REFORM

THE MYTH OF A PROGRESSIVE REFORM

Railroad Regulation
in Wisconsin
1903–1910

STANLEY P. CAINE

MADISON
THE STATE HISTORICAL SOCIETY OF WISCONSIN
1970

LIBRARY OF CONGRESS CATALOG CARD NUMBER:
LC 75-630131
STANDARD BOOK NUMBER:
87020-110-7

EUROPE: W. S. HALL & CO., INC., LONDON, AMSTERDAM, NEW YORK
CANADA: HARVEST HOUSE, LTD., MONTREAL
INDIA: THACKER & CO., LTD., BOMBAY

MANUFACTURED IN THE UNITED STATES OF AMERICA BY
IMPRESSIONS, INC., MADISON, WISCONSIN

Acknowledgments

I was aided and supported by persons too numerous to mention in the writing of this study. Dr. E. David Cronon of the University of Wisconsin, who advised me throughout my graduate career, gave invaluable help by shoring up a faltering writing style and encouraging me in my work. He supervised the initial writing of this study as my doctoral dissertation with concern and insight, ferreting out many errors in logic and composition. Dr. David P. Thelen of the University of Missouri aided me greatly in the conception of the project. The staff of the State Historical Society of Wisconsin showed remarkable sensitivity to my needs, making available at my convenience the materials necessary to complete the study. Miss Mary Ellen Packard, a student at Lindenwood College, was extremely helpful in the revision and preparation of the final manuscript. I am most thankful to my wife Karen, who encouraged me during the long process of writing and diligently proofread the study several times. Her insight helped make the manuscript understandable. Remaining errors in logic and composition are solely my responsibility.

To Karen

Contents

PORTRAITS OF THE FIRST FOUR MEMBERS OF
THE RAILROAD COMMISSION OF WISCONSIN
FOLLOW PAGES 128, 160

Introduction

The literature concerning historical trends in early twentieth-century America is replete with biographies of prominent political figures and studies of fights for reform legislation. While much of this writing is extremely helpful, it does not deal with the important question of the ultimate effect of the "progressive movement" upon American society. Too often assuming that legislation automatically brought about intended changes, historians have concerned themselves primarily with the efforts to achieve reform. They have seemed to feel that if the configurations of the struggles for new measures could be divined and appropriate credit given to those leaders who were most instrumental in enacting such reforms, then the movement itself could be fully understood.

This study takes a different approach. It attempts to trace the evolution of a progressive reform from its origins through its adoption by self-conscious reformers, its institutionalization as a law, and its early administration. Concentrating upon the reform itself, it seeks to evaluate the shifting roles of interested Wisconsin groups and to assess the concrete effects of the reform crusade. While the rhetoric of reformers has been used as an expression of the principles underlying the fight, for the most part such oratory has been viewed functionally, in terms of what it contributed to molding the climate of opinion concerning the issue. By the same token, the arguments of those who opposed such reform aspirations are evaluated in terms of their effect on the fight itself. More objective gauges have been devised to determine the actual effects of the crusade whenever possible.

The subject under study is the fight for increased railroad regulation in Wisconsin from 1903 to 1910. The struggle for effective regulatory legislation in Wisconsin stretches back to the 1870's. While these early origins are touched upon, the first section of the inquiry concentrates primarily on the "progressive" stage of the fight—the three years between 1903 and 1905 during which Robert M. La Follette assumed control of the crusade and pushed through legislation designed to usher in a new commercial order in the state. Although the Railroad Commission of Wisconsin, the progeny of this reform effort, is still in operation as the Wisconsin Public Service Commission, the study of the administration of the regulation act is confined primarily to the period from the formation of the Commission in June, 1905, through December, 1910. These first five-and-one-half years of the Commission's existence can be called the "formative years" in that agency's life. During that time, under the dynamic leadership of B. H. Meyer, the Commission evolved most of the precedents by which it was to abide for many years. When Meyer left the Commission in December, 1910, to join the Interstate Commerce Commission, the "Meyer years," during which the concept of regulation in Wisconsin took form as an administrative reality, ended both literally and figuratively and the agency passed into a new, more routine phase.

Within these chronological limits, the boundaries of the study are defined by the desire to trace the evolution of a reform idea and test its efficacy. Hence while other parts of La Follette's reform program are mentioned, they are dealt with only as they relate to the fight for a railroad regulation bill. By the same token, no attempt is made in the latter part of the study to give a balanced picture of all aspects of the Commission's work. Rather, the focus remains on the degree to which the new agency implemented the principles which motivated men to fight for regulatory legislation.

Because of the complexity of the fight over regulation and the clarity with which reform leaders stated their principles, the pivotal years in the Wisconsin regulation experience offer fertile ground for the study of that aspect of the progressive era which has too long been neglected — the process of implementing the hopes and ideals of the political and economic reformers. The Wisconsin effort is important, however, not only as a case study but also because it had much broader implications nationally in the early part of this century. The elevation to the Interstate Commerce Commission of B. H. Meyer, the chief figure on the Wisconsin Commission, meant that the national body was fully exposed to precedents developed in Wisconsin. More important, the major piece of legislation under study was enacted during the governorship of Robert M. La Follette, one of the most prominent national leaders of the "progressive movement." After the passage of the act, La Follette, anxious to assume a wider role, declared that his legislative program had been accomplished. He quickly assumed a seat in the United States Senate, where he soon gained prominence on the basis of his reputation for standing uncompromisingly for "the people" against "the interests." While serving in Washington, he defined as one of his major tasks that of making the Interstate Commerce Commission as effective as the Wisconsin Commission, which he claimed to have fathered. Because of the characterization of the Wisconsin railroad commission as a "model" commission by La Follette and many others, reformers in other states as well as national figures sought to use the Wisconsin pattern to achieve effective regulation elsewhere. In the years after 1905 the importance of the Wisconsin law and the work of the Wisconsin Commission was therefore magnified.

The crucial importance of the Wisconsin experience in regulation also makes it an interesting place to test recent historiographical trends. Historians such as Gabriel Kolko and Robert Wiebe recently have issued a bold new challenge to the traditional conception of the progressive era as one in which crusaders pushed through antibusiness legislation designed to bring reckless corporations to heel.[1] Kolko's reinterpretation is particularly provocative as it relates to the subject of railroad regulation, for Kolko totally reverses the conventional interpretation, arguing that the carriers themselves were responsible for most of the agitation for regulation, since they viewed regulation as a way of rationalizing their industry and dampening competition. While Kolko confines his analysis to regulation at the federal level, the implications of

[1] Gabriel Kolko, *Railroads and Regulation* (Princeton, 1965); Gabriel Kolko, *The Triumph of Conservatism* (New York, 1963); Robert A. Wiebe, *Businessmen and Reform* (Cambridge, Massachusetts, 1962).

his theory for state regulation are clear also. Thus a test of the
Kolko thesis in Wisconsin, which is often construed as a model
progressive state, and which moreover furnished one of the bell-
wethers for federal regulatory legislation, may shed important
light on the limitations of recent historiography on this central
issue in the early twentieth century.

✿   ✿   ✿   ✿   ✿

During the process of research, I confronted several obstacles
which bore directly on the study itself. The most profound problems arose during my study of the work of the Wisconsin Railroad
Commission in its early years of operation. These difficulties,
common to all who seek to study policy making by administrative
agencies, related directly to the rather limited and parochial function served by regulatory agencies. Whereas legislative decisions
are clearly visible, and embodied in laws, resolutions, and other
public pronouncements, policies evolved by administrative agencies are much more difficult to discover. Burdened with the major
task of handling complaints and questions case-by-case and day-
by-day, administrators usually do not promulgate policies in the
same manner as do legislative bodies. Therefore only through
close examination of the manner in which the agencies approach
their tasks and the trends evident in their many, somewhat isolated
decisions can one discern what policies such bodies are following.
William Boyer, in a study of administrative policy making, notes:
"The discovery of such policies is a challenge to both the lay citizen
and the agency itself."[2]

While this difference in the method of policy making makes
administrative studies more difficult than those which center on
legislative behavior, an even knottier problem is the assignment of
causation to administrative trends. Because legislative affairs are
often intriguing and newsworthy, numerous correspondents busy
themselves every day seeking out interviews and even exploiting
secret sources of information in an effort to penetrate the legislative
policy-making process and discover who was really responsible for
making particular decisions and what their motives were. But
administrative agencies do their work in a much more private

[2] William W. Boyer, *Bureaucracy on Trial* (Indianapolis, 1964), 112.

atmosphere, with little attention given to participants or decisions. Often even the major decisions of such bodies are ignored or relegated to the back pages of newspapers, with little or nothing to indicate why such decisions were made.

The lack of publicity given the work of such agencies creates profound problems in divining public reaction also. While the major groups which deal with regulatory agencies regularly keep abreast of their decisions and are quick to react to these judgments, the ordinary citizen seldom hears about the work of the agencies. Hence from the time of the creation of regulatory commissions, little is heard from the public concerning their work. Ironically, despite the fact that most commissions are at least ostensibly established to aid "the common man," the climate of opinion surrounding them is more likely to be set by large interests—often the very interests these commissions were established to curb. While politicians interested in reform can keep the spirit of their crusades alive by pressuring the regulatory agencies to fulfill objectives and informing the public of the work of the commissioners, in the case of Wisconsin this was not done. As a result, evidence concerning the public reaction to the Wisconsin Railroad Commission's early work is extremely difficult to find.

These difficulties should not obscure the fact that the everyday decisions of such administrative bodies frequently have more impact on society than do laws promulgated by legislatures. This is particularly true in the area of government regulation, for, no matter how detailed the legislation which authorizes regulation, lawmakers cannot anticipate all of the varied situations which a regulatory commission will face. Nor is there any assurance that the commission will interpret the statute in a manner which the framers intended. Hence any study of the evolution of regulatory policies must necessarily give some attention to the administration of the legislative mandate.

All of these generalizations applied to the Wisconsin experience, but because of the nature of the regulatory legislation passed in 1905 there were added reasons why the implementation of the act was so vitally important. Aware that no regulation bill could be approved without the consent of more moderate legislators, spokesmen for the La Follette administration were forced to temper their demands in order to secure enough votes to pass a measure. The more conservative interests in turn pushed through provisions designed to safeguard their future under the new order. The result was a legislative mandate engendering several theories of regulation which often worked at cross purposes to one another.

The Railroad Commission of Wisconsin was charged with the somewhat contradictory task of creating a more equitable rate system for the state without disrupting elements in the current structure which were major causes of the existing inequities. It was to eliminate discriminatory practices—but without tampering with the numerous special rate structures. It was to transform the rate system of the state—but without establishing entirely new rate schedules for the various railroads in the state. Because of this confusion of the regulatory mandate, the numerous procedural and substantive precedents laid down by the first Wisconsin railroad commission were ultimately decisive in determining the outcome of the conflict over railroad regulation in Wisconsin.

STANLEY P. CAINE

Lindenwood College
January, 1970

THE MYTH OF A
PROGRESSIVE REFORM

Robert La Follette and the Wisconsin Reform Tradition

1 The history of relations between the state government and the railroads in Wisconsin during the first sixty years of rail operations resembles that of an unstable marriage, in which each partner is acutely aware of the necessity of the other but restive because of the burdens imposed by their peculiar relationship. For the most part, government played the role of the petulant wife, anxious to assert her independence from her husband's dominance but unwilling to cut herself off from the many and varied benefits she enjoyed while in his good graces. The state sought a modicum of control and independence, but seldom was willing to risk the total alienation of the carriers. In turn, the carriers, like a domineering husband, granted occasional concessions and at times even seemed destined to lose control of their affairs but through the use of subtle and overt pressures, succeeded in the end in retaining their position of ultimate authority and power.

From the outset of railroading in Wisconsin the carriers had the upper hand, for they had a service to offer the region which was indispensable for the area's growth. Although they often called upon the government for aid, for the most part the railroads grew and flourished independent of and sometimes in spite of the activities of state officials. By developing a constituency dependent upon them for economic benefits, the roads became an independent political force in Wisconsin, a kind of "private government" able

3

to demand and secure influence in the councils of the duly-elected state government.[1]

The key to the development of this new relationship is the mercuric growth of railroad traffic in Wisconsin. When George Wallace Jones of the Wisconsin territorial delegation in 1837 presented a petition from a village in Grant County calling for a survey of a railroad route from Milwaukee to San Francisco, which would pass through the town, he was greeted with "a great laugh and hurrah in the house." Within a decade, however, the first railroad company to build in Wisconsin, the Milwaukee and Mississippi, had been chartered, and by 1851 it had initiated the state's first train service on a run from Milwaukee to Waukesha.[2] When the Civil War began there were nearly 900 miles of track in the state; by 1890 the figure exceeded 5,500 and was headed for a high of 7,963 in 1916.[3]

The notable thing about this rapid growth was the degree to which it was achieved without the help of state government. The Wisconsin state constitution included a provision which specifically forbade the state to lend money or credit for the financing of such ventures. The eagerness of citizens in the state to gain railroad services, however, opened up numerous other sources of aid to the entrepreneurs. Towns throughout the state borrowed profusely to facilitate building in their locales. Many individuals, principally farmers, invested heavily in the new enterprise which promised them more direct access to markets and goods. While eastern capitalists were more circumspect in their interest during the early decades of the railroad boom in Wisconsin, after 1870 they too contributed substantially to railroad building. As in many western states, however, the core of capital formation was the federal government, which in the late nineteenth century ceded to the various railroads in the state some 2,874,000 acres, nearly one-twelfth of the area of the state.[4]

---

[1] See Marver H. Bernstein, *Regulating Business by Independent Commission* (Princeton, 1955), for a discussion of the concept of "private governments" and regulatory commissions.
[2] William F. Raney, "The Building of Wisconsin Railroads," in the *Wisconsin Magazine of History*, 19:387 (June, 1936).
[3] *Ibid.*, 388.
[4] *Ibid.*, 388–390.

The early years of railroading in Wisconsin saw the development of numerous small enterprising carriers, many of them seeking to serve only one particular section of the state. Soon, however, the national pattern of steady consolidation was reflected in Wisconsin, and by the first decade of the twentieth century railroading in the state was dominated by three major companies, each of which included Wisconsin traffic as a part of operations spanning many states. The largest of these was the Chicago and North Western Railway which not only boasted of the most mileage of any of the roads operating in Wisconsin by 1910 but also owned controlling interest in the Chicago, St. Paul, Minneapolis and Omaha Railway which carried substantial state traffic. The Chicago, Milwaukee and St. Paul was nearly equal to the Chicago and North Western in size and influence, while the Minneapolis, St. Paul and Sault Sainte Marie Railway constituted the third major operation in the state, having grown substantially in size and influence in 1909 when it purchased the Wisconsin Central Railway, the only distinctively Wisconsin road of any size.[5]

Although state aid was of little moment in the development of the railroad systems in Wisconsin, the rapid growth of the state's first real "big business" not unexpectedly had profound effects upon the political as well as the economic development in the state. In the spirit of the "Gilded Age," Wisconsin people in the late nineteenth century "came to regard the state legislature as a counter over which private groups could acquire legal rights and privileges, without undue squeamishness about the methods employed by lobbyist or legislator."[6] Taking full advantage of this congenial view, the railroads, often joined by the state's large lumber interests, came to dominate Wisconsin politics in the latter third of the nineteenth century.

The natural partnership between lumber and railroad interests was of enormous mutual benefit. As lumbering became increasingly important and lucrative in the years after the Civil War, the most prosperous of the mill owners began to branch out into related

[5] See James P. Kayser, *The Railroads of Wisconsin* (Boston, 1937), for a good statistical summary of the growth of railroad companies in Wisconsin.
[6] Robert S. Hunt, *Law and Locomotives: The Impact of the Railroad on Wisconsin Law in the Nineteenth Century* (Madison, 1958), 33.

fields, such as land speculation, shipping, wholesaling, and even retailing of lumber products, in an effort to extend their operations. Quite naturally their interest in railroading grew also. Railroads to them were a necessity, for they hauled logs to mills and lumber to market whenever the river system was inadequate. Beyond that, they offered a lucrative place to invest profits from their major enterprise and a convenient means of obtaining highly valuable tracts of timberland which were often part of land grants to expanding railroads.[7]

The major vehicle used by railroad men, lumbermen, and other entrepreneurs to dominate Wisconsin state politics in the late nineteenth century was the state's Republican party. During most of this period the Republican party operated under the autocratic control of three men: Philetus Sawyer, a wealthy lumberman who rose to a position of power and influence in the United States Senate; Henry Payne, president of the Wisconsin Telephone Company, consolidator of street railways in Milwaukee, builder of interurban electric lines, and railroad president; and John C. Spooner, a lawyer who protected large business interests in the state and who also became a powerful force in the United States Senate. Working through such co-operative political figures, large business interests were able often to use the state, and occasionally, the federal government to gain needed lands or concessions. In return, they "repaid the politicians with their support, which made the party not only strong but also respectable."[8]

In spite of the powerful alliance between railroads and politicians, public sentiment developed early for controls on the activities of the arrogant carriers. Protests dated back to the 1850's when Byron Kilbourn, the president of the La Crosse and Milwaukee Railway, bribed top state officials in order to get a large land grant, then saw his road fold in the Panic of 1857 which drove every railroad in the state into bankruptcy. As a result about 6,000 farmers who had mortgaged their farms to aid in construction of various roads lost some $5,000,000.[9] The pattern of arrogance and irrespon-

[7] Richard N. Current, *Pine Logs and Politics, A Life of Philetus Sawyer, 1816–1900* (Madison, 1950), 104–105, 131–132.
[8] *Ibid.*, 236, 240.
[9] Raney, "The Building of Wisconsin Railroads," 391.

sibility exhibited during the 1850's was intensified in the following decades as the railroads gained in strength and tightened their hold on the state's shippers. These attitudes were facilitated by the absorption of numerous small roads into several giant systems which lessened competition and permitted arbitrary and exorbitant rate increases.[10]

It is, therefore, no distinct surprise that in the decade after the Civil War the demands for effective regulation of the state's carriers became more and more intense. This reform sentiment, which culminated in the early 1870's, was linked both in form and purpose to the demands heard in a number of midwestern states for tighter controls on the railroads. The Potter Law, the result of Wisconsin's first crusade for regulation, would be classified as a "Granger law." The label "Granger law," however, is no more accurate in describing the true origins of the act in Wisconsin than it is in other midwestern states.[11] While support for a stringent antirailroad bill in Wisconsin "crossed party lines, economic interests and geographical location," and did include farmers, the campaign was in fact led by a group in the Milwaukee Chamber of Commerce, the organization which would prove to be the most consistent champion of economic reform in Wisconsin in the next decades.[12]

The Potter Law, passed by the Wisconsin legislature in 1874, arranged all passenger and freight traffic into classifications and set maximum rates that could be charged for items within each category. A three-man board of railroad commissioners was established to implement the provisions of the law—handle complaints, review classifications, and ascertain pertinent facts concerning railroad finance.[13] There is a marked difference of opinion among

[10] Hunt, *Law and Locomotives*, 98.

[11] See Harold D. Woodman, "Chicago Businessmen and 'Granger' Laws," in *Agricultural History*, 3:16–24 (January, 1962), and George H. Miller, "Origins of the Iowa Granger Law," in the *Mississippi Valley Historical Review*, 40:657–680 (March, 1954).

[12] Dale E. Treleven, "Commissions, Corners, and Conveyance: The Origins of Anti-Monopolism in Milwaukee" (unpublished master's thesis, University of Wisconsin, 1968), 44–46, 121.

[13] William L. Burton, "The First Wisconsin Railroad Commission: Reform or Political Expediency" (unpublished master's thesis, University of Wisconsin, 1952), 107–108.

8   THE MYTH OF A PROGRESSIVE REFORM

those who have studied the law extensively concerning the meaning of its provisions. Robert Daland, in 1949, argued that the railroad men themselves controlled the writing of the Potter Law.[14]
Noting the unprecedented controls imposed upon the state's carriers by the law, however, William Burton, in a 1952 study, asserts
that the law was "the most drastic of all legislative attacks on
corporate power."[15] In a more recent study Dale Treleven, center-
ing his attention on the tariff schedules to which all roads were
impelled to conform, and which were commonly considered to be
the most rigid feature of the bill, takes a middle position. Noting
that reformers demanded a rate schedule which was "far more
stringent," he argues that the final statute represented "a mild
reform measure in response to intensive pressure by railroads."[16]

In retrospect, the Potter Law was probably both too stringent
and too lenient. The legislated rates may have been more to the
liking of the railroad lobbyist than the reformer, but whatever the
case, the more important fact was that they created a dangerous
inflexibility in freight rates on the very items which were most
vital to the Wisconsin economy.[17] On the other hand, the commission established to administer the act was totally devoid of independent enforcement powers, having been denied even the power
to initiate proceedings to enforce the principles of legislation.

Thus, as a result of a curious combination of factors, the Potter
Law was doomed from the outset. In its short two-year life, the
principle of the state's right to regulate the carriers was firmly
established, through an epic decision by the Wisconsin Supreme
Court which gave both legal and popular sanction to the idea.[18]
Through a concerted campaign by the railroads, however, the
majority of the attention was focused on the shortcomings and
weaknesses in the statute.

The state's railroads assumed a totally arrogant posture toward
the new law, refusing to abide by provisions which they considered

[14] Robert Daland, "Enactment of the Potter Law," in the *Wisconsin Magazine
of History*, 33:45–54 (September, 1949.)
[15] Burton, "Wisconsin Railroad Commission," Introduction.
[16] Treleven, "Commissions, Corners, and Conveyance," 118–119.
[17] Hunt, *Law and Locomotives*, 127.
[18] *Ibid.*, 12.

damaging to their stockholders while, at the same time, using the law as a scapegoat for decision-making. Alexander Mitchell, the president of the Milwaukee and St. Paul Railroad, for example, refused to build more storage facilities for grain shippers in Milwaukee until the people of Wisconsin ceased their war against the carriers. As a result many pro-regulation businessmen who were fearful of further losses in their fight with Chicago for the grain trade began to agitate for repeal of the law.[19]

This pattern was repeated throughout the state. Although the evidence indicates that the law itself had only a slight effect on the earnings of the major roads in the state, the carriers propagated the notion that the law seriously threatened their operations and might even force them to shut down.[20] Convinced by such assertions, people were prone to attribute any curtailment of services directly to the law itself.[21]

In the end a combination of things crippled this first experiment in regulation: the defects in the Potter Law itself, certain unrelated economic factors, including a brief depression, which affected the health of the railroad industry, and, perhaps most important, the canny propaganda efforts of the carriers.[22] In a mood for reassessment, the state legislature scrapped the Potter Law in 1876 and replaced it with a measure which effectively returned all policy-making duties to the carriers, including the all-important task of rate-setting, and reduced the three-man commission to a single railroad commissioner who functioned primarily as a bookkeeper. While a shadow of regulatory continuity was retained in the 1876 law and much more helpful information concerning railroad affairs was garnered by the commissioner in the next three decades, for all practical purposes regulation on the state level was not a reality again until 1905.

The thirty-year lag between regulatory attempts is in part attributable to the railroads' continuing efforts to thwart new reforms by distorting the Potter Law experience. "The 'Granger laws' have served the purpose of a 'bloody shirt' to conceal incompetence in

---

[19] Treleven, "Commissions, Corners, and Conveyance," 131–134.
[20] *Ibid.*, 131.
[21] Hunt, *Law and Locomotives*, 128.
[22] *Ibid.*, 126.

railway management for twenty years at least," argued Albert Stickney, the iconoclastic president of the Chicago and Great Western Railway, in 1891.[23] In Wisconsin the Potter Law became this "bloody shirt." Whenever the subject of regulation was broached, the sad story of the Potter Law was quickly resurrected. This tactic was especially effective in the 1890's when numerous attempts to pass regulation bills failed partly if not principally because of a continuing fear on the part of legislators and businessmen of a repetition of the economic calamity which this initial regulatory legislation was said to have sparked.[24] It was still being used in 1903 when La Follette joined the regulation crusade. Stalwarts like Elisha Keyes, the battle-hardened veteran of three decades of political in-fighting, and the *Milwaukee Sentinel* combined forces to retell once more the evils of the Potter Law experiment and warn of the dangers of trying such a thing again. They branded the current batch of reformers "latter day Potter law advocates" who sought to give the governor "power to 'govern' the railroads."[25] "It is the part of wisdom to draw on the experience of the past and . . . picture . . . the evil fruit born by arbitrary interference and ill conceived regulation of the railways in the early seventies," wrote Marvin Hughitt, president of the Chicago and North Western Railway. "Such patriotic expressions . . . will hasten the return to sounder views."[26]

The beleaguered administration group, understanding the magic effect of this argument out of the past, countered with arguments that the Potter Law had in fact been effective and was being misrepresented.[27] They also recalled the 1875 Wisconsin Supreme Court decision which affirmed the right of the state to regulate railroad transportation as a proof of the legality of their crusade. This fight, waged over a regulation attempt thirty years earlier, was a key factor in La Follette's final state reform campaign.

[23] A. B. Stickney, *The Railway Problem* (St. Paul, 1891), 210.

[24] Emanuel L. Philipp, *Political Reform in Wisconsin* (Milwaukee, 1910), 210.

[25] *Milwaukee Sentinel*, March 16, 17, 1903.

[26] Marvin Hughitt to Keyes, March 23, 1903, in the Elisha W. Keyes Papers. Unless otherwise noted, all manuscript collections are in the State Historical Society of Wisconsin.

[27] Robert M. La Follette, *Granger Legislation and State Control of Railway Rates* (Madison, 1904).

Although the continued reference to the Potter Law experience pointed out the continuity of the regulation struggle from the 1870's into the twentieth century, other more direct ties existed between the fight La Follette led and the past. The 1903 and 1905 legislative struggles over regulation simply marked a climax of battles over regulation which had been carried on in every session of the Wisconsin legislature since 1887. Most important to La Follette's phase of the campaign was a continuity of personnel, for at the feet of experienced reformers the governor obtained the knowledge which allowed him to carry on an intelligent and persuasive campaign on this issue. In the difficult years of the late nineteenth century before the powerful La Follette coalition embraced the issue, two giants, Albert R. Hall and Edward P. Bacon, dominated. No more unlikely combination could be conceived.

Albert Hall was a small, self-effacing bachelor who lived with his sister on a large farm outside of Knapp, Wisconsin, husbanding his funds in spite of the fact he was independently wealthy. Though conservative and ordered in his personal life, his politics were strictly radical. The nephew of Oliver H. Kelley, founder of the Granger movement, he spent the final decades of the nineteenth century in mortal combat with forces which he felt threatened the position of the underdog in society.[28] He brought to the regulation fight the righteous indignation of the small man who distrusted large corporations and was determined to bring these irresponsible giants under close public supervision. In the decade prior to La Follette's governorship, Hall's activities on behalf of railroad regulation as a Wisconsin assemblyman were crucial.

Beginning in 1891, Hall brought before the assembly at every session a plan for sterner regulation of common carriers. First he championed joint resolutions asking that a "state railroad appraisal commission" be appointed to assess the railroads of the state and learn whether the carriers were asking an unfair return on their investment through excessive rates.[29] In 1895 Hall hardened his

[28] *Dunn County News,* November 15, 1906; Hall's mother to Albert Hall, June 7, 1873; article entitled "Worcester Expects 25,000 People at Grange Convention" (box 1), both in the Albert R. Hall Papers. The letter from Hall's mother describes the family's involvement in the Granger movement, and the article notes the relationship between Kelley and Albert's sister Carrie.

[29] *Wisconsin Assembly Journal,* 1891, Joint Resolution No. 57 A, 1003.

plea, demanding now the formation of a permanent regulatory commission with powers to draw up an entirely new rate structure for all roads within the state.[30] In support of such measures fellow legislators learned to expect to find on their desks data showing comparative rates for equal distances in Wisconsin and neighboring states which told an eloquent story of discrimination against the shippers of their state.[31] When ignored by his colleagues, the indomitable little reformer was wont to go straight to the people, organizing referenda in towns throughout the state in support of his measures.[32]

Whether attacking railroad rates or condemning the abuses of railroad passes and the undertaxation of carriers, Hall was a pillar of strength at a time when the causes he espoused were so highly unpopular that few were willing to support his efforts. "I remember then that we were a hopeless minority; sometimes ridiculed, and often punished indirectly because of the attitude we assumed on 'Rate Commission' and 'Anti-Pass'," recalled one of Hall's few supporters.[33] On the occasion of his death in 1905, the leading progressive organ would proclaim: "He was the father of reform in the state. . . . He has done more than anyone else first to arouse the conscience of the state and create the public sentiment that finally stirred the people to demand their own."[34] Others later heralded him as "the father of the 'Progressive' movement in Wisconsin," "La Follette's mentor," and the man "largely responsible for making La Follette the power he has been in State and National affairs."[35] But in the pre-La Follette 1890's, none spoke so highly. His was a lonely, principled vigil.

While Hall's roots were deep in the soil of Wisconsin reform, Edward Payson Bacon could boast of an even earlier involvement. Born in upstate New York in 1834 the eldest son of a tailor, Bacon

---

[30] *Wisconsin Assembly Bills,* 1895, No. 146 A and 148 A. Also see Hall to Frank A. Flower, November 13, 1894, in the Hall Papers.

[31] *Wisconsin State Journal,* January 21, 1903.

[32] Philipp, *Political Reform in Wisconsin,* 209.

[33] D. O. Mahoney to Esch, February 16, 1905, in the John J. Esch Papers.

[34] *Milwaukee Free Press,* June 3, 1905.

[35] Nils P. Haugen, *Pioneer and Political Reminiscences* (Evansville, Wisconsin, 1929), 97; James A. Frear, *Forty Years of Progressive Public Service* (Washington, 1937), 33; "Autobiography of John Strange," dated May 23, 1922, p. 26, in the John Strange Papers.

was forced to quit school at the age of seventeen to help support his family. He began as a freight and ticket clerk with the New York and Erie Railroad in a small town in New York, but within four years he was chief clerk of the freight department in New York City. After a short stint at the same post in Chicago with the Michigan Southern and Northern Indiana Railroad, he moved to Milwaukee where he spent the next nine years organizing and supervising the administrative offices of the Milwaukee and Mississippi Railroad. During that time he originated systems of accounting and methods of conducting freight and passenger departments which were accepted generally by the western roads. Equipment he devised for handling coupon tickets in passenger departments was used far into the twentieth century. In 1865 he left railroading to found the Milwaukee firm of Bacon and Everingham which engaged in the grain trade. Later organizing the E. P. Bacon Company, he extended his operations to Chicago as well as Milwaukee and became known as the leading grain trader in the Middle West. Here too he innovated, instituting many important changes in grain trading methods.[36]

When the inventive Bacon left railroading to enter the grain trade, he took with him a clear understanding of the importance of freight rates and traffic patterns in determining the success or failure of his new enterprise. It is not surprising, therefore, that the young grain merchant soon became a conspicuous leader in the quest for effective regulatory machinery.[37]

For Bacon the struggle for tighter railroad regulation was simply the first of many reform campaigns. While earning a national reputation as a proponent of railroad regulation, he also took time to help organize the Milwaukee YMCA, to serve as a member of the Beloit College board of trustees, where he established several scholarships, to champion a drive to make the fathers of illegiti-

[36] *Dictionary of American Biography* (New York, 1928), 1:476; *Dictionary of Wisconsin Biography* (Madison, 1960), 19.
[37] It is not clear when Bacon first became involved in the fight for railroad regulation. Evidence indicates, however, that it was quite early. A fellow Milwaukeean, Edward D. Holton, in remarks to the National Board of Trade in 1886, referred to Bacon as one who "has for years led a controversy in our State on the question of regulating home traffic among our own people." Treleven, "Commissions, Corners, and Conveyance," 56.

mate children responsible for their support, and to participate in many other efforts toward social betterment.[38]

Although his reform interests were catholic, Bacon's major preoccupation was stricter government regulation of railroads. In working toward this goal he was often joined by his close companion, Robert Eliot, a fellow grain merchant who possessed the same consuming interest in the endeavor. This tandem of Bacon and Eliot, the former more charming and appealing and the latter abrupt and businesslike, was a formidable duo in decades during which the ideal of regulation was realized in Wisconsin and throughout the nation.

When these men spoke for stricter controls, they usually spoke as representatives of the Milwaukee Chamber of Commerce, the long-time champion of governmental supervision of railroad practices. Milwaukee between 1880 and 1910 underwent a transition from a commercial-based community to a manufacturing one. One aspect of this change was a steady decline in the importance of the Milwaukee grain market as Minneapolis and Chicago, taking advantage of superior locations and promotional abilities, secured more and more of the commerce which formerly came through the Wisconsin port city. Having earlier benefited from an excellent port and the proximity of much wheat farming, the development of a more efficient rail system eastward through Chicago and the gradual disappearance of wheat from the farms of Wisconsin and southern Minnesota as a result of an agricultural transition seemed to spell doom for many a grain merchant in Milwaukee.[39]

As early as the 1870's the Chamber of Commerce had shown its deep concern about rate structures by spearheading the agitation which led to the passage of the ill-fated Potter Law. Evidently chastened by the failure of this initial experiment, the Chamber was relatively silent in the years following the repeal of that law. But by the mid-1880's, with men like E. P. Bacon at the helm, the

---

[38] *Dictionary of American Biography*, 1:476; *Dictionary of Wisconsin Biography*, 19; Edward P. Bacon to La Follette, January 5, 1905, in the Robert M. La Follette Papers.

[39] William E. Derby, "A History of the Port of Milwaukee" (unpublished Ph.D. dissertation, University of Wisconsin, 1963), particularly 280, 289, 291, 347.

Milwaukee group launched an intensified fight for stiffer controls, charging that discriminatory rate policies rather than the other more impersonal factors were largely responsible for the flow of grain away from Milwaukee. Given an equitable rate structure, it argued, the major Wisconsin city could compete on even terms with Minneapolis and Chicago.[40]

While pushing for more effective government regulation of the carriers, the Chamber of Commerce did not abandon hope of gaining concessions from the roads themselves. Year after year, in extended conference and through detailed communication, the Chamber and the executives of the major railroads sought a common ground which would settle matters short of an acrimonious legislative fight. While on occasion agreement seemed near, a lasting resolution never was achieved.[41]

Although the channels of communication to the roads were kept open, it is clear that men like Bacon and Eliot expected little to come from such negotiation. They therefore spearheaded efforts in both Washington and Madison designed to compel changes in railroad policy. When hearings on the pending Interstate Commerce Act were held in Washington in 1886, Bacon and Eliot testified before the Senate Select Committee on Interstate Commerce, arguing for a co-ordinated structure of state and national regulatory commissions to insure better control of railroad rates.[42] Immediately after the Commission's formation the Chamber brought before the body the first of several complaints against the major railroads. It was repeatedly frustrated, however, primarily

---

[40] *Ibid.*, 353.

[41] Boxes 2 and 3 of Milwaukee Chamber of Commerce Papers contain minutes of several conferences and numerous letters between chamber committees and railroad representatives. See "Report to the Chamber by the Chamber committee," February 7, 1885, in the Milwaukee Chamber of Commerce Papers, Milwaukee County Historical Society, for the most hopeful report which reads in part: "Satisfactory results can be accomplished in the remedying of evils complained of, by future amicable negotiations under existing laws, without seeking legislative action, which in the present unfavorable condition of financial affairs might operate seriously to the detriment of railway interests."

[42] *Report of Senate Select Committee on Interstate Commerce* (49 Congress, 1 session, Senate Report no. 46, pt. 2, serial 2357, Washington, 1886), 3:692–713. Eliot's name misspelled "Elliott."

because of the limitations placed upon the Commission by an unsympathetic Supreme Court in the 1890's. Angered by this turn of events, Bacon undertook a vigorous campaign for legislation to give the Interstate Commerce Commission sufficient power to do its work and make its decisions stand.

The new campaign began in 1899 when he organized the League of National Associations, which was pledged to broaden the powers of the Interstate Commerce Commission, and which included the Millers' National Association, the National Association of Manufacturers, the National Board of Trade, the National Grange, and some fifty other national organizations. With the name changed to the Interstate Commerce Law Convention, Bacon's organization became in the next five years "the major merchant spokesman for railroad regulation." By 1902 the organization had sufficient prestige to champion the Corless-Nelson bill (called the "Bacon bill" in deference to its author), which envisioned tighter rate controls on the carriers. Frightened by the growing strength of his organization, representatives of the New York Central and Pennsylvania systems invited Bacon, Eliot, and Frank Barry of the National Board of Trade to a conference where a compromise measure was formulated. Before final passage, however, the railroad group reneged on its promise of good faith and deleted the bulk of Bacon's demands, leaving simply an antirebate measure, the Elkins Act.[43]

Promising "vigorous efforts at the next session of Congress," the determined Bacon continued to build up the size of his organization until in 1905 over 500 organizations were members.[44] Now seventy years old and suffering from ill health, the indomitable Bacon was still a formidable opponent with his full, pure white Van Dyke beard and distinguished features reminiscent of a latter-day Jeremiah.[45] "Peter the Hermit," his foes called him and were wont to attempt to downgrade all efforts to pass new regulatory measures

[43] Kolko, *Railroads and Regulation*, 93; Wiebe, *Businessmen and Reform*, 51–52; *Dictionary of American Biography*, 1:476.

[44] Wiebe, *Businessmen and Reform*, 52.

[45] Ray Stannard Baker, "Railroads on Trial," in *McClure's*, 26:544 (March 1906).

by labeling them "a joint campaign of our friends Bacon and Moseley [secretary of the ICC]," or "really the bill of Mr. Bacon . . . and Mr. Prouty, of the Interstate Commerce Commission."[46] All their efforts were doomed to failure, however, for now that he possessed the proper organizational strength, the elderly reformer personally convinced President Theodore Roosevelt to support his crusade. The Hepburn Act of 1906, the eventful result of reform agitation in the early years of the twentieth century, was due more to the efforts of Bacon than those of any other man.[47]

The victory gained in the Congress in 1906 represented the height of achievement for Bacon and his colleagues in the Chamber of Commerce. The problem of obtaining proper state regulation of carriers, however, also concerned them greatly during these two decades. It was in fact in the legislative in-fighting in the Wisconsin capital that the Milwaukee men won their spurs as skilled lobbyists. By 1885 the Chamber was actively discussing its intention to push for a strengthening of the token regulation in Wisconsin. Bacon and a few Milwaukee associates failed in 1887 in their initial attempt to push a regulation bill through the Wisconsin legislature. In that effort, however, for the first time each member of the legislature was furnished with a tabular statement comparing rates from points in Wisconsin to Milwaukee on the major state lines with those of surrounding states for like distances, a technique and argument passed on by Bacon to Hall and then to La Follette.[48]

In 1889 the Milwaukee Chamber group returned to Madison, this time ready for a full-fledged battle on the issue of state regulation. After seeking the advice of commission members in surrounding states, they decided on a bill which virtually duplicated that passed by Congress in 1887, secured a sponsor, and undertook a vigorous campaign on behalf of the "Taylor Bill." Hampered by a lack of zeal on the part of the sponsor of the legislation, H. A.

[46] *Regulation of Railway Rates, Hearings before the Committee on Interstate Commerce, United States Senate* (58 Congress, 3 session, Washington, 1904–1905), 3:1954, 2503, 2515.

[47] *Dictionary of American Biography*, 1:476.

[48] Bacon to Haugen, June 23, 1888, in the Nils P. Haugen Papers. See also Bacon to Atley Peterson, June 18, 1888, enclosed in letter to Haugen.

Taylor, they were unable to break through the rock-ribbed conservatism of the state senate and failed in their first concerted bid.[49]

State railroad reform efforts in the decade of the 1890's were championed primarily by Hall with occasional support from Bacon and the Milwaukee group, as the attentions of the Chamber men turned to actions before the Interstate Commerce Commission, which they felt offered promise of more substantial relief from their plight.[50] The ties between Hall and the Milwaukee group remained strong, however, and when, in 1901, Bacon and his aides shifted their emphasis again to the passage of new legislation to perfect the regulation process, Hall was responsive to their advice. Heeding their contentions that he stood no chance of passing the sort of hard-line regulation bill he had proposed for three consecutive sessions, Hall modified the legislation, striking out all commission powers to set initial rates for all commerce within the state. The modified bill was promptly buried by the first legislature serving under the young, ambitious Governor Robert M. La Follette—with no word of help or comfort from the executive office.[51]

The crusade for railroad regulation had been brought to the threshold of the executive mansion. Techniques of persuasion had been formulated, legislation had been tried and tested, and important economic groups had been enlisted in its support. One final task remained for the dedicated group of reformers, that of interesting the ambitious governor in their reform enterprise. The men with the economic insight sought ties with the man who possessed political power.

In 1901 prospects for such a coalition must have seemed dim indeed to the Hall-Bacon group. The year before La Follette had persuaded Hall to withdraw his demand for a regulation plank in the Republican platform, and now he had ignored the concerted attempt by the combined forces of Hall and Bacon to pass even the more moderate kind of regulation bill in the legislature. ("Can you tell me anything about the Hall R. Bill?" E. A. Edmonds, a

[49] Eliot to La Follette, January 19, 1905; Eliot to La Follette, February 11, 1905, both in the La Follette Papers; *Wisconsin Senate Bills*, 1889, No. 19.
[50] In a speech in 1904 Hall admitted Bacon preceded him. *Milwaukee Free Press*, November 5, 1904. See also *Wisconsin State Journal*, May 5, 1903.
[51] Eliot to La Follette, June 4, 1904, in the La Follette Papers.

close supporter of the young governor, had written in February, 1901.[52] "Beyond the fact that such a railway bill as you mention has been introduced, I am not informed with regard to it or its prospect for favorable consideration," La Follette had replied.[53])

Later the governor would explain that although "he was as keen for railway regulation in Wisconsin as anyone could be," the need to build "our structure of reform step by step" was the reason why he headed off Hall's efforts to include regulation in his first gubernatorial platform. Anyway, he explained, "[Hall] wanted to make a record." He dismissed the 1901 bill as "not such a measure as I should have been willing to make a fight for as a law covering the subject."[54]

Neither explanation rings true. In 1900, of course, it was not the governor's decision whether or not railroad regulation would become a reform issue in Wisconsin, only whether he would embrace it as part of *his* reform program. The first decision had been made long before he was an important political figure. Perhaps in attempting to understand why La Follette did not embrace the issue in his first successful bid for the governorship, one can most profitably begin by recalling the concerted effort of the young lawyer and his friends to gain the support of key railroad men during the campaign. Nor can the 1901 excuse be accepted. A more candid reply might be that the governor was chary to support measures which he did not personally champion, and he was neither ready nor willing to cope with the complexity of regulation in his first term. The 1901 Hall bill, for which he was not "willing to make a fight," was the basis for the kind of legislation he himself sponsored several years later!

In spite of such a lack of concern on the part of La Follette, the reform group had reason to feel efforts to interest the governor might eventually succeed for, in the case of the Milwaukee cadre, their zeal was matched by a growing political strength and influence. Although La Follette could afford to ignore the blandish-

[52] E. A. Edmonds to La Follette, February 19, 1901, in the La Follette Papers.
[53] La Follette to Edmonds, February 25, 1901, in the La Follette Letterbooks.
[54] Robert M. La Follette, *Autobiography* (Madison, 1911), 238–240.

ments of Albert Hall who, in spite of the esteem in which he was held by many, was essentially a loner, he could ignore less easily the urban-based sector of the reform movement. Bacon's Interstate Commerce Law Convention counted within its membership many of the important business and agricultural groups in Wisconsin and Bacon himself was becoming an increasingly important figure on the national scene.[55] Beyond this, the Milwaukee group had purchased considerable stock in the *Milwaukee Free Press*, founded in 1901 as a spokesman for La Follette and reform causes. Although it is impossible to tell how much of a stake the merchant reformers had in this paper, from all indications their shares were sufficient to give them considerable influence over the paper's editorial policy.[56] The governor, alert to the need for support of as broad a section of economic groups as possible, in search ultimately of a national career, and highly dependent upon the *Free Press* for publicity and support, could scarcely ignore the blandishments of men who held keys in all these areas.

From the outset of La Follette's governorship the old-line Chamber of Commerce men had been courting the governor, offering him advice and support in a plethora of tasks. One sporadic correspondent, Robert Eliot, was characteristically dogmatic and tactless in his approach. "In your inaugural message you made some grave errors which boomerranged [*sic*] upon us and cast us down," he wrote concerning the development of the taxation issue.[57] Not until La Follette was in the midst of the regulation fight and found Eliot's letters extremely helpful did he finally take this expert's advice seriously, learn to spell his name correctly, and write more than perfunctory replies.[58]

---

[55] Wisconsin members of the Interstate Commerce Law Convention as of May, 1905, included nineteen important commercial organizations. Senate Committee on Interstate Commerce, *Regulation of Railway Rates*, 2766.

[56] Eliot to La Follette, November 9, 1901; Johnson to La Follette, July 19, 1902; Ralph McKenzie to La Follette, January 11, 1905. McKenzie wrote La Follette that Johnson "makes Myrick [editor of the *Free Press*] do about as he wants him," and later that "they have an executive committee to run the *Free Press* of which Johnson the partner of Bacon is the 'main guy'." McKenzie to J. J. Hannan, December 7, 1904; McKenzie to La Follette, February 23, 1905, all in the La Follette Papers.

[57] Eliot to La Follette, November 9, 1901, in the La Follette Papers.

[58] The first correct spelling occurred January 3, 1903, in response to a letter

More effective was George H. D. Johnson, E. P. Bacon's younger partner, who, having apparently joined the Chamber movement during the 1890's, had early assumed an important role as a statistician and theorist. Patient and resourceful, he had constructed many of the painstakingly accurate comparison tables which were the basis of the numerous appeals made before the Interstate Commerce Commission and by Hall in the Wisconsin assembly.[59] Like the other Milwaukee man, he had many reform interests. (His primary concern during La Follette's tenure as governor, other than the regulation issue, was a plan to prohibit the sale of liquor within a specified distance of schools.)[60]

Whether Johnson knew La Follette before 1901 is not known. It is clear, however, that he understood the young reformer's temperament much better than did Eliot, for whereas Eliot was prone to preach and teach, Johnson praised and cajoled. Johnson's tactic won the Milwaukee group its first chance to enlist the governor's support.

Johnson had early written the governor in praise of his stand on the direct primary, but his most persuasive and ingratiating letter was not addressed to La Follette but to *The Outlook*, a national publication which had gotten itself embroiled in a local Wisconsin controversy. In reply to a letter accusing La Follette of being a demagogue, Johnson had fired off an equally vigorous rejoinder strongly defending the governor, asserting, "to those who know him best he is a frank and able and honorable man."[61] "A clear and forceful statement of the situation," declared La Follette in expressing his appreciation of the Milwaukee merchant's gesture.[62]

Alert to his chance, Johnson pressed his advantage that summer. After enlisting the aid of Hall, he broached the problem of regulation for the first time, linking the issue to tax reform to which the governor was already committed. "If proper tax laws are passed without any restriction on rates, there is a strong probability that

---

enclosing valuable information concerning regulation in Illinois. La Follette to Eliot, in the La Follette Letterbooks.

[59] Hall to La Follette, December 16, 1902, in the La Follette Papers.

[60] G. H. D. Johnson to Hoard, January 25, 1905, in the W. D. Hoard Papers; Johnson to La Follette, January 25, 1905, in the La Follette Papers.

[61] Letter to the editor, *The Outlook*, 70:883–884 (April 5, 1902).

[62] La Follette to Johnson, April 7, 1902, in the La Follette Letterbooks.

the railways will take revenge upon the people of the state by advancing rates for transportation, which are already much higher than in surrounding states where proper restrictions have been placed upon the railways to prevent excessive charges," he warned. Urging this broader issue as a fertile theme for the impending campaign, Johnson noted he would be in Madison during the coming nominating convention and would be pleased to arrange the details of this plank of the platform if desired. Just in case, the thorough Johnson enclosed a proposal for such a platform plank demanding firmer regulatory legislation on the state and national levels.[63] Put off by La Follette's reply that he would give his proposed resolution "to some member of the platform committee capable of securing consideration for it,"[64] two days later the Milwaukee reformer sent along a revised resolution stripping the proposed legislation of the provisions for initial rate-making for commissions but retaining the demand for added strength in regulation.[65]

Meanwhile, however, Hall had unexpectedly poured cold water on Johnson's scheme. Noting that support for stiffer national legislation should surely be given, Hall argued that the inclusion of the regulation issue at this late date might seriously injure La Follette's chances for re-election as governor in view of the obvious opposition which would come from manufacturers and railroads. Later such a measure must be passed, but for now he counseled caution.[66]

Whether Hall's advice deterred the governor or whether La Follette still simply lacked interest, no encouragement was offered to the Milwaukee man and no regulation plank was included in the 1902 platform. He may have learned his first lesson, however, for six months later when he embraced the issue he would justify regulation on the grounds Johnson had advised.

In the fall of 1902, while the governor campaigned for tax reform and the direct primary, the *Milwaukee Free Press* launched a full-scale attack on the Wisconsin railroads, charging, by the use of familiar graphs and tables, that rates were uniformly higher in

[63] Johnson to La Follette, July 9, 1902, in the La Follette Papers.
[64] La Follette to Johnson, July 10, 1902, in the La Follette Letterbooks.
[65] Johnson to La Follette, July 12, 1902, in the La Follette Papers.
[66] Hall to La Follette, July 11, 1902, in the La Follette Papers.

Wisconsin than in surrounding states. Although the *Free Press*'s offensive might possibly have been part of a plan by the administration to set the stage for a later regulation campaign, from all appearances it seems to have been an independent crusade, with the Milwaukee cadre supplying the data for the comparative tables used in the articles.[67] Now the governor, content to ignore regulation, would read in his favorite newspaper of the launching of a new phase of the vital state reform movement for which he, the self-styled premier reformer, had not lifted a finger.

Occasionally during his fall campaign the governor gave some indications of interest in the regulation issue, warning he would not allow increased taxes levied on the railroads to be passed on to the users of the carriers.[68] This theme, however, receded into the background during the campaign. Although state newspapers began to take sides on the regulation issue,[69] the administration campaigners on the hustings took little note of the issue.

By the time La Follette had won a conclusive victory in early November, the new assault on state railroad rates was in full force. Urged on by friends[70] and the flow of events, the governor at last seriously contemplated adding this issue to his crusades.

It must have been with a feeling of irony that Albert Hall, newly retired after over a decade of lonely battling for regulation, read his most recent letter from the governor in early December. "Dear Albert," it began, "I wish you would send me everything that you have in hand bearing upon the rate question and establishment of a commission. Do not think anything too unimportant to send down."[71] Hall's reply reviewed briefly the history of his lonely fight for regulatory legislation, mentioned the role of the Milwaukee group, and enclosed appropriate tables and references for possible

---

[67] See Commissioner Graham Rice to G. H. D. Johnson, October 6, 14, 1902, Railroad Commissioners' Letterbooks, volume 14, in the Wisconsin Public Service Commission Records, Wisconsin State Archives, State Historical Society of Wisconsin, for Rice's response to Johnson's repeated requests for technical rate information.

[68] *Vernon County Censor*, October 8, 1902.

[69] *Ibid.*, October 22, 29, 1902; *Milwaukee Sentinel*, November 9, 1902.

[70] W. L. Bennett to La Follette, November 24, 1902, in the La Follette Papers.

[71] La Follette to Hall, December 9, 1902, in the La Follette Letterbooks.

use in a new regulation fight. Apologizing for the disorganized way
in which the figures were sent, he suggested that La Follette write
to Johnson for better copies of such rate comparisons.[72] Coinci-
dentally the very day Hall replied La Follette found on his desk
a letter from Johnson himself urging the governor to include in his
inaugural message to the legislature a recommendation for regulatory legislation—and declaring he already had planned a campaign
for such a measure. The governor was simply being asked to give
this independent campaign a needed lift. "The papers of the state
having taken up the subject with so much interest, and there having
been so many expressions by businessmen, notably those at Oshkosh, regarding the discriminations against Wisconsin shippers,
it would appear that the present is a very favorable time to endeavor to secure the needed legislation," he argued.[73]

The governor was obviously bemused. Although he had begun
inquiries concerning regulation, his early correspondence with key
legislative figures concerning the coming session failed to mention
the regulation issue. Now, faced with the prospect of the popular
reform issue again being agitated before the legislature he claimed
to control, and without even perfunctory aid from the executive
mansion, he sent Adjutant General C. R. Boardman, a loyal administration man, to interview Oshkosh businessmen to see if Johnson
really had such strong potential support. Boardman's optimistic
report apparently congealed the governor's thinking.[74] He immediately instructed Halford Erickson, commissioner of labor and industrial statistics, to secure comparative rate information on a wide
variety of farm materials shipped in Illinois and Iowa as well as
Wisconsin. "It seems to me it would greatly strengthen *our* case
to do so," he declared.[75] Convinced, the governor adopted the regulation cause, issue, and method, from longtime exponents. ("By the
opening of the session of 1903," he later explained, "the consideration of the control of railway transportation rates in connection

[72] Hall to La Follette, December 16, 1902, in the La Follette Papers.
[73] Johnson to La Follette, December 16, 1902, in the La Follette Papers.
[74] Boardman to La Follette, December 24, 1902, in the La Follette Papers.
[75] La Follette to Halford Erickson, December 27, 1902, in the La Follette
Papers. (Emphasis added.)

with railway taxation, had made its way into public discussion and awakened such general interest that the time seemed ripe to secure this important legislation.")[76] Appropriately, Erickson scurried off to Milwaukee to borrow tables and learn the finer points of this sort of tabulation from the veteran reformers at the Chamber of Commerce.[77] A new phase in the fight for railroad regulation had begun.

The background to the fight for effective regulatory legislation in Wisconsin in the first decade of the twentieth century points up a weakness evident in many studies of reform movements. In the development of such a crusade, often a glamorous figure appears at an opportune moment and seems to personify the reform itself with his dynamic self-assurance. Too often looking at the success of the movement, scholars forget that once there was a time when the reform was an unpopular idea being promoted by a small cadre of dedicated men, or even one man, who only in moments of great optimism could hope that some day the crusade would achieve victory. And seldom do they note how often the men present for the final institutionalization of the issue were nowhere to be seen in the dark days when the issue was neither popular nor politically viable.

A case in point is the movement for railroad regulation in Wisconsin and the career of Robert M. La Follette. In 1905 when a railroad regulation measure, which remains the basic legislation to this day, was finally passed, the young Madison lawyer was the governor of the state. In 1903 and 1904 he had fought with a self-conscious gallantry to pass a regulation law which would once and for all make the common carriers subject to the will of the state. On passage of the bill he would proclaim it a great victory for the people—and for his administration—and later, in his *Autobiography*, he would take almost total credit for the development of the issue and its enactment into law. In the aftermath all would be impressed with the courage and fortitude of the man and the achievements of "his administration," while forgetting to search

---

[76] *Milwaukee Free Press,* July 31, 1903.
[77] Johnson to La Follette, December 30, 1902, in the La Follette Papers.

for the real roots of the issue he helped formalize into law and for the real heroes, who did their work when times were less propitious and credit less likely to come.

There is, in a sense, an inevitability about such distortions if the roots of a reform lie primarily in the thinking of forward-looking men, for often few clues are left by which such musings can be traced. In the case of railroad regulation in Wisconsin, however, no such excuse can serve, for long before La Follette became interested in it this idea was introduced into the political realm and attempts were made to institutionalize it. The true irony of Wisconsin railroad regulation is not that La Follette took an old idea and dressed it up as his own, but that he hitched a ride on a reform train which stretched far into the past, then made it look like he was the engineer.

The Price of Indecision

2 La Follette's commitment to the issue of railroad regulation on the eve of the 1903 legislative session confronted him with a host of new problems. Having long neglected this area of reform, he lacked the basic tools to deal with the question in the kind of depth and detail required for adequate leadership. More important, although he boasted a large personal and political following, he could not be sure how much of this support would be forthcoming for the new economic reform he had embraced. As a result, while the governor immediately became the nominal leader of the regulation crusade in 1903, the Milwaukee group remained an essential part of the campaign, for it involved the men with information and the semblance of a political organization.

In the early days of January the governor set about acquiring the knowledge and the support necessary for success. The problem of information was most easily dealt with. James A. Frear, who had helped in the 1889 campaign, as well as Albert Hall and the Chamber of Commerce men were available with advice about the dimensions of possible solutions of the regulation question in Wisconsin.[1] It would take time, but the governor could confidently expect to master the theoretical aspects of the regulation issue.

More difficult was the problem of rallying political support, for here was an area where the longtime reformers had failed and

---

[1] James A. Frear to La Follette, December 22, 1902, in the La Follette Papers.

27

where La Follette had a reputation for success. Whereas Albert
Hall by necessity had been satisfied to live on the edge of the
legislative stage gathering support for his unpopular cause from
those fugitive lawmakers who had strong commitments to reform,
La Follette could not settle for this sort of haphazard organization
if he hoped to succeed. At the outset, however, he had to be content
to work with a core of legislative leadership which, largely due to
the Milwaukee group, was already committed to the regulation
cause in 1903. Frank A. Cady, an influential assemblyman from
Grand Rapids, who had voted against the 1901 Hall bill, promised
to lead the regulation fight in the lower house, while ambitious
Irvine Lenroot, in search of the speakership of the assembly, also
showed interest in the issue. Frear, under pressure from La Follette
and Hall, agreed to assume a leading role as a member of the
assembly committee on railroads. In the senate, always a stumbling
block for reform causes, hopes lay with Lieutenant Governor James
O. Davidson, the presiding officer, a man with a record of support
for railroad regulation. Perhaps he could use his power and position
to insure the appointment of a senate committee on railroads which
would be sympathetic to a regulation plan.[2]

At the outset able advisers and a core of a strongly committed
legislative leadership existed for the governor to draw upon. His
problem was to use these means to sway the rank and file.

With the aid of his advisers, who deluged him with detailed rate
tables and other information which made a strong case for regulatory legislation in Wisconsin, La Follette composed his inaugural
message to the legislature featuring the issue of regulation. Even
while he conferred with Thomas H. Gill, a longtime supporter and
chief counsel for the Wisconsin Central Railroad, about repayment
of a loan and the draining of a mine they had invested in jointly,[3]
the governor formulated final plans for an all-out attack on the
railroads of the state.

When Robert La Follette had anything at all to say he was
long-winded, and on January 15, 1903, the governor had a new

[2] George H. D. Johnson to La Follette, December 30, 1902, in the La
Follette Papers; Frear, *Forty Years of Progressive Public Service*, 34.
[3] La Follette to Gill, January 1, 1903; Gill to Johnson, February 9, 1903,
both in the La Follette Papers.

cause to plead. The result was the longest speech "so far in state history."[4] Aided by twenty-one complex rate tables, the fruits of the union between the Milwaukee Chamber of Commerce reformers and La Follette's personal staff, the governor retold the familiar story of how Wisconsin had long been discriminated against by unregulated carriers while Illinois and Iowa shippers enjoyed the benefits of strict state regulation of railroad rates. Speaking almost autobiographically, La Follette declared, "While it has been commonly understood that the railways of the country have overridden law, and, in a measure, controlled legislation, it is doubtful whether any considerable number of people of Wisconsin have until very recently had any conception of the enormity of the wrong which they have suffered in discriminating rates at the hands of railroads throughout this Commonwealth." Railroad rates, he declared, were "a tax upon the commerce of the country." They affected every man who ever bought or sold anything—and it was time that this tax was more equitably levied in Wisconsin.

The governor proposed two solutions to the problem. Either the legislature could fix by law all maximum transportation charges, or it could appoint a commission to study the situation, and then render a decision establishing reasonable rates within the state. He chose the latter as the more reasonable of these two drastic solutions.[5] In so doing he lined up his forces on the side of strong government intervention in the area of railroad rate making. His mood was belligerent, and his proposals made it inevitable that a bitter fight would follow.

It was no surprise to opponents of regulation to learn that in the 1903 session they would be forced to fight another battle. As early as the latter part of November the venerable E. W. Keyes had seen clouds on the political horizon. "It may be that the session of 1903 will resemble . . . the session of 1874," he warned a La Crosse businessman, "as the public mind seems to be under the impression that the railroads need overhauling."[6] Storm warnings also went

---

[4] Albert O. Barton, *La Follette's Winning of Wisconsin* (Des Moines, 1922), 235.
[5] *Wisconsin State Journal*, January 15, 1903.
[6] Keyes to A. E. Bleekman, November 25, 1902, in the Keyes Letterbooks.

out to the president of the Milwaukee Road that the legislature "will be an ugly lot."[7] Forewarned, the railroads and large manufacturers readied their forces for a more vigorous struggle than usual.

Particularly determined were the chief manufacturers in the state. In 1901 some of their number had been forced to descend on Madison in protest in order to stem a tide which seemed likely to bring regulation to Wisconsin. Certain that such restraints would mean an end to the special privileges they had long enjoyed, they resolved to fight a better organized holding action in 1903 if necessary in order to retain their natural advantages. Hence when, in early January, Frank K. Bull, millionaire president of the J. I. Case Threshing Machine Company of Racine, one of the largest manufacturing concerns in Wisconsin, called a meeting in Milwaukee for the purpose of "protecting and furthering the interests of every branch of manufacturing in the state," nearly every substantial manufacturing firm responded. Seventy manufacturers, representing the interests of twenty-six cities and towns, congregated in the Hotel Pfister in Milwaukee where, supported by the messages of many others who were unable to attend, they vowed a fight to the finish against increased taxation for railroads and state railroad regulation.[8] Christened the Wisconsin Manufacturers' Association, this group posed a formidable obstacle to any plans for strict regulation.

Whether the railroads or the large shippers knew yet that the governor planned to take personal charge of the newest regulation fight is uncertain. For Keyes, who at that time was one of the most important political contacts the major railroads had in the state, it was enough that the legislature itself looked like an unfriendly delegation and that "the anti-railroad Ishmaelite," Bacon, was actively trying to gain conservative support for his railroad regulation plan.[9] The election of a more reform-minded legislature in November, 1902, plus the stepped-up activity of the Milwaukee reformers, who carried the powerful *Free Press* with them, was perhaps enough to cause other conservatives to look to their laurels.

[7] Keyes to A. J. Earling, December 10, 1902, in the Keyes Letterbooks.
[8] *Milwaukee Free Press,* January 10, 1903.
[9] Keyes to W. H. Stennett, December 30, 1902, in the Keyes Letterbooks.

After the powerful La Follette threw himself into the fray, their plans and hopes took on a new urgency.

While the governor shocked antiregulation forces into a new sense of urgency, he was by no means prepared in early January to wage a full-scale legislative battle on the issue which he himself had subscribed to for a scant month or so. The cram course he had taken in December had allowed him to speak intelligently about the issue of regulation in his inaugural, but it would not suffice for the more difficult task of law making. An order for six of the most important books on railway regulation started his search for a deeper knowledge of the subject,[10] but more important were his attempts to establish close personal ties with experts on the regulation issue.

The cementing of relations with the Milwaukee group, including a more friendly attitude toward Eliot and the induction of E. P. Bacon himself as a top administrative adviser, proved the key to this process. Not only could they offer much essential advice but by bringing them into the administration's inner circle the governor also linked himself to the many regulation experts who worked with Bacon's Interstate Commerce Law Convention.[11]

Closer ties with the Milwaukee group in turn led La Follette to look toward the west for expert advice on regulation. For years the Wisconsin reform campaign had been built upon comparing abused Wisconsin with well-regulated Iowa, and through the years Bacon had forged strong ties with leading advocates of regulation in Iowa. It was normal, therefore, that when the governor was inducted into the crusade, he too turned there for help. Earlier he had written Governor Albert Cummins regarding his state's law, but Cummins was a scant help beyond the disconcerting observation that the Iowa Commission "at the present time . . . is almost dormant and exercises but a tithe of the influence and authority that it formerly did."[12] (La Follette would conveniently forget this

[10] La Follette to A. D. McClurg Company, January 19, 1903, in the La Follette Letterbooks.
[11] Robert Eliot to La Follette, January 25, 1903, in the La Follette Papers, La Follette to Eliot, January 27, 1903, in the La Follette Letterbooks, Johnson to La Follette, February 11, 1903, in the La Follette Papers.
[12] Albert Cummins to La Follette, February 10, 1903, in the La Follette Papers.

comment which undermined the comparison between regulated Iowa and unregulated Wisconsin, an image he made much of in the next two-and-one-half years.) Contacts made with ex-Governor William Larrabee, Frank Campbell, and Interstate Commerce Commissioner Peter A. Dey, all experts on the Iowa experience, and all apparently friends of the Bacon group, proved of great value, however, since they could appraise the existing legislation and suggest a plan for effective regulation in their sister state.[13]

While the governor accumulated advice and information on regulation, the price he paid was time. After stirring up the sparks of antirailroad feeling in January, La Follette seemed slowly to lose his advantage. "The fact that six weeks are gone with no visible evidence of the issue (beyond Governor La Follette's argument in his message) makes it doubtful if it can become a law this session," noted Amos Wilder, the seasoned editor of the *Wisconsin State Journal*, in mid-February.[14]

It was perhaps in response to such warnings that the La Follette-controlled assembly committee on railroads on March 6 came forth with a preliminary proposal for regulation in Wisconsin, bill 623A. Essentially Albert Hall's 1901 compromise proposal, the measure was clearly conceived simply to offer a basis for beginning legislative debate on the issue of regulation. Three basic issues dominated discussion concerning the establishment of a regulatory commission in Wisconsin: whether a commission should be elected by the people or appointed by the governor, whether the commission should have the right to make up new schedules of rates or simply change rates which were brought to its attention by complaints, and what role special rates would have under a regulatory statute. Bill 623A muddied the waters in all three of these areas.

Skirting the important question of whether an able group of expert commissioners could best be chosen directly by the people or by the governor, the measure called for one elected commis-

---

[13] La Follette to Frank Campbell, February 13, 1903, in the La Follette Letterbooks, Johnson to La Follette, February 17, 1903, in the La Follette Papers, La Follette to William Larrabee, February 21, 1903, in the La Follette Letterbooks, La Follette to Johnson, February 21, 1903, in the La Follette Letterbooks.

[14] *Wisconsin State Journal*, February 17, 1903.

sioner and two appointed by the chief executive. Apparently the
railroads retained the right to make their own rates initially, but
strong prohibitions against any kind of discrimination caused
carriers and shippers to question the extent of their freedom in this
area. Although temporary and indecisive, the bill at last opened up
the matter of regulation for discussion and political maneuvering
in the legislature. With its introduction the first La Follette fight
for railroad regulation in Wisconsin began in earnest.

As opponents of regulation awaited the administration's first plan
implementing the governor's inaugural call for strict regulation,
they were clearly apprehensive. Particularly bothersome to them
was the evidence that La Follette was contemplating embracing
the Iowa regulation plan which called for a commission empowered to establish an entirely new schedule of rates for intrastate
commerce. "If a commission can arbitrarily fix the rates for [freight
and passengers], what is to prevent it from going farther, and by
its own motion control the prices on all commodities of general
use?" asked the *Monroe Sentinel*.[15] *Railway Age*, a spokesman for
the carriers, expressed worry at rumors that the pending Wisconsin
bill "goes much further than the framers of the radical Iowa law
thought wise."[16]

The apprehension among antiregulation forces proved a spur to
their organizational efforts. Having early achieved a coalition of
an important segment of their group in the formation of the Wisconsin Manufacturers' Association, they now made constructive
use of the long delay occasioned by the administration's reluctance
to advance a legislative proposal. The introduction of 623A on
March 6 triggered the last alarm. When, in late March, hearings
on the first reform proposal were convened, the fruits of careful
work by opponents quickly became evident.

As hearings opened on March 16, the many-faceted attack
planned by opponents of administration plans began with martial
discipline. Petitions from all points in the state began to flow into
the legislature in opposition to any plans to disrupt the status quo

---

[15] As quoted in the *Milwaukee Sentinel*, February 27, 1903.
[16] *Railway Age*, 35:727 (February 27, 1903).

through railroad regulation.[17] The *Milwaukee Sentinel*, surprisingly reserved and objective during the early months of La Follette's efforts, broke forth with a stinging indictment of the governor's initial plan. Commenting on irascible old Elisha Keyes' prominently displayed letter to the editor linking the 1903 attempt with a similar attempt in 1874 which resulted in disaster, the *Sentinel* charged that the new plan sought to "take over the management of all the railroads." Interestingly enough, the *Sentinel* pointed to the plan for the appointment of two commissioners and the election of the other as the most suspicious of the provisions of the bill. Well aware of the history of regulation struggles in the state, the *Sentinel* asked: "Suppose, for the sake of illustration, that the law in question should be passed, and Governor La Follette should appoint as two of the commissioners A. R. Hall . . . and E. P. Bacon. . . . Does anyone doubt that the history of the state under the Potter law would be repeated?" Branding Hall and Bacon "corporation baiters," the stalwart organ charged that under their leadership "the adjustment of the relations between the transportation companies and the merchants and manufacturers of Wisconsin would be attempted on the theory that might makes right."[18] Although ideology did not serve, the *Sentinel* preferred to keep corporate fortunes in the hands of the people—and out of the grasp of the feared La Follette.

In support of this barrage of well-timed opposition, when the assembly committee on railroads opened its doors and began hearings on the administration bill, over two hundred manufacturers or their representatives flowed in and so packed the hearing room that the proceedings had to be moved to the assembly chamber. In general these large shippers echoed the broad concern expressed by Keyes and the *Sentinel*, that regulation by commission would mean regulation by radical elements, but they stated their complaint in more specific terms. Whether it was the president of the La Crosse Plow Company, the secretary of the Wisconsin Furniture Manufacturers' Association, or a representative of the Milwaukee brewers (the list of those who testified spreadeagled the

[17] *Wisconsin Assembly Journal*, 1903, beginning on 542.
[18] *Milwaukee Sentinel*, March 16, 17, 1903.

state and an impressive section of the state's economy), the message the witnesses brought was the same—the railroads had established a complex structure of special rates under which manufacturing thrived in Wisconsin, and this system could be altered only at their peril. A commission, these men feared, would not or could not tolerate such special tariff schedules.[19]

The rates they referred to were indeed a very important part of the Wisconsin transportation system. Over the years manufacturers and other large shippers who often used the railroads had adjusted their relations with carriers to such an extent that they planned upon various special tariff schedules for the transporting of the bulk of their products to market. Chief among these were concentration rates, transit rates, and commodity rates. Concentration rates benefited industries such as lumbering by allowing materials harvested to be shipped free to a central point if the cargo was then shipped en masse to a single processing point. Large shippers of produce such as wheat could count on transit rates which allowed shipment to a processing point and then on to a terminal market under a single long haul rate rather than two higher local tariffs. Commodity rates, the most important of the special classifications, were granted on a wide range of raw materials essential for manufacturing, and meant that the goods could be shipped to processing points at greatly reduced rates.

The assembly committee quickly got to the core of the apprehension which brought the manufacturers to Madison when Frear asked the president of the La Crosse Plow Company: "Would this bill injure the manufacturers if the commodity rates are preserved?" "No," he replied. "Not if the commodity rates are preserved to competitive points."[20] As if to underline the extreme doubts the group had about this prospect under a regulatory commission, however, Thomas Kearney, representing the Wisconsin Manufacturers' Association, later declared wryly: "If you can get a commission which will leave things as they are no one will object. . . . But the people will not pay $3,600 a year to each of three men to maintain things as they are." Railroads could make special rates

[19] *Wisconsin State Journal*, March 18, April 1, 1903.
[20] *Milwaukee Free Press*, March 18, 1903.

by private contract, he added, but "the legislature has not the power to grant a commission the right to fix one rate for one class and another rate for a different class of shippers."[21]

It was surely no coincidence that when Burton Hansen, general solicitor for the Milwaukee Road, took the stand on behalf of the carriers he echoed the shippers' fears, arguing that the entire structure of special rates would be torn asunder if the bill passed.[22] Railroad men, who had many reasons to fear strong regulation, exploited the argument which they counted on to garner sufficient statewide opposition to the regulation drive. They were cultivating a grass-roots movement of the most exotic variety.

In contrast to the lockstep discipline with which the antiregulation witnesses went through their paces, the administration forces exhibited a continuing lack of decisive leadership which had been evident in the tentative nature of its initial legislative proposal. Unable to summon to its cause the same sort of representative sample of state opinion as opponents had mustered, it settled for a heterogeneous crew of advocates, each of which had a different approach and a different axe to grind.

On hand was Thomas C. Richmond, a Madison lawyer and progressive Democrat, who spoke for no group in the state. (Two years later, seeking more influence as an advocate of regulation, Richmond received permission to speak for the butter makers of Wisconsin by promising to represent them without remuneration.[23]) "Tom's the only man who could throw Bryan back on his rhetorical haunches," remarked the *Wisconsin State Journal*.[24] Unfortunately this oratorical ability was about all the flamboyant Richmond brought to the hearings. While arguing vigorously the right of the state to undertake regulation and hurling charges of wholesale rebating on the part of the state's railroads, Richmond principally succeeded in provoking a near fist fight with the normally mild mannered Burton Hansen. The broad question of the legality of state regulation had been resolved long before 1903. The question

[21] *Ibid.*, March 19, 1903.
[22] *Ibid.*, April 15, 1903.
[23] *Proceedings of Fourth Annual Meeting of the Wisconsin Buttermakers' Association*, 1905, 35.
[24] *Wisconsin State Journal*, July 21, 1903.

now concerned kind and amount, and here Richmond had nothing to offer.[25]

Another principal witness was Frank Hall, onetime Methodist preacher and now a Madison lawyer, whom apparently no one had expected to take a role in the struggle. After seeking an opportunity to speak, Hall began with the startling admission that he had begun to study the question of regulation only two days prior to his appearance. Speaking on behalf of "the people," Hall lashed out at commodity rates as "a delusion and a snare and an instigation of some power that arbitrarily assumes to portion out the kingdoms of the earth, not according to natural laws, but according to their own devices."[26] It is not hard to imagine the consternation of manufacturers, and perhaps administration representatives, as Hall confirmed the worst fears of the opponents of regulation.

In the wake of such testimony, the burden of advocacy fell on E. P. Bacon, who shouldered it manfully if not entirely convincingly. Responding to the charge that the only demand for the measure came from a few grain men in Milwaukee, the eloquent Bacon argued that regulation was primarily for the small men who suffered, as producers and consumers, from exorbitant rates charged by the carriers. The manufacturers who "have been brought here in a senseless panic to oppose the bill" have nothing to fear, he declared, for commodity rates would not be touched by the new measure. The farmer, however, who sent his goods to market where commission men deducted the excessive freight charges from the price they paid, or the consumer who was forced to pay a higher price for the necessities of life because of excess transportation costs needed stronger government regulation. "The state," he argued, "should protect the men who are not able to protect themselves."[27]

Before the committee Neil Brown, a Wausau lawyer representing lumber interests who opposed regulation because of their dependence on the carriers, insisted that the large shippers were the only ones rightfully concerned about railroad rates. Chairman Charles

---

[25] *Ibid.*, April 14, 15, 1903.
[26] *Ibid.*, March 19, 1903; *Milwaukee Free Press*, March 23, 1903.
[27] *Milwaukee Free Press*, April 16, 1903.

W. Gilman, a spokesman for the administration, challenged Brown's claim. "Is not the farmer, who actually pays the freight, a fit person to ask for the passage of this or another law if he believes the legislation is demanded and right?" he asked.[28] Although appropriate in context, Gilman's remark served to point up the essential weakness of the administration's position. Neither the efforts of a disinterested Madison lawyer nor the pleadings of a longtime reformer from Milwaukee could adequately substitute for authentic voices of support from throughout the state. The opposition had summoned to the capital important businessmen, many of whom were prominent politically in their areas. Augmented by a group of ex-political luminaries including ex-Governor Edward Scofield, they presented an impressive argument against any change in the status quo.[29] Aided by a steady flow of petitions from throughout the state pleading "it is wise to let well enough alone,"[30] and by a series of articles in the *Milwaukee Sentinel* in which kingpins in many of the most important economic centers in the state expressed their unyielding opposition to the kind of legislation the La Follette forces proposed,[31] opponents possessed considerable leverage in dealing with impressionable assemblymen.

In contrast the thinness of the pro-La Follette ranks was even more apparent. Disregarding Frank Hall, the *Sentinel* argued that Richmond, Bacon, and two committee men, Gilman and Frear, "may be considered as representing in their persons all of the elements in this state that favor the passage of this particular bill." They dismissed Richmond as a "populist," Bacon as "a grain dealer who is seeking a business advantage," and Frear and Gilman as simply representatives of the governor. Harking back to the lonely efforts of Albert Hall and Bacon in the previous decade, the *Sentinel* declared confidently, "The situation is not changed except that Mr. Hall has dropped out of the fight and Governor La Follette has taken his place."[32]

[28] *Ibid.*, April 15, 1903.
[29] Keyes to Stennett, March 27, 1903, in the Keyes Letterbooks.
[30] See *Milwaukee Free Press*, March 17, 1903, for a typical petition.
[31] *Milwaukee Sentinel*, April 16–18, 1903.
[32] *Ibid.*, March 29, April 13, 16, 1903.

The governor had anticipated for a number of weeks that the administration forces would give the impression of weakness and disunity, and in vain he had done all that was within his power at that late date to counteract such an impression. Galvanized by the impressive show of opposition from large shippers and carriers, in mid-March La Follette had fired off letters to friends asking them to organize *"at once"* prominent supporters of regulation in their areas who could exert strong pressure on assemblymen to support the administration bill.[33] "The work should be done thoroughly to convince the members that there are interests involved other than those represented by the corporation lobby and a few favored patrons of these public service corporations," he declared.[34]

At the same time La Follette sought a better delegation of regulation advocates to appear before the assembly committee. His most fertile source failed, however, for Johnson wrote that his friends thought it too short notice to find a representative attorney to appear and help counter legal arguments, and Johnson himself was unable to find anyone else to appear at the hearings.[35]

By early April, the administration increased its efforts to counter the grass-roots campaigning of the opposition which resulted in a constant flow of antiregulation petitions into the committee and the legislature. Charles Gilman sent form letters throughout the state urging supporters to read an enclosed petition at town meetings or other large gatherings, secure a positive vote, and report the results to their assemblymen.[36]

These strategies, plus a more concerted attempt to obtain favorable publicity for the legislation in the newspapers of the state, all essentially reactions to moves of the opposition, made up the bulk of the administration's efforts to reverse the balance of power on the regulation question. By mid-April the La Follette forces seemed to realize the extent of their failure. Proregulation mail had reached many legislators in considerable quantity and proregula-

---

[33] La Follette to Walter Owen, March 16, 1903, in the La Follette Letterbooks.

[34] La Follette to Johnson, March 16, 1903, in the La Follette Letterbooks.

[35] Johnson to LaFollette, March 19, 1903, in the La Follette Papers.

[36] See copies of form letter from Charles Gilman, April 3, 1903, in the La Follette Papers.

tion petitions from groups throughout the state were introduced daily by compliant solons, but such efforts were clearly inadequate, for in the halls and hearing rooms of the capitol, the antiregulation forces were winning more friends and votes through a vigorous campaign of private pressure and public argumentation.

In view of these developments some reform newspapers were ready to concede the struggle for that session.[37] But the pugnacious governor and his most ardent followers had no intentions of retiring from the field in such a sorry state. In fact, in a very literal sense, the governor had only begun to fight. Because of the haste with which he had embraced the campaign, the governor had never really been able to pull together all the threads of the issue in the early months. His vigorous address in January had basically been broad principles backed by canned documentation furnished him by the Milwaukee group, and the first administration bill had simply been a rehashing of earlier efforts.

After the initial legislation was introduced, La Follette sought a measure which would better express his feelings concerning the role of state government in insuring equal public transportation for all. Well-marked copies of the initial effort, bill 623A, in the governor's personal correspondence during late March show his intense interest in transforming the first bill into something to which he could wholeheartedly commit himself.[38] By mid-April, he was prepared to put his characteristic stamp on the regulation struggle by amending 623A.

On the very day of the introduction of the first administration bill, that outspoken old campaigner Robert Eliot submitted a typically tactless but insightful criticism of the initial effort, in which he forecasted both of the basic changes the governor would eventually authorize. Singling out the paragraph banning discrimination or preferential treatment to "any particular description of traffic," the Milwaukee merchant noted that this clause alone had brought "thirty or forty of the leading manufacturers of the state" to Madison in 1901 to protest and was bound to have the same effect again. Although the clause did not in fact prevent com-

[37] *Jefferson County Union*, April 10, 1903.
[38] See folder for March 26–31, 1903, in the La Follette Papers.

modity rates, he urged that the quoted words be stricken out to avoid confusion. At the same time, Eliot pointed out the extreme irony of the clause in the bill, taken from the Iowa law, which declared the present tariffs reasonable and just until changed by the commissioners, in view of the fact that "what we are seeking to attain by this legislation is a material reduction from these excessive, unjust rates."[39]

The events of the next few weeks showed the irascible Eliot to be an able prophet on the special rate issue as manufacturers descended on Madison in much larger numbers than they had in 1901 protesting the intention to abolish commodity rates and other essential rate adjustments. Particularly after Frank Hall had muddied the waters by labeling commodity rates "a delusion and a snare," the administration was forced to take positive action to recoup the tremendous losses of support it had experienced in the business community. The governor embraced an amendment written by Bacon and Eliot which specifically stated that nothing contained in the bill "shall be construed or applied to prevent the granting by railway companies of commodity rates, provided such rates do not discriminate against persons or places."[40] The bar against "discrimination" and "any undue preference or advantage" to persons or locations included in the amendment indicated how grudgingly some of the reformers granted this chance for special rate agreements which might result in the sort of abuses they sought to eliminate.[41]

While apparently taking a step backwards by yielding on the special rate issue, in truth La Follete contemplated a stronger measure. As Eliot had ably pointed out, the initial bill, in granting the basic equity of the existing rate structure, ran directly contrary to the convictions which the governor had expounded on publicly during the early months of 1903. Although such a clause was logical in Iowa, where a set of tariffs had been established under the Iowa law, in Wisconsin it simply meant approval of the railroads' own tariffs. Convinced that the people of Wisconsin would

[39] Eliot to La Follette, March 6, 1903, in the La Follette Papers.
[40] Eliot to La Follette, March 21, 1903, in the La Follette Papers.
[41] See *Wisconsin Assembly Bills*, 1903, Substitute for No. 623A, Section 31.

receive justice only when the rate-making power was wrested from the greedy hand of the carriers and vested in an impartial board representing the public, La Follette sought a stronger remedy.

Advice and precedent supported a stronger stand. The laws of neighboring states, including Iowa, plus most of the earlier regulatory attempts in Wisconsin all provided for a commission which would draw up entirely new schedules of rates which the railroads would be required to follow. Advice from Judge S. H. Cowan of Fort Worth, Texas, a member of Bacon's executive committee of the Interstate Commerce Law Convention and a leading national expert on regulation, also strengthened La Follette's resolve. Cowan argued the conditions of economic life which caused the carriers to desire excessive rates and the shippers to demand unremunerative rates without sufficient competition to allow a fair rate to emerge made it "a grave necessity" that "every community" have "some impartial body to fix by law the rates of freight to be applied, so as to make the same reasonable both as to the carrier and the shipper." Without such a body, he argued, "the theory of the common law that freight rates should be just and reasonable is a mere figment of the imagination."[42] Indications were that the Milwaukee group agreed with Cowan's assessment.

As early as January, George H. D. Johnson had written La Follette that "the principal reason" why a system under which a commission was given authority to fix "either distance tariffs or maximum rates" had not been advocated previously was the "expected opposition of the railroad companies rather than any disapproval of the system itself." Arguing that it now looked as if the carriers might oppose any regulation attempt, he suggested they go ahead and incorporate "the Iowa system."[43] Apparently convinced, like Johnson, that some opposition was inevitable, La Follette advocated a harder approach. "The board shall prepare, as soon as practicable, schedules of reasonable maximum rates for the transportation of passengers and property between the various stations on the lines of the several railroads within this state" began a radically amended section 24 of the new bill.[44]

[42] *Milwaukee Free Press,* March 17, 1903.
[43] Johnson to La Follette, January 9, 1903 in the La Follette Papers.
[44] *Wisconsin Assembly Bills,* 1903, Substitute for No. 623A.

Armed this time with a bill which he had personally helped draft, La Follette looked for a way to initiate this new phase of the regulation crusade. Perhaps the issue could still be won if the urgency of passing such a bill could be dramatized in some way. The aging Albert Hall suggested a means to execute the reversal of form. Noting that Minnesota was currently collecting additional license fees from the railroads after an investigation which showed that the railroads had failed to report earnings which they had returned to shippers in the form of rebates, Hall argued: "If Minnesota is collecting license fees on earnings that were rebates Wisconsin can. . . . We are entitled to a Million dollars."[45] La Follette took an immediate interest and received more information from Hall, along with urgings to put the matter before the legislature.[46] Seeing this new approach as a fine way of dramatizing the need for closer scrutiny of railroad affairs, La Follette set about composing a message implementing Hall's suggestion.

The problem now was timing. Having hit upon an idea which might swing the balance in favor of regulation, the governor sought the optimum time to launch the new assault. After last minute consultations with Bacon and Johnson, La Follette took the fight to the legislature on April 24, knowing that the assembly's committee on railroads stood ready to introduce the more vigorous substitute bill on the heels of his speech. Thus the crucial last week began.

The tactic adopted by La Follette seemed to be a surprise to his foes who had expected a new attack from the executive mansion, but not of this variety. Completely ignoring the commission issue, in a special message to the lower house La Follette asked the legislature to authorize the state bank examiner to make a careful examination of the books of the railroads to see if they were paying their full share of license fees. Minnesota, he noted, had found the carriers remiss and chances were very good that their conduct was no more ethical in Wisconsin.[47]

The effort was well-timed for, in that year of Elkins Act agitation when everyone decried the evils of rebating, the inference

---

[45] Hall to La Follette, March 25, 1903, in the La Follette Papers.
[46] Hall to La Follette, April 15, 1903, in the La Follette Papers.
[47] *Wisconsin State Journal*, April 24, 1903.

that the railroads, as well as the shippers, were using the system to their advantage was a serious indictment. Even the violently anti-La Follette *Milwaukee Sentinel* had to yield to the governor's demand, admitting that the combination of Minnesota evidence and the firm antirebate position of the Republican party made it imperative that the examination the governor requested be made.[48] When Chairman Gilman reported out the substitute railroad commission bill shortly after the governor's address was heard, it seemed to see the light of day in a more congenial and receptive atmosphere.

Since a vote on the new measure was slated for Thursday, April 30, a long strenuous week followed for both sides, for neither could afford to rest on its laurels. Encouraged by the approval given to his first effort, La Follette planned a second assault, this time addressing himself directly to the major issue at hand. Amazed by the apparent gains made by the administration, the antirailroad forces sent out a distress call for a new show of grass-roots opposition.

The final drive for votes began on April 28, when the governor, in his second special message within five days, leveled a scathing attack on the "railroad lobbyists" who sought to retain their own privileged positions without thought for the small man by opposing adequate government control of freight rates. Proclaiming that an increase in taxes would surely mean an increase in freight rates, he demanded that a commission be authorized with the power to set maximum rates, in order to impel the carriers to bear the new burden themselves and to redress the balance which saw the Wisconsin shippers paying more than Iowa and Illinois men. Even the shippers who were getting rebates could expect a better deal under commission rule, he declared.[49]

The antiregulation shippers, however, were having none of this. Back they came to Madison determined to quell this last-ditch attempt by the administration. The senate chamber had scarcely been emptied for the day on April 29 before 151 business representatives, one representing 165 manufacturers from Sheboygan

[48] *Milwaukee Sentinel,* April 27, 1903.
[49] *Wisconsin State Journal,* April 29, 1903.

and others claiming to speak for large blocks of manufacturing interests, filed into the chamber and adopted a carefully worded protest to the assembly "on behalf of Wisconsin manufacturers and businessmen against the passage of the railway commission bill." They had resolved to make their stand against the bill before the administration-controlled lower house in an attempt to choke off the bill even before it reached the more friendly senate. They declared,

> The producers of Wisconsin have, after many years of labor and effort, succeeded in bringing about the adoption by the railroad companies of the state of such commodity, group, and concentration rates as are best fitted to develop their business and promote the growth of the state. We believe that any attempt to disturb this system of transportation rates will unsettle the business affairs of the state, endanger investment, and interfere with the development of our industries.

The framers of 623A and its amendments did not understand or appreciate the importance of special rates in the state, the group charged. Nor did the amended version which specifically approved the continuation of special rate structures suffice. "A mere blind, a legal delusion," it labeled the provision referring to these rates, for "how can the same rate be made from two points at different distances from a common center or market under an act which prohibits the granting of any preference or advantage to one locality over another?" Such an effort to legalize commodity rates and at the same time prohibit discrimination between localities and commodities "illustrates the folly of attempting to regulate the transportation business of the state by the hard and fast rule of the law," they argued.

> This is not an Iowa question or an Illinois question, or a political question. It is a Wisconsin business question . . . and our experience in supplying the markets of the other states where railroad rates are established by law convinces us that the rates in this state are more equitably adjusted, and that all interests are better served than where the rates are fixed by railroad commissions.[50]

⁰ *Milwaukee Sentinel,* April 30, 1903.

It did not take long the following day to learn who had won the war of words. When Gilman moved that the assembly consider 623A, the motion was rejected 43–50, with seven members not voting. Apparently hopeful of avoiding an all-out defeat, administration Assemblyman E. E. Le Roy proposed an amendment which would result in a referendum on the question in April of 1904. This time it was 56 against, 37 for, and 3 not voting. When the administrative substitute bill was balloted upon, it was simply for the record—59 against, 34 for, and 3 not voting. The La Follette forces had been dealt a stunning blow in their stronghold, with many a "progressive" assemblyman abandoning the cause under heavy pressure from their business constituents.[51]

While elated opponents of regulation kept the Park Hotel bar open after hours and Emanuel L. Philipp, leader of the antiadministration forces on the regulation issue, led the group in singing "In the Good Old Summer Time,"[52] La Follette and his colleagues had to face up to a demoralizing defeat. La Follette would later argue that he did not "expect" the regulation bill to pass in 1903. "I hoped to make such a hot fight for regulation that before the session was over the railroad lobby would be most happy to let our taxation bill go through, if thereby they could prevent the enactment of a law creating a commission to regulate them," he declared.[53]

While La Follette's statement perhaps contains a kernel of truth, its oversimplifications smack of convenient hindsight. Unquestionably the governor entertained doubts that, in view of his late start, he could succeed in marshalling sufficient support for the issue, but because he did not feel assured of triumph did not preclude him from making an all-out effort to win this fight in 1903. As early as March 16, before the hearings on the regulation bill had begun, as prejudiced a source as the *Milwaukee Free Press* freely admitted that "the railroad lobby," as it called it, had already conceded the ad valorem issue and was intent on defeating regulation. So in the last decisive six weeks of activity the struggle was by no means a diversionary tactic, but a genuine confrontation.

[51] *Wisconsin Assembly Journal*, 1903, pp. 1002, 1006, 1007.
[52] *Milwaukee Free Press*, May 1, 1903.
[53] La Follette, *Autobiography*, 280.

In the aftermath of the assembly defeat of the regulation bill, Elisha Keyes quipped: "It is an old saying that Providence is generally on the side of the heaviest battalions. In this fight our battalions were the stronger, and therefore Providence must have been on our side."[54] It was in the fight for the loyalties of the legislative battalions that La Follette lost this initial regulation battle. In retrospect two major factors seem to have swung the balance against the administration. The first fatal decision was made in the summer of 1902 when La Follette refused to make regulation a part of his fall campaign. Having failed to plead the issue in the previous campaign, the administration's claim that "the people" demanded regulation had a hollow ring to it. In the final days of decision impressionable assemblymen could see no evidence that their constituents had expressed themselves positively on this issue. Assemblyman Joseph M. Cowling, in the final debate before the fateful April 30 vote, noted, "With control of that convention, with the introduction of planks on taxation and primary election, if the matter had been agitated at that time and demand had existed and was so general as we are being led to believe here, certainly a plank on freight rates could have been injected into that platform as well as the two which were. We heard nothing about it; the people have not studied the matter in detail. . . ."[55]

Left without any sort of popular mandate to guide them, some of the most loyal administration assemblymen fell prey to the demands of influential business interests who demanded that they reject the bill as dangerous and ill-conceived. Having failed to exploit the issue in the fall, the the governor was unable, partly because of inexperience and indecision, to launch a belated campaign for support which would counter this impressive body of well-co-ordinated opinion. As a result, down to the final day of voting only one unified voice was apparent and that opposed the governor's plan. "The businessmen of my district are protesting against the bill, and telling me personally and by letter to be against it. How can I do otherwise?" asked one legislator. Others pleaded the same case, arguing that although they supported regu-

[54] Keys to Roswell Miller, May 2, 1903, in the Keyes Letterbooks.
[55] *Milwaukee Sentinel*, May 1, 1903.

lation, they could not stand up against the concerted pressure of the business interests in their districts. Among them was the down-hearted Frank Cady who, after early committing himself to leading the regulation fight, became the opposition's prize catch under heavy pressure from the large manufacturing interests of his district.[56]

The governor's job was now clear. If he wished to triumph in the struggle for regulation, he would have to marshal enough popular support to drown out the voice of special interest with demands of the people for a better kind of justice in transportation rates. The only other alternatives were compromise or defeat.

[56] *Wisconsin State Journal,* May 1, 2, 1903.

The Politics of Re-election

3 The assembly defeat of the administration's regulation measure left La Follette in an awkward position indeed. Having borne the humiliation of finding his newest reform scheme unacceptable to the body which he claimed to control, he stood at an important juncture in his political career with his reputation as an effective reform leader seriously in question. He had succeeded in pushing through an ad valorem taxation bill in 1903 which reshaped Wisconsin's tax system, but he had failed to win a clear victory in either of the two other legs of his tripod of reform. The direct primary bill, an issue in which the governor had been interested for a much longer time than railroad regulation, had been put off by a legislative compromise which called for a referendum on the issue in November, 1904. The regulation measure had been roundly defeated in that bastion of progressive politics, the assembly. Nearing the close of the 1903 legislative session, the last to be held during La Follette's second term as governor, the chief executive faced the unsavory prospect of an abbreviated and none-too-successful political career if he abided by a well-established state tradition and retired as governor at the end of that term.

To a less ambitious and industrious man this combination of circumstances and precedents might have seemed overwhelming, but to La Follette they simply seemed to demand a new and more vigorous approach. In search of higher political goals, the governor conspired to use the events in such a way as to generate the demand

49

that he break precedent, secure another gubernatorial term, and complete the reform program he espoused. The eighteen months stretching from May, 1903, through November, 1904, showed La Follette at his best as a master politician and popular leader.

In May of 1903, as the Wisconsin legislature moved toward adjournment, La Follette began a new phase of his crusade for strict railroad regulation. Having failed to put through such a measure primarily because of little evidence of grass-roots support, the governor began immediately a campaign to reshape the thinking of Wisconsin people of all persuasions in order to make the demand for regulatory legislation in 1905 compelling and convincing and his own re-election in 1904 a necessity. As a first step in this new campaign La Follette sought some evidence of legislative interest in the regulation issue upon which to build this new campaign and help erase some of the damage done by the decisive assembly rebuff.

"This bill is to be the chief card of the campaign," noted the perceptive *Wisconsin State Journal* on the eve of the fatal April 30 assembly vote. "If the administration's own Assembly refuses it, its value as an issue will be greatly discredited."[1] Once such a rejection had occurred, La Follette and his colleagues could only grope for ways to make the best of a bad situation. While the *Free Press* weakly observed that the vote showed the "independence" of the assembly and argued that "had the bill been better understood" the vote would have been different,[2] the administration sought means of escaping the political dilemma in which it found itself.

Some, particularly the far-sighted and battle-hardened E. P. Bacon, had perceived even before the stunning defeat of the rate bill that the administration ought to have a viable alternative if the main plan failed. Hence on the day after the defeat the Milwaukee reformer presented to La Follette a completely new bill for the governor to consider. Reflecting the practical bent of its framer, the bill was an Elkins-like antirebate measure altered to fit the state situation. Noting the persistent denials on the part of railroads and manufacturers that they gave or received rebates and the

---

[1] *Wisconsin State Journal*, April 27, 1903.
[2] *Milwaukee Free Press*, May 3, 4, 1903.

advocacy of such a measure by the antiadministration *Milwaukee Sentinel,* Bacon argued that "a bill of this character will be likely to pass both branches of the legislature with very little, if any, opposition."[3]

Although such a plan appealed to men like Bacon who were primarily interested in concrete economic gains in the area of regulation, La Follette had different priorities. He had to rebuild his coalition and his prestige. For these purposes the Bacon plan, designed to appeal to a broad spectrum in order to achieve a small victory, would not suffice. The ambitious governor needed not a small victory in 1903 but a large victory in November, 1904.

In search of a better way to dramatize his continuing distrust of the railroads, the governor tried a new twist to an old argument. La Follette had based his initial efforts to drum up support for regulation on the allegation that if the railroads were made to pay their proper share of state taxes, they would simply pass the added burden on to their patrons in the form of higher rates. This argument, never really abandoned, was now revived and updated with additional "information."

On May 7 the governor sent another special message to the legislature setting forth his new proposal. Noting that for the first time coal dealers, bidding for contracts to stock the state institutions for the next year, had included a provision in which they reserved the right to raise their price during the year if freight transportation costs went up, La Follette charged that this was clear proof that the railroads intended to raise coal rates if and when their taxes were increased. And, he added, "we may be certain that advances made at this time are not to be confined to coal rates, but will extend to all classes of freight, where the same does not affect favored shippers."[4] To combat this inevitability, La Follette demanded the passage of a measure to prohibit any increase in railroad rates in force June 15, 1902.

It is extremely unlikely that the new clause in the coal bids had such sinister roots. Such riders, which allowed for adjustments up or *down,* were common in adjoining states and were in full accord

---

[3] Bacon to La Follette, May 1, 1903, in the La Follette Papers.

[4] *Wisconsin State Journal,* May 8, 1903.

with an Interstate Commerce Commission ruling that all freight rates were subject to change on ten days' notice. Shippers from outside the state bidding for the Wisconsin contracts had also added the clause, although they would not be affected in the least by changes in intrastate rates. Beyond this, it was highly unlikely that the railroads would knowingly choose to antagonize the Wisconsin state government at this time. As the *Milwaukee Sentinel* argued, "Should the managers of the railroads doing business in Wisconsin contemplate advancing their freight rates at this time of anti-corporation agitation, when charges had been iterated and reiterated that the rates already are too high, they would thereby qualify themselves for admission to the home for the feeble minded."[5]

Most important, however, it is doubtful that the railroads even anticipated large losses from the new form of taxation which they would need to recoup in some other fashion. Publicly and privately, important railroad executives had expressed confidence that the ad valorem tax system would not add significantly to their taxes. President A. J. Earling of the Milwaukee Road in a public statement asserted how pleased he was with the new law, and Roswell Miller, chairman of the board of the Milwaukee Road, had earlier voiced the same sentiment privately. "I do not know how it will come out," he had commented, "but if it is adopted and works fairly I am satisfied we will pay less taxes than we pay now, because I believe railroads are the sole interests in the State of Wisconsin that pay full taxes."[6] The addition of this clause in the bids for coal contracts appears to have been a routine change in business procedures rather than the first overt act in the perpetration of a conspiracy. While it may have stemmed from the instability of the rate system brought on in part by the widespread cries for stricter regulation, there is no evidence that the carriers had proclaimed their intentions to raise coal rates to defray higher taxes.

In spite of the underlying weaknesses in La Follette's newest appeal, it struck a responsive note, for the governor had warned of

[5] *Milwaukee Sentinel,* May 15, 1903.

[6] *Ibid.,* May 13, 1903; Roswell Miller to Keyes, May 4, 1903, in the Keyes Papers.

such a railroad plan for some time. "It has long been thought by most everybody that any extra money the state takes from the railroad corporations in taxes will be recouped in increased charges for freight," noted the moderate *Wisconsin State Journal*.[7] By resolving to prevent such an eventuality, La Follette enlisted the support of many who suspected his more extensive regulation plans.

With this new tool the governor won back the assembly to his side, for it quickly approved the new measure. The senate committee on railroads, however, wasted no time in exposing the many weaknesses in the bill. It noted, in addition to some of the contradictions mentioned above, that the rates operative on June 15, 1902, were totally unsatisfactory to some shippers because of a temporary rise in charges which had taken place around that time. Furthermore, it declared, "An inflexible, maximum rate, founded upon conditions as they existed June 15th, 1902 or any other specified date, would tend to hamper the shippers of this state in competition with those of adjoining states, by preventing the proper adjustment between railroad companies and shippers to meet changed conditions."[8] The senate, following the committee's lead, defeated the measure 20 to 10.

In spite of the senate rejection, La Follette had won a partial victory. "There is no shadow of doubt . . . that the governor wants to force the branch of the legislature of which he is reputed to have had control to go on record in some manner in favor of further state regulation of transportation," declared the *Sentinel* at the outset of the struggle.[9] And this was undeniably the case. In subsequent campaigning La Follette would conveniently feature this vote by the upper house as proof that the corrupt, corporation-dominated senate was the major obstacle to the achievement of more equitable regulation. In this manner he conveniently downgraded the defeat he had suffered in the lower house on the major regulation effort of that session.

La Follette achieved one lesser victory for regulation before the

---

[7] *Wisconsin State Journal,* May 13, 1903.
[8] *Wisconsin Senate Journal,* 1903, Special Report of Committee on Railroads, 1138–1139.
[9] *Milwaukee Sentinel,* May 9, 1903.

1903 legislature adjourned, although the circumstances surrounding it gave it the flavor of another rebuff. Having failed to secure the regulatory measures which he most desired, in the final weeks of the session the governor resurrected his appeal for an investigation to determine whether or not the railroads were reporting all of their gross earnings for tax purposes. In support of his April appeal a bill had been introduced calling for the formation of a three-man commission composed of the attorney general, railroad commissioner, and state bank examiner to investigate the matter. In those desperate days toward the end of the session when it was "any port in a storm" from the administration's standpoint, the measure was dragged out of committee and passed by the assembly. Once again, however, in the senate the measure experienced more difficulty. When reported out of the committee on assessment and collection of taxes, which was chaired by John M. Whitehead, an archenemy of La Follette, the bill had been significantly altered. Arguing that the railroad commissioner had sufficient power to handle all railroad grievances and should be given sole responsibility for such an investigation, the committee amended the measure to put sole investigatory responsibility on the railroad commissioner.[10] The measure passed.

In the 17 to 8 vote which approved the measure, the majority was made up largely of hard core anti-La Follette men, while senators like George B. Hudnall, James J. McGillivray, Oliver G. Munson, George Wylie, and Herman C. Wipperman, all strong La Follette supporters, were among the eight dissenters.[11] Apparently, in taking the power of investigation away from the pro-La Follette attorney general and state bank examiner and giving it to John O. Thomas, the able but politically ambivalent railroad commissioner, the senate had frightened the administration supporters. Fearing a plot against reform by stalwart forces, they opposed the amended measure.

The La Follette forces in the assembly, faced with a *fait accompli,* made the best of a bad situation by approving the amended senate measure. Subsequently the governor would take full credit for the

[10] *Wisconsin Senate Journal,* 1903, pp. 1216–1218.
[11] *Ibid.,* 1261.

measure and use information gleaned from the investigation to good advantage in his next campaign. In truth, however, the anti-La Follette forces had furnished the impetus to pass the measure while La Follette men bridled at the changes made by the stalwart senate committee.

Albert Barton relates that at the close of the legislative session, a group of La Follette supporters came to the governor's office at two o'clock in the morning where the governor was busily signing bills prior to leaving on a 4 A.M. train to begin a lecture tour. Approaching George Wylie, one of his most loyal supporters, the governor threw his arms around his neck and exclaimed: "Well, we didn't get all we wanted, but we did pretty well, and we have enough left over for another campaign."[12]

The statement aptly expresses how the eternally optimistic Robert La Follette saw circumstances in the late spring of 1903. Although his many efforts to achieve some sort of clearcut legislative success in the area of regulation had all gone awry, he still had an issue around which to build a new campaign. Because railroad regulation promised economic gains for voters throughout the state, the governor could anticipate even greater response to this new appeal than he had received from crusades built on tax reform or the direct primary if only he could bring the urgency of the issue home to the voters.

Throwing down the gauntlet, *Railway Age,* a leading spokesman for railroad interests, commented smugly in mid-May that it had been evident even to the pro-administration assembly that "the proposed rate commission was opposed by all classes of shippers throughout the State, excepting certain grain handlers in one city."[13] The governor's future depended on his ability to build a broader base of appeal for the sort of regulatory measure he so fervently desired.

Having failed to center the investigation of railroad earnings in a committee which he could trust, in May La Follette replaced the deputy railroad commissioner with John M. Winterbotham, a junior member of the governor's law firm, who could be counted

---

[12] Barton, *La Follette's Winning of Wisconsin,* 262.
[13] *Railway Age,* 35:856 (May 15, 1903).

on to funnel helpful information to the governor. This personnel change spotlighted a renewed effort by the administration to open all possible channels of information concerning railroad abuses for use in a new phase of the governor's railroad regulation campaign. While the office of the railroad commissioner would prove a major clearing house for statistical data concerning the railroads, the job of processing and organizing such information remained with the cadre of Milwaukee merchants headed by Bacon, Johnson, and Eliot. Throughout the summer La Follette consulted with them and received numerous letters with pertinent information concerning traffic abuses in the particular areas through which he traveled, complete with the familiar tables of figures which he would use to drive his point home. When the economies of rate comparison became particularly complex, personal assistance was available to the governor to make the data understood clearly.[14]

With such a wealth of information and analysis available to them, La Follette and his political colleagues confidently undertook a hard-driving offensive against the railroads and their alleged compatriots, "the corporations." The administration sent printed information to important political figures of both parties throughout the state presenting the case for further regulation.[15] C. W Gilman, chairman of the assembly committee on railroads, wrote an impressive plea for regulation in the pro-La Follette *Milwaukee Free Press* which marked the beginning of a concerted effort by the Milwaukee reform paper to inform the public of the penalties Wisconsin was paying for the lack of sufficient railroad regulation. Whether publicizing Minnesota Commission action ("What a Freight Commission does in one state"), or publishing one of a long series of tables comparing freight rates from some small Wisconsin hamlet to Milwaukee with rates for a comparable distance in Iowa ("What does Dartford think about it"), the subject of rate regulation dominated the *Free Press* throughout the latter half of 1903.[16]

[14] Claude A. Tupper to La Follette, September 5, 1905, in the La Follette Papers
[15] James A. Frear to J. J. Hannan, June 23, 1903, in the La Follette Papers
[16] *Milwaukee Free Press,* June 21, 27, September 1, 1903.

The dissemination of printed information on regulation was auxiliary to the major flow of events in 1903, however, for the ubiquitous La Follette on a purposeful lecture tour commanded the spotlight. First in Chautauqua addresses and later on the stump at county fairs where Secretary of State Walter Houser aided him on occasion, La Follette hammered out a new, more pervasive theory of the importance of rate regulation.

After a stirring inaugural of the new crusade in a Chautauqua address in Lake Champlain, New York, in which the governor condemned "the overbalancing control of city, state and national legislatures, by the wealth and power of public service corporations" as "the greatest danger menacing republican institutions today,"[17] the orator returned to his home state to cultivate support by elaborating on this theme.

Robert La Follette prided himself on being the friend of the small man, particularly the small farmer. The governor, who was most effective on rural platforms and most at home among farm people, considered his control of the rural vote the key to his continuing political success. In the crisis time of 1903, therefore, the compact little orator chose to share programs with plow horse races and speak from the backs of hay wagons in an effort to increase grass-roots support for himself and his new issue.

Although often asserting that the railroads planned to recoup their tax losses through higher rates and employing the subtle distortion of blaming the state senate for the defeat of regulation, the governor featured a new sort of attack on the common carriers. He charged the railroads with reducing the value of farm property in Wisconsin. His effort at the Langlade County fair in Antigo was typical. After reciting in detail the number of acres in the county planted to oats and the number of bushels harvested, La Follette argued: "This is an average of 31 bushels to each acre. As it costs you 1.23 cents per bushel more to produce and market your oats here, on account of exorbitant freight rates than it does in Iowa, your loss from this source amounts to over 38 cents per acre." Declaring that the lower profits reduced the value of the land to

[17] *Ibid.*, July 19, 1903.

a corresponding degree, he concluded that the acreage of the county was worth $40,239 less than it ought to be. This, he proclaimed, was the tax the farmer was forced to pay to the railroads in the form of exorbitant rates—more taxes than he paid to government on the same land.[18]

Repeating this performance with appropriate statistical alterations throughout the state, La Follette argued regulation by commission was the only possible way to bring justice to the farmer. "Wisconsin," he argued, "is far behind its surrounding states. . . . Many other states regulate the rates, and in every [case] such regulation has resulted in more favorable conditions to the shipper."[19] Never losing sight of his personal objective, the governor's pledge at Chippewa Falls was echoed on many occasions: "It matters not what the future has in store, it matters not how many defeats it may bring, there is one man in the state who will continue this fight until this question is settled and until all get a fair deal from the railroad corporations."[20]

Quite naturally the opponents of La Follette and his regulation schemes fought back in the face of such virulent attacks. Led by Emanuel Philipp, they countered the figures used by the administration with other rate comparison tables which they circulated throughout the state in sympathetic newspapers. Their accounts showed that in fact Wisconsin rates were lower than those in Iowa in the area where it really counted, the cost of getting produce to market.[21] Insofar as they dealt primarily with interstate rates when they compared costs for equal distances (Fond du Lac, Wisconsin, to Chicago versus Low Moor, Iowa, to Chicago, etc.),[22] they did not meet La Follette's argument at all, for he was considering rates under the control of the Iowa commission in contrast to those in unregulated Wisconsin. Still the other side of the question was kept before the public. A leading railway journal also took up the cudgels, arguing that La Follette proved nothing until he revealed

---

[18] *Ibid.*, September 9, 1903.
[19] *Ibid.*, September 3, 1903.
[20] *Ibid.*, September 19, 1903.
[21] Philipp, *Political Reform in Wisconsin,* 227
[22] Philipp to John Hicks, October 8, 1903, in the Emanuel L. Philipp Papers.

more clearly how the average value of farm lands in Wisconsin compared with other states and whether in and of itself, the Wisconsin roads were making higher profits than were warranted.[23]

Conspicuously absent from these rebuttals was any condemnation of the idea of regulation by commission. Even while fighting relentlessly against the regulation plan the administration submitted to the 1903 legislature, opponents had been careful not to oppose all kinds of regulation. Instead they focused upon the dangerous elements of the particular measure La Follette was promoting. Speaking very critically in early September, 1903, the *Wisconsin State Journal* commented: "The only new thing the governor offers is a railroad commission. Most everyone will accept a railroad commission."

Although a bit exaggerated, the *Journal's* comment summed up the dilemma facing the governor's opponents. Aware that many who opposed La Follette tacitly favored some sort of check upon the activities of the railroads and equally aware of the unyielding opposition to strict control by a large number of business interests, particularly manufacturers, opponents sought a middle ground by confining their fire to the methods employed by La Follette in arguing for a strong regulation. Commenting on the campaign, Elisha Keyes advised United States Senator John C. Spooner to ignore the issue of a regulatory commission while campaigning for the stalwart wing "until we are compelled to consider [it]. I do this because I know that it will save our campaign and our candidate from considerable embarassment [*sic*]."[25]

The dilemma facing those who sought to contest La Follette on the regulation issue was well expressed in a University of Wisconsin debate in December, 1903. The question was phrased: "Resolved, that the state of Wisconsin should enact a law providing for the appointment of a commission to fix maximum reasonable freight rates on all articles whose shipping point and destination lies within the state." The N. O. Whitney club, taking the negative, won the debate by arguing that although it did not object to a commission

[23] *Railway World*, 29:1083 (September 19, 1903).
[24] *Wisconsin State Journal*, September 5, 1903.
[25] Keyes to Spooner, November 15, 1903, in the Keyes Letterbooks.

with the power to review rates, it objected to any commission empowered to "fix" rates initially.[26] None could profitably oppose all kinds of regulation by the end of 1903.

Faced with the necessity of separating the La Follette regulation program from the larger issue, the efforts of the opposition floundered. "I am somewhat pessimistic about the warfare with lafollette [sic]," commented the chairman of the board of the Milwaukee Road. "He seems to be pretty strongly entrenched with the people."[27]

In December of 1903 the railroads of Wisconsin issued new schedules of freight rates, with considerable reductions in some areas. Conspicuously lower were the rates on coal, the commodity around which La Follette had centered his fight for a rate ceiling the previous spring. Reformers soon argued that the governor was directly responsible for the rate reductions and that every speech La Follette had made during 1903 was therefore worth "many thousands of dollars" to the people.[28] Since the new schedules were initiated in the same month in which the railroads discussed ways of economizing on operations in order to survive financially "harder times this winter than they have experienced in decades," the reduction indeed must have stemmed from a strong feeling of urgency.[29] "It is supposed," observed the astute Wisconsin State Journal, "that the reductions will have a political bearing and upset the force of the comparison put out by the administration. When in discussion one man quotes an apparent injustice, the other fellow can reply 'old rates; not new.' "[30] The pessimism of the railroad men seems to have spurred concrete measures to undercut the new administration program.

When La Follette officially began campaigning for the 1904 election at the end of January, he could look back on an apparently successful round of public appearances in the latter part of 1903. Although he had no concrete way of measuring the gains he had

[26] Wisconsin State Journal, December 5, 1903.
[27] Roswell Miller to Keyes, December 3, 1903, in the Keyes Papers.
[28] Milwaukee Free Press, December 30, 1903; Lower Freight Rates Demanded for Wisconsin (Milwaukee, 1904), 8.
[29] Wisconsin State Journal, December 30, 1903.
[30] Ibid., December 31, 1903.

made, the impressive response to his many efforts at county fairs and other public gatherings most certainly was a tonic to the sensitive governor, while the recent cuts in railroad rates, whether politically inspired or not, were used as another proof of the efficacy of his precampaign oratory.

In 1904 new challenges developed, however, primary among them being the transformation of a well-cultivated antirailroad attitude into votes and support for the governor and a slate of compliant legislators. During the early months of 1904 it would be decided whether or not the governor had enough support to warrant nomination for a third term.

The governor began his final gubernatorial campaign in a fitting manner. Returning to rural Wisconsin, he initiated his drive for a third-term nomination with a ringing denunciation of those who implied that the Potter Law had been a destructive experiment. Labeling the 1874 effort "just" and "a step in the right direction," La Follette made a strong bid for the sort of farmer support which had insured the success of that measure three decades earlier. "Corruption may find its ready instruments in the slums and purlieus of crowded quarters of the larger centers of population," he declared, "but the wholesome work that brings wholesome rest in the outdoor life of the farm, the long hours of patient toil in the fields and woods, the quiet evening with books and family at the close of the day, all conduce to that reserve of judgment, that mental poise and balance, making the farmer the most intelligently critical, conservative and cautious citizen of the country." The men of the soil had been right when they demanded regulation in the 1870's, and they would be right in insisting on regulation now, he argued.[31] Printed copies of this oration together with an article in the *Free Press* by W. O. Taylor, governor during the Potter Law experience, which praised the regulatory measure,[32] were widely circulated in a concerted attempt to clear the air for the final discussion of current priorities.

The key role E. P. Bacon played in securing this statement of

[31] Robert M. La Follette, *Granger Legislation and State Control of Railway Rates* (Madison, 1904), 18.
[32] *Milwaukee Free Press*, February 28, 1904.

support from the ex-governor prefigured the increasingly important role the Milwaukee merchant was to play in determining the governor's political future.[33] No longer simply a technical adviser, in the spring of 1904 Bacon spearheaded the final phase of the well-co-ordinated campaign to "draft" La Follette for a third term. First he released a widely circulated joint letter signed by W. D. Hoard, Charles F. Ilsley, Isaac Stephenson, Albert R. Hall, L. S. Hanks, and himself, a group of influential men who represented a cross section of economic and political interests, calling for renewed support for the governor in order that he could finish his reform tasks. He then pressed the general appeal by sending petitions throughout the state asking for a show of grass-roots support for La Follette.[34] Personal appeals from Hall and Hoard followed as administration supporters sought to close ranks in favor of La Follette's third-term candidacy.[35]

Following close on the heels of this well-contrived demand for a La Follette draft, the administration released the first results of the examination of railroad accounts which had been authorized the previous year by the legislature. In the report the railroad commissioner, John Thomas, alleged that the four major railroads in the state had failed to report almost $1,700,000 in gross earnings for tax purposes, and that one had, at the last minute, added rebate figures to its 1903 report in order to avoid a similar discovery for that year. In an apparent administration attempt to stymie shipper opposition, Thomas significantly added, "This office is in receipt of information giving the names and addresses of shippers who it is claimed are getting rebates regularly."[36] The timing of the report, coming during the final stages of planning for the Republican convention, was unabashedly political. ("We have had in mind since our employment that the principal amount of the concealed earning would be included in the freight reductions," wrote one of the

[33] Bacon to La Follette, February 4, 1904, in the La Follette Papers.
[34] *Milwaukee Free Press*, March 7, 1904. See the La Follette Papers, Box 95 for Bacon-La Follette correspondence. Albert Hall to La Follette, March 21, 1904, in the La Follette Papers.
[35] Hall letter, May 2, 1904, in the Hall Papers; Hoard letter, March 24, 1904, in the Hoard Papers.
[36] *Wisconsin State Journal*, April 11, 1904.

investigators, ". . . and that these would constitute the most valuable ammunition to be used in the coming campaign.")[37] Combined with the well-organized plan to draft the governor, the release nicely united candidate and issue in a striking way at the proper time. "The complete expose by the report of the state railroad commissioner has made the necessity of a rate commission more apparent if freight rates in Wisconsin are to be open and fair to every merchant and manufacturer alike," asserted the *Free Press.*[38] (Ironically, one La Follette supporter complained, "That R. R. report, of the R. R. Commissioner [*sic*], rather staggered them up here: And for all these sins of omission and commission the Gov. is responsible.")[39]

While the anti-La Follette press accused the administration of "grandstanding" because of the timing of the news,[40] none would question that this latest exposure left the railroads in a weaker position to fight administration plans. In January, even before the railroad commissioners' first report was released, the railroads had discontinued the practice of issuing free transportation to shippers who shipped livestock to Chicago, an action which incurred the ire of many small farmers, the very people La Follette was seeking to draw more closely to his banner.[41] Some of the good will won by the carriers in December through rate reductions was lost early the next year through inept administration.

In the face of these setbacks, opponents of La Follette-type regulation stepped up efforts to down the governor and his program. Bringing together many arguments used in 1903 to counter the governor's rate comparisons, Emanuel Philipp, leader of the antiregulation forces, published an impressive booklet entitled *The Truth About Wisconsin Freight Rates* which used similar accounting to prove that Wisconsin shippers were actually enjoying lower rates to important markets than were shippers of neighboring states. The essential arguments in the booklet were reiter-

[37] Stephen W. Gilman to John W. Thomas, August 1, 1904, in the La Follette Papers.
[38] *Milwaukee Free Press,* April 14, 1904.
[39] B. J. Morse to W. D. Hoard, April 14, 1904, in the La Follette Papers.
[40] *Wisconsin State Journal,* February 9, 1904.
[41] *Ibid.,* January 14, 1904.

ated in anti-La Follette papers throughout the state. At the same time the opposition gave particular attention to building up the support of the large shippers and manufacturers who had played such a crucial role in turning the tide in the 1903 legislature. Questionnaires were addressed to manufacturers throughout the state which asked intimidating questions and gave decisive answers. ("Would it not ruin your business if you were obliged to operate it on a mileage tariff? Answer. Yes.")[42]

Hopeful that such arguments would again spur these important business interests in the state into action, La Follette's opponents watched anxiously the results of the caucuses throughout the state.[43] Perhaps the continued support of the manufacturers, coupled with that of railroad employees (who had been pretty much ordered to oppose the governor),[44] and sundry other groups in Wisconsin who disliked La Follette because of his principles or methods, could prevent the governor from fulfilling his dream of a precedent-setting third term in the statehouse.

The May Republican State Convention was hardly the kind of democratic exercise for which the prophet of reform had so often expressed a fondness. Unsure of his ground because of expected opposition from a large number of Republicans, La Follette insured his nomination by packing the convention held in the University Armory with administration supporters and barring the stalwarts through the use of special tickets and brawny football players. As a result the more conservative wing marched down the street to the Opera House where they held their own gathering.

The events surrounding this breakup of the Republican party imply a deep division between the two factions. An interesting commentary on the nature of the factors which split the party, however, is the similarity with which the two groups viewed the major campaign issue. Arguing that "justice" demanded reasonable rates, the La Follette-controlled "Republican State Convention" pledged itself to enact a law creating a railway commission "empowered to fix and enforce reasonable transportation charges so

[42] Robert Eliot to La Follette, April 25, 1904, in the La Follette Papers.
[43] "Burnham" to P. H. Spooner, April 18, 1904, in the Philipp Papers.
[44] *Milwaukee Free Press*, April 15, 1904.

far as the same may be subject to state control," while eliminating discrimination and placing "every shipper similarly situated on the same footing as his competitor in the matter of transportation rates."[45]

Meanwhile, the bolting "National Republican Party" declared that "railway corporations are the creatures of the state and subject to regulation by the state."

> We favor the enactment of law supplanting existing legislation which, while leaving the railway companies free to adopt their rates and regulations to the interests of the sections, cities and industries to the end that the developments of the state may be thereby increased, will prohibit under heavy penalties unjust discrimination as to persons or places by secret preferences. . . .

To implement such a law, the stalwarts supported the creation of a railroad commission of three elected members "with full powers to investigate conditions, to originate actions (either upon complaint or its own initiative) and to enforce (in the courts and by such other means as may be provided by law) a strict observance of legal restrictions upon the exercise of corporate power."[46]

Soon the weak Democratic party would also enter its bid for support with a plank calling for a ban on "unjust discriminating freight rates" and favoring the election of a commission to "examine, investigate and ascertain" through cost and earning analysis the "true condition of every such corporation" and report periodically to the governor and legislature on its findings.[47]

The coincidence of platform planks was the final eloquent expression of the state of the regulation question. While the fight surrounding La Follette's candidacy was bitter and disagreements concerning the powers a regulatory commission should have were profound, all political groups gave notice that there was no longer any question that some form of regulation was soon coming to Wisconsin. By seizing upon an issue which had been fought and won in many states and which was a prominent national question,

---

[45] *The Blue Book of the State of Wisconsin* (Madison, 1905), 1020.
[46] *Ibid.*, 1044–1045.
[47] *Ibid.*, 1027.

La Follette had disarmed many of his opponents and insured support for some sort of railroad reform in his state. Not incidentally, he had also kept intact his own political future.

The similarity in the positions of the major political groups in 1904 made the ensuing campaign a puzzling one with the shadow-boxing of accusation replacing the more fundamental sort of issue-centered debates which had characterized earlier campaigns. The turn of events which had seen the La Follette forces stake a claim to an election issue only to find that everyone agreed such a reform was needed had disturbed many in the administration hierarchy. While they continued to feature their major argument concerning the discrimination to which the Wisconsin shippers were subjected because of excessive rates, the governor and his political colleagues also sought to distinguish their position from those taken by opposing elements. Their major weapon was to question the sincerity of the pronouncements of the stalwarts and Democrats.

Condemning the "paltry pretense of the rump platform," the administration charged that the stalwarts "valued platform promises as lightly as a thief does property rights."[48] The more conservative Republican leaders "are simply representing the railroads in this contest, and they are prepared to strike any attitude that will bring them votes. The railroads understand this very fully," they charged, for "they are in on the deal."[49] Noting also that the stalwarts and Democrats both entertained more moderate views concerning the powers which a regulatory commission should possess, the La Follette forces argued that they alone stood for the formation of a really effective commission with the strength necessary to "fix and establish reasonable rates." The difference, declared Irvine Lenroot, was that a commission established under La Follette's leadership would assume sufficient "power to give relief without . . . the aid and consent of any railroad corporation."[50] Whether set forth in *Lower Freight Rates Demanded for Wisconsin,* a lengthy answer to the stalwarts' *The Truth About Freight Rates,* or by the governor and his top aides in their barnstorming throughout the

[48] *Milwaukee Free Press,* September 7, 1904.
[49] *Lower Freight Rates Demanded for Wisconsin,* 26.
[50] *Milwaukee Free Press,* October 29, 1904.

state, the message was the same. Only a pro-La Follette legislature under the leadership of the "fearless champion of a just cause" could be trusted with the delicate task of enacting effective regulatory measures.[51]

But even the normal process of rate comparison, the method employed by reformers for over a decade to prove that Wisconsin shippers were being treated unfairly, became more difficult for the administration. Because of the extensive alterations in rates by the railroads in the previous December, La Follette found it more difficult to obtain useful rate information, in spite of careful scrutiny by proadministration men in the office of the railroad commissioner aided by Halford Erickson, commissioner of labor and industrial statistics. "Since the reduction, a case for Wisconsin can only be made by careful selection," wrote the apologetic Erickson in the face of the governor's persistent demands for more persuasive rate comparisons. "I always try to give you the best and safest rates for each place. If sometimes they fail to make a case it is because of existing traffic conditions."[52] Erickson's candor was apparently not matched by other aides. When La Follette read evidence garnered in the railroad commissioner's office which "proved" that Emanuel Philipp, leader of the opposition, had received sizable rebates from railroad companies, Ray Stannard Baker published the charge in a muckraking article in *McClure's*. In an ensuing lawsuit, Philipp won a $15,000 judgment against the journal for libel.[53]

Although hampered by this lack of clearcut issues and information which would set their stand off from those of other political contestants, the La Follette wing pushed hard to achieve the kind of election victory which would insure a more positive verdict on regulation in the 1905 legislature. Vowing to "clean up the legislature," La Follette set about exposing those lawmakers who had opposed his reform plans the previous year. With the same persistence and thoroughness which characterized his county-fair

---

[51] See *Lower Freight Rates Demanded for Wisconsin,* 45 and *passim.*
[52] Halford Erickson to La Follette, October 5, 1904, in the La Follette Papers.
[53] See Robert S. Maxwell, *Emanuel L. Philipp, Wisconsin Stalwart* (Madison, 1959), Chapter 4 for a full discussion.

campaigning of the previous year, the governor stumped districts throughout the state where key races were in progress, "read the record" on recalcitrant legislators, and demanded their ouster. In spite of the split in the party and the confusion resulting from the convergence of issues, La Follette fought mightily for a base of support which he might use in the completion of his reform program in the next legislature.

The troubles experienced by La Follette in his fall campaigning were petty compared to those of the stalwarts. Having bolted the regular party structure, they found themselves in the anomalous position of dissenting with only the fragments of an organization. Their slate of candidates was particularly unexciting. Keyes, the dean of the old guard politicians, wrote in regard to the stalwart candidate for governor, "Cook is a pinhead, and the fight should come between Bob and Peck [the Democratic candidate]."[54] Matters were made worse when Samuel Cook finally quit the race and ex-Governor Edward Scofield had to be rushed in to fill the breach. Under such divisive strain, the optimism of the late spring ("The Stalwart Japs are besieging the Russian La Follette stronghold of Port Arthur and it will surely fall")[55] died in the cool of autumn. As the stalwart organization crumbled, individual candidates were forced to fend for themselves. Many supported a rate commission but advocated election of its members in a gesture of defiance toward the governor, but others chose to ignore the issue.

"Nobody with any conception of the situation in Wisconsin today will be found to predict anything less than a plurality of 75,000 for Governor La Follette next year," wrote the partisan *Milwaukee Free Press* in August, 1903. "He will probably lead the national ticket by 10,000 to 15,000."[56] When the zany 1904 campaign was over, La Follette, running far behind the national ticket and garnering fewer votes than any other victorious candidate for state office, managed to poll a plurality of about fifty thousand votes. The primary election referendum won, however, and the administration seemed destined to control both houses, so the claims of

[54] Keyes to H. A. Taylor, September 23, 1904, in the Keyes Letterbooks.
[55] Keyes to Marvin Hughitt, May 25, 1904, in the Keyes Letterbooks.
[56] *Milwaukee Free Press*, August 26, 1903.

decisive victory echoed by the administration supporters were perhaps warranted. The governor had sought to break tradition and, in spite of the indifferent margin of his victory, had accomplished it. Before him lay the task of redressing the defeat suffered in 1903. The passage of a strict railroad regulation bill would complete La Follette's reform program and offer an excellent base for an expansion of his reform activities to the national scene.

Half a Loaf

4 In the weeks following the election of 1904 the governor had little time to savor his unprecented third-term victory. Instead, he faced for the second time the task of making the issue into a policy and that policy into law. It was little consolation to La Follette and his colleagues that all sides in that confusing year had supported regulation of a sort, for the campaign had made it abundantly clear that the depth of regulation desired by various political and economic groups differed greatly. Hence the widespread public assumption that a railroad commission would be established by the next legislature only increased the burden felt by the governor and his supporters. They knew that the rocks and shoals of consensus politics could weaken the resolve of many a legislator and ultimately batter the life out of the particular kind of regulation law which they felt was imperative.

The differences concerned the power which should be granted the proposed commission. Friendly advice by some political supporters, tendered publicly in editorials in the *Free Press* and privately through correspondence, was to compromise the issue and allow the railroads control over initial rate making with the commission limited to modifying specific rates if and when complaints were made.[1] La Follette, however, had long ago committed himself to a stronger sort of commission. In the spring of 1904 a

---

[1] *Milwaukee Free Press*, December 11, 1904; Robert Eliot to La Follette, December 22, 1904, W. D. Connor to La Follette, January 5, 1905, both in the La Follette Papers. Wrote Eliot: "The principal howl of our opponents has been against the primary rate-making power."

more compliant underling, probably Halford Erickson, had drafted for the governor an ambiguous reply to a Sheboygan shipper which, after discussing the rate-making function of a commission, asserted: "There are, no doubt, other ways in which reasonable rates can be fixed. For instance, the commissioners might let the railroads establish the rates and then upon investigation reduce these to a reasonable basis." La Follette struck out the quoted words, leaving the assertion that a railroad commission would "undoubtedly" have the duty of establishing "reasonable rates on the traffic between stations within the state." Although the letter admitted that the law would limit the ways in which the commission might proceed to accomplish this task, it closed with the notation that the Iowa and Illinois commissioners fixed maximum rates and their rates were lower than those in Wisconsin.[2] This commitment to a rate-setting commission was further bolstered in the fall campaign.

Still, in the late months of 1904 the governor was cautious and rather noncommitttal about the kind of law he would propose for passage in 1905. Perhaps remembering the stunning defeat he had suffered in 1903, he carefully weighed the sort of demands he could make on the new legislature and the degree of regulatory powers which would be sufficient to make a commission effective. In order to obtain the best advice possible on how to proceed, the governor, in mid-December, again sought expert help. Enclosing copies of the strong administration bill of 1903, which called for a commission charged with responsibility for setting maximum rates for all railroads operating in the state, he queried eight noted experts on regulation concerning changes which should be made in the 1903 proposal.

The inquiries went to Iowans Frank Campbell and William Larrabee, who had been helpful in 1903, to John H. Reagan of Texas, who had been instrumental in setting up the strong Texas commission, to Interstate Commerce Commissioner Charles A. Prouty, who admired the Texas commission above all others, and to Albert Hall, E. P. Bacon, and John R. Commons, all of whom

---

[2] See reply to A. D. DeLand, March 7, 1904, in the La Follette Papers, La Follette to A. D. DeLand, March 7, 1904, in the La Follette Letter-books.

wished the Wisconsin commission to be as strong as possible. A personal envoy was sent to A. B. Stickney, the eccentric president of the Chicago and Great Western, who felt government should take over the rate-making function from the railroads, and whose writings had greatly influenced La Follette's thinking.[3] Detailed replies from seven of the eight men—Stickney had nothing new to offer—came quickly back to the executive mansion, all of them commenting favorably about the bill but many suggesting ways of strengthening the measure even more, particularly by allowing the commission to write schedules of absolute rates rather than simply maximum rates.[4]

At the same time, John M. Winterbotham, the deputy railroad commissioner and longtime La Follette supporter, took an extensive fact-finding trip to Texas at the governor's request, which included interviews with Reagan and O. B. Colquitt of the Texas commission. The full transcript of a long interview between Colquitt and Winterbotham, in which Colquitt spoke highly of the effectiveness of the strict Texas regulatory measure, was forwarded to the governor. He too advised that the commission be given power to fix absolute rates. Winterbotham recommended that Wisconsin follow the lead of Texas and pass a strong commission bill.[5]

[3] See Decemberer 19, 1905, letters from La Follette to each of these men. See *Freight*, 1:93 (May 1, 1904), for Prouty's opinion of the Texas commission. A. Munster to La Follette, December 30, 1904, in the La Follette Papers, describes a visit with Stickney. La Follette felt the three best books on regulation were *The Railway Problem* by A. B. Stickney, *The Railroad Question* by William Larrabee, and *State Railroad Control* by F. H. Dixon. The last two concern the Iowa regulation experience. La Follette to Hubert H. Jones, February 28, 1905, in the La Follette Letterbooks.

[4] Frank Campbell to La Follette, December 26, 1904; William Larrabee to La Follette, December 22, 1904; John Reagan to La Follette, December 24, 1904; Hall to La Follette, December 25, 1904; Bacon to La Follette, December 26, 1904; Charles A. Prouty to La Follette, January 16, 1905; undated Commons Memo (box 83), all in the La Follette Papers.

[5] "Minutes of the conference held between Hon. J. M. Winterbotham, Deputy Railroad Commissioner of the State of Wisconsin, and Hon. O. B. Colquitt, member of the Railroad Commission of Texas, on December 26, 1904, concerning the workings and operation of the Railroad Commission Act and the Stock and Bond Law, of the State of Texas," December 26, 1904, in the La Follette Papers; *Milwaukee Free Press*, December 24, 1904.

Reinforced by the recommendations of these experts, the governor decided upon a course which would result in a radically new order in Wisconsin transportation costs. Throughout the next months he and his subordinates continued to write to knowledgeable men throughout the country in search of information and ways in which to achieve this goal. In the case of regulation, the Wisconsin Idea was made national.

Ironically, the La Follette men made a contribution to an Iowa fight for better rates, which was going on at the same time, by sending the neighboring reformers copies of the *Truth About Wisconsin Freight Rates* by Emanuel Philipp, which purported to prove that Wisconsin's rates were in fact lower than those of Iowa. "Believing that you can make use of some of these to advantage, there is sent you for distribution a dozen copies of the pamphlet," wrote La Follette's private secretary to the secretary of the Council Bluffs Commercial Club.[6] These Midwest reformers knew how to play both sides of the street!

On November 11, W. D. Connor, the Republican state chairman, asserted that the La Follette forces could count on seventy votes in the assembly and nineteen in the senate, majorities large enough to insure the success of any administration plans.[7] La Follette too was confident, declaring "we have both branches of the legislature," but he worried about rumors of "a break in our ranks."[8] He therefore set about making sure his new reform ship remained seaworthy. A December 10 caucus of all administration senators in Madison, called to reinforce his control over that traditionally troublesome wing, instead showed his suspicions to be warranted. Only fifteen senators attended and pledged support, while two others seemed certain to co-operate. Seventeen was, however, the barest of majorities and raised an ominous possibility of defeat if,

[6] J. J. Hannan to W. G. Reed, February 9, 1905; La Follette to A. F. Barnard, February 4, 1905, both in the La Follette Letterbooks; *Milwaukee Sentinel*, January 9, 1905.

[7] Carroll Lahmann, "Robert Marion La Follette As Public Speaker and Political Leader, 1855–1905" (unpublished Ph.D. dissertation, University of Wisconsin, 1939), 919.

[8] La Follette to Lincoln Steffens, November 14, 1905, in the La Follette Letterbooks.

as the *Free Press* suspected, the railroads were ready for "the most bitter of any contest they have yet waged."[9]

Faced with an uncertain political situation in the upper house of the legislature but reinforced by expert advice, La Follette began the final phase of his most bitter fight, the attempt to bring effective railroad regulation to Wisconsin.

La Follette's 1905 inaugural address was for the most part typical and predictable. It was long (112 pages, 3 hours), catholic (including such questions as better protection of game), and it emphasized the principal issue of 1904, railroad regulation (42 pages were devoted to it). In his treatment of the regulation question, however, he made two significant revisions. Responding to the advice of experts, he now demanded a commission empowered to establish absolute rates rather than simply maximum rates. And he equivocated a bit on how the commission should use its powers. "While the commission should doubtless be clothed with power to promulgate entire schedules of rates and classifications, it may well be questioned whether such action upon its part should be made mandatory. It would appear to be the more prudent course to make it the duty of the commission to establish rates with respect to any one product or shipment or to particular lines of merchandise or to specified commodities, as from time to time their importance may demand consideration." Such a course, he explained, would, of course, allow the commission to afford relief quickly before it completed the investigation of the commerce of the entire state and "under such a course the commission would proceed in a conservative way, having due regard to the pressing needs of shippers upon the one hand, and fair consideration of the rights of the transportation companies upon the other."[10] Caught between the advice of trusted experts that his strong program was, if anything, too compromising and the urgings of those who saw in his program an implicit threat to the business community, La Follette tried to straddle the fence. The commission should have more power but exercise it in a cautious way.

On January 25, La Follette accepted the legislature's choice of

---

[9] *Milwaukee Free Press,* December 11, 1904.
[10] *Ibid.,* January 13, 1905.

him as United States Senator to replace John V. Quarles, a luckless Republican moderate who desired a second term but was thwarted by the governor's rising ambitions. "If we are in a position to get the state legislation for which we have contended, we are likewise in a position to get the right kind of a United States senator at Washington," the governor had written ex-governor Hoard in late December. "Our organization will never have a greater necessity to secure a strong man for senator than now. If we are not careful now, we will not have much interest in what takes place four years from now. . . ."[11] In a characteristically egotistical way, La Follette saw himself as the only man sufficient to every task. He had ordained himself that "strong man" who would make "the right kind of a United States senator." Seemingly, he was also sizing up the Presidency when the equally dynamic and self-assured Theodore Roosevelt finished his second term.

But first he felt it essential to accomplish his program, so he straddled. Speaking of "certain things" he stood for in government, he proclaimed in accepting the Senatorship: "I can not at present see what I could do as governor for this legislation after this session should terminate, if there were failure either in whole or in part, which I might do equally well, and, perhaps, more effectively, as a United States senator." But if, he continued, "there should appear any conflict in the obligation I entered into when I took the oath of office as governor and that of United States senator-elect then I shall ask you to receive it from me and place it in other hands of your own choosing."[12]

The governor would not go to Washington until the present session of the state legislature was over and then only under certain conditions. Many would argue throughout the session that he had committed himself not to leave Wisconsin until a railroad commission bill was passed, and this seems to be so. Conveniently deleted from the message, however, was a reference to the necessity for "the establishment of a railway commission *with commensurate power to meet the platform promises.*"[13] The governor, it seems,

---

[11] La Follette to W. D. Hoard, December 26, 1904, in the Hoard Papers.
[12] *Milwaukee Sentinel,* January 26, 1905.
[13] See original copy of acceptance speech (box 116), in the La Follette Papers.

was not ready to stand too strongly on principle when Washington beckoned. Instead, he was ready to make the best of an ambiguous situation. Throughout the session rumors that La Follette would not step down if certain provisions were not included in a regulation bill would crop up, but seasoned politicians seemingly saw through the threats. "He belongs to the class that never resigns," quipped Keyes.[14] In spite of his conditional reply to the legislature, the governor forfeited a significant amount of leverage on the state level by making himself a lame duck.

The senatorial election boosted the confidence of the governor and his supporters. When combined with an impressive triumph in the legislature on a bill to expand the statute of limitations on actions designed to impel railroads to pay the remainder of their back taxes on unreported earnings uncovered by the Thomas investigation, it renewed the administration's faith that this session would bring the railroads to heel.[15]

Charged with new confidence, on February 10 supporters of the administration introduced in both wings of the legislature plans which pointed to a commission whose duty it would be to establish an entirely new schedule of rates for all freight and passenger traffic in the state. In the assembly the administration-dominated committee on railroads introduced a measure which was a virtual copy of the Texas regulation bill. In the senate two such proposals were introduced, one by William H. Hatten, chairman of the railroad committee, which was identical to the assembly proposal and the other by James A. Frear which was identical to the administration bill which had been roundly defeated by the assembly in 1903.[16] The administration was obviously determined to make a fight for the strongest possible kind of regulatory legislation.

In the opposition camp there had been considerable apprehension ever since La Follette's victory in November. Having battled hard to prevent a clear-cut victory for the men who supported strict regulation of common carriers, stalwarts began to fear the worst, particularly after the communications between the strong Texas

[14] Keyes to John Spooner, January 25, 1905, in the Keyes Letterbooks.
[15] *Milwaukee Free Press*, February 3, 1905.
[16] See No. 444A, No. 268S, No. 319S.

regulatory commission and the administration became public. Con-
juring up visions of Texas-type restriction on Wisconsin railroads,
newspapers which opposed La Follette began to predict the total
ruin of the state's commercial and industrial system if the governor
were allowed to carry out his plans.[17]

Spurred on by such intense apprehensions, opponents of the
administration's regulation plans concentrated on promoting an
alternative regulatory measure designed to satisfy the public desire
for tighter controls without depriving the railroads of the broad
freedom and discretion which they deemed so necessary for their
well-being. In December, 1904, the *Milwaukee Sentinel,* chief
spokesman for the more conservative wing of the dominant Republican party, advanced the first concrete proposal for regulatory
legislation based on the model advocated in the stalwart platform
of that year. Praising the Quarles-Cooper bill, a national measure
sponsored by two Wisconsin Congressmen and written, ironically,
by arch-rival E. P. Bacon, the *Sentinel* suggested that such a
measure, adjusted to fit the needs of the state, would provide the
proper amount of supervision over railroad affairs. Comparing this
national measure, which sought to give the Interstate Commerce
Commission the power to change rates on complaint from shippers,
with the La Follette program, which called for a board empowered
to establish a completely new schedule of freight and passenger
rates, the conservative newspaper declared the former proposal
"just and fair," the latter "confiscation."[18]

In January, 1905, key figures who opposed La Follette's more
radical regulation plans began to give their public support to the
kind of legislation the *Sentinel* advocated. First Emanuel Philipp,
a leader of the shipping interests and political factions who opposed the governor, in a lengthy consideration of the regulation
question, proclaimed: "The difference between giving the commissioners power to fix the rates and giving them power to correct
them if they proved to be unfair or unreasonable, is all the difference between the failure of the Potter law and the best judgment
of the great majority of the modern students of the transportation

---

[17] *Milwaukee Sentinel,* January 31, February 1, 1905.
[18] *Ibid.,* December 1, 1904.

problems."[19] Later, replying on behalf of the railroads to La Follette's strongly worded inaugural, Burton Hanson, general solicitor of the Chicago and North Western Railway, concurred. "The powers of the commission involve the whole event of failure or success in the regulation of the railways."[20]

Spurred on by this new unity of purpose, opposition leadership undertook a concerted attempt to garner the support of important political and economic groups for their cause. They were clearly hopeful that the more moderate stand would allow them to undermine the governor's plans once more. And it was not long before their fondest hopes seemed to be materializing.

In early 1905 the highly conservative Frank K. Bull, president of the Wisconsin Manufacturers Association, prepared to lead his organization in another drive against any sort of regulatory legislation. On February 27, however, he yielded to the demands of more moderate members who saw the handwriting on the wall and agreed to poll the membership before initiating such a campaign. The response to his circular letter was so surprising that the executive committee of the association, on March 7, agreed to oppose vigorously the La Follette plan but to join the growing ranks of those who supported a weaker sort of commission measure. "It would be to the general interest of the manufacturers of the state to protest against any commission having full power to make rates, on its own initiative . . . but to favor a commission which should look into the matter of alleged discrimination with a view of correcting any such abuses, if found and . . . to take up and adjust rates only on complaints with the idea of justice to shipper, consumer and carrier alike," declared Bull in voicing the significant change in attitude of the key manufacturers group.[21]

The reunification of the coalition which had successfully combatted La Follette's plans in 1903 around a more moderate stand brought new hope to all who feared the governor's regulation

---

[19] *Ibid.*, January 11, 1905.
[20] Burton Hanson, *A Reply to Those Portions of Governor La Follette's Message of 1905 Which Relate to Railways* (Chicago, 1905), 25.
[21] Frank K. Bull to Jesse C. Coogan, February 27, 1905, in the La Follette Papers; *Milwaukee Free Press*, March 11, 1905.

plans. In the face of the administration's February 10 legislative proposals, which embodied all of the provisions the opponents most feared, an almost unseemly confidence pervaded the camp of the opposition. Although the *Sentinel* declared that the bills "could not be worse," through the crucial month and a half which followed, railway publications, the stalwart press, and the private expressions of leading opponents of the La Follette plan expressed a cautious confidence that their measures would eventually prevail.[22]

By March, La Follette's opponents were set to wage their campaign for a different sort of regulation. On March 2, Senator Andrew L. Kreutzer, longtime opponent of the governor, introduced a substitute to the administration bill which called for a commission to investigate complaints of discriminatory or excessive charges with the power to set a new rate when deemed necessary. The job of initial rate making remained with the railroads. Quite naturally, the opposition flocked to its support. "A decided improvement" and "a step toward a rational solution of the railroad commission problem" declared the *Milwaukee Sentinel,* while *Railway Age* juxtaposed its "fairness and intent to conserve all interests," with the attitude of "passion and desire to injure" evident in the La Follette bills.[23] Now the opponents of strict regulation had a legislative proposal around which to rally their forces.

Encouraging as these events might be, an even greater source of joy to the anti-La Follette group was the evidence of disarray in the administration camp. Having early noted the absence of key senators, including William Hatten, from discussion leading up to the introduction of the administration measures on February 10, the *Sentinel* remarked confidently that the bills did not express the views of Hatten nor the members of the all important senate railroad committee. Such feelings, also echoed in other quarters, laid the basis for hopes that senators whom the administration confi-

---

[22] *Milwaukee Sentinel,* February 11, 12, 1905; *Railway Age,* 39:224 (February 17, 1905); *Railway Gazette,* 38:273 (March 24, 1905); Keyes to Hughitt, February 12, 1905, in the Keyes Letterbooks.
[23] *Milwaukee Sentinel,* March 4, 1905; *Railway Age,* 39:334 (March 17, 1905).

dently depended on would defect when the chips were down.[24] "Stalwart members are fraternizing somewhat with the Half-breeds with a view to tone them down," reported Elisha Keyes.[25]

The administration was indeed in trouble. Aware of the crucial importance of seizing the initiative, particularly in view of the debacle of 1903, the governor early undertook an effort to consolidate the bulk of his support in order to avoid the need for a rush to regain support as he had had to do in the last legislature. His program, apparently borrowed from the opposition efforts of two years previous, was twofold: to overwhelm the senate with testimony from a cross section of Wisconsin leadership of major economic groups, and to deluge the legislature with petitions from throughout the state affirming their strong support for the La Follette regulation program. The governor failed to achieve completely either aim.

W. D. Hoard was the "representative farmer and dairyman" La Follette wanted to testify for the bill before the senate committee, while E. A. Edmunds, a prosperous lumberman, was asked to speak on behalf of the large manufacturers and shippers. John Barnes, an able lawyer, was told to "provide yourself with a client" and come to counter the arguments of the railroad attorneys.[26] The hope was that such articulate and sympathetic voices would destroy the notion once and for all that no one except politicians and perhaps a few Milwaukee grain merchants supported the kind of regulation plan which the administration advocated. Although none of these men lacked sympathy for the plan, all refused to make an appearance for one reason or another.[27] The burden of testimony, therefore, fell once again largely on the same cast of characters which had appeared in 1903 although W. D. Conner

---

[24] *Milwaukee Sentinel,* February 9, 11, 1905; Keyes to Hughitt, February 12, 1905, in the Keyes Papers.
[25] Keyes to Hughitt, March 1, 1905, in the Keyes Letterbooks. The term "Half-breed" refers to those who composed the La Follette wing of the Wisconsin State Republican party.
[26] La Follette to Hoard, February 27, 1905; La Follette to Edmonds, February 20, 1905; La Follette to Barnes, March 3, 1905, all in the La Follette Letterbooks.
[27] Hoard to Grant Thomas, March 17, 1905, in the Hoard Letterbooks; John Barnes to La Follette, February 25, 1905, in the La Follette Papers.

chairman of the La Follette-dominated state Republican party, made an appearance as a "shipper." The Milwaukee men, particularly Bacon, with the aid of sympathetic administration legislators like Frear made some telling points, but the attempt at catholicity failed miserably.

Nor was the petition campaign fully successful. While it brought many signatures, the results did not begin to reach the legislature until late March, when the administration was already moderating its demands in the face of growing opposition.

Had La Follette controlled the legislature as administration supporters boasted, such failures would have been immaterial. The truth was, however, that the La Follette "machine" was in a state of near collapse. Early signs of trouble could be seen in the refusal of some senators, who were counted on by the administration, to attend the caucus called to formulate plans to pass a regulation measure of the sort La Follette wanted. Although the administration succeeded in organizing both houses in early January, in an interview one of the "administration" senators who had attended the December caucus, Herman C. Wipperman, advocated a commission of a far different type than La Follette anticipated, illustrating the lack of discipline under which these men felt they operated.[28] As the 1905 session wore on reports of defections by senators whom the governor had counted on began to pour into Madison, and La Follette began to wonder whether any sort of regulation bill could be passed.[29]

Worry as he might about the possible defection of senators like Wilcox, Stevens, Froemming, or Merton, these concerns were dwarfed by the implications of the defection of Senator William H. Hatten, the man handpicked to lead the administration program to victory. As the governor lost control of the rate regulation question the indomitable Hatten decided to run his own committee and write his own bill.

As early as October of 1904 the perceptive Amos Wilder of the

---

[28] *Milwaukee Sentinel,* January 14, 1905.
[29] B. C. Wolter to E. E. Mills, March 27, 1905; E. E. Mills, to La Follette, March 28, 1905, both in the La Follette Papers; La Follette to E. C. Little, March 29, 1905, in the La Follette Letterbooks; "Shaw" to Stone, March 30, 1905, in the James A. Stone Papers.

Wisconsin State Journal had remarked that "the railroad commission bill . . . must be fathered by some more tolerant leader [than La Follette] who is willing to live and let live politically."[30] This mantle fell on Hatten, who indeed was a singular man. Born in New York state in 1856 but having moved to Wisconsin at the age of seventeen, the ambitious Hatten had spurned the pleasures of youth—he never drank, smoked, danced, played cards, or married —and set his sights on building a timber empire. In the next two decades he acquired large tracts of lumber and a number of mills in the South (including a lumber company in Philipp, Mississippi, named after Emanuel Philipp), while developing large holdings in Wisconsin and other areas also. By the 1930's he could boast of ownership of large properties in Tennessee, Louisiana, Oregon, Washington, Michigan, Minnesota, British Columbia, and California, where he owned a stand of the finest redwoods in the state. Real estate holdings in Chicago, millions of dollars in securities and control of a number of banks had swelled his fortune, until in the 1920's he was said to be worth from $15,000,000 to $16,000,000. When he died in 1937, his Wisconsin estate alone was valued at $3,000,000, although he died of malnutrition and bronchial pneumonia, the apparent victim of an overarching greed which not only caused his own death but the sufferings of many employees from miserably low wages and poor working conditions. Looking down into his grave, the Reverend A. W. Sneesby pronounced a final judgment: "His greatest interest seems to be the making and holding of wealth."[31]

In 1905, when Hatten emerged as a powerful independent force, such miserly eccentricities were not apparent, only the taciturnity, toughness, and single-minded brilliance which had already made him a millionaire. John R. Commons later described him as "the most capable negotiator in my experience," while La Follette himself described him as a "very strong man."[32] Tall, spare, and handsome, he was a figure to be dealt with in any situation.

[30] *Wisconsin State Journal,* October 20, 1904.
[31] *Dictionary of Wisconsin Biography,* 163; *Milwaukee Journal,* April 22, 23, 24, 1940.
[32] John R. Commons, *Myself* (Madison, 1964), 125; La Follette, *Autobiography,* 296.

Probably more than any other important economic group in the state, the lumbermen were suspicious of all plans for strict regulation of railroads. Highly dependent on the carriers to get their products to market and often favored by special agreements with the roads, they feared the disruption of good relations and a fruitful collaboration which the La Follette plans seemed to indicate. It was apparently this suspicion, born of his role as a leading lumber producer and fed by a fear of the Potter Law debacle as he saw it,[33] which led Hatten to seek a path different from that which La Follette advocated. Whatever his motivation, Hatten, although labeled an "administration man," exhibited a distressing independence from the outset of the 1905 fight.

Although he had attended the administration caucus in December, on the eve of the meeting he had made it clear that he intended to stand upon his own principles by proclaiming publicly he would not consent to a purge of such stalwarts as Whitehead from important committee posts in the next legislature.[34] Such sentiments endeared him to the stalwart *Milwaukee Sentinel* and as the jockeying for position in the final regulation fight began, it put its faith in Hatten's good judgment as a legislator and a businessman as the key to thwarting the administration's regulation plan.[35] Hatten did not let the conservative journal down.

While Hatten had formally introduced the administration version of the strict regulation measure in February, astute observers were not fooled by his sponsorship. In particular, it appears that James Frear, who was perhaps closer to La Follette than any other senator, suspected the worst and thus introduced his own version of a strong regulation measure. Unwilling to see the administration's plans undermined if and when the "Hatten bill" was abandoned by its namesake, Frear set his own course.

After the 1905 struggle was over Hatten would openly admit that the bill he introduced was simply a "dummy," something to occupy the senate while his committee hammered out a more moderate bill.[36] Long before that time, however, Hatten had made it abun-

[33] *Milwaukee Free Press*, February 19, 1907.
[34] *Milwaukee Sentinel*, December 12, 1904.
[35] *Ibid.*, February 7, 1905.
[36] Philipp, *Political Reform in Wisconsin*, 231.

dantly clear that he would not support the administration plan.
On February 24, in a virtual repudiation of the measure he had
introduced two weeks earlier, Hatten publicly predicted that the
bill "when amended so as to more clearly express the intent of its
framers" would leave the initiative of rate making and classification
with the carriers and not endow the commission with powers to
change rates "until it shall find after . . . hearing and investigation
that the existing rate is unreasonable and unjust."[37] He then undertook an independent campaign of personal inquiry, writing experts
of all persuasions, including leading railroad figures and important
businessmen, in an effort to gain final approval of a bill built along
more conservative lines.[38]

Needless to say, Hatten's overtures met an enthusiastic response
from those who had hoped for just such a break in the administration ranks. By early March railroad men were claiming they had
won over a key administration man "whose name will carry weight
throughout the state," strengthen the opposition, and put the
administration forces into a panic.[39] The reference was most likely
to Hatten, for it was reliably reported that he had contributed to
the writing of the Kreutzer bill,[40] the measure around which the
opposition to La Follette's program was gathering as an initial step
in moderating the regulation plans for Wisconsin. Apparently sensing that Hatten, in deserting the administration measure and turning toward the opposition, had taken the crucial votes with him,
E. P. Bacon, ever alert to the flow of legislative power, began
sending his regulation information to Hatten hoping to have an
impact on him, while the Milwaukee man on occasion forgot to
send the governor the same data.[41]

The establishment of Hatten as an independent force outside the
realm of administration control posed difficult new problems for
La Follette and his colleagues, who needed success so badly in

---

[37] *Milwaukee Free Press,* February 25, 1905; see also *Milwaukee Sentinel,*
   February 16, 1905.
[38] Charles McArthur, Northwestern Land Agency agent, to Hatten, February
   24, 1905, in the La Follette Papers; Hatten to Hoard, March 13, 1905, in
   the Hoard Papers.
[39] *Milwaukee Free Press,* March 6, 1905.
[40] *Vernon County Censor,* March 8, 1905.
[41] Bacon to La Follette, March 25, 1905, in the La Follette Papers.

that legislative session. In 1903 the governor would have been quite content to win in the assembly, lose in the senate, then go to the people with a plea that they turn out the corrupt, corporation-controlled senators. But now there was no time for moral victories for, with the United States senatorship in his hands, he needed some sort of regulation bill in order to be free to go to Washington and begin a new career. An adamant supporter of strong regulation, James Frear, argued publicly that "in Wisconsin it is today a question of whether or not a commission can be secured with power to fix absolute or maximum rates upon its own initiative in order to remedy a condition disclosed by the discrimination of railway companies against Wisconsin and in favor of other states."[42] But the administration, now convinced such a stand was untenable, sought a suitable compromise through which it might regain control of the measure. As evidence mounted that the senate would not tolerate a strong measure, administration spokesmen began to trim. By late March they were arguing that they had never really intended to give a commission the power to fix rates initially.[43]

On March 30, in an apparent attempt to stop the pernicious defection of supporters of the administration on the rate issue, the La Follette-controlled assembly committee on railroads introduced a substitute to the harsh bill of February 10 which stripped the proposed commission of its original rate-making powers and relegated it to the role of investigating and revising rates found to be unreasonable or discriminatory. It also added explicit assurances that commodity rates and other special tariffs were legal and could be continued. The measure, apparently the result of long hours of work by Senators Hatten and George Hudnall, and Assembly Speaker Irvine Lenroot, represented a major defeat for La Follette and the more vigorous sort of regulation espoused by him and practiced in many other states. The bill passed the assembly by a wide margin on April 18. No longer need the carriers fear that the rate-making power would be wrested from their hands completely. The pendulum had swung toward the right.

---

[42] *Freight*, 3:124 (March, 1905).
[43] J. D. Beck to Esch, March 15, 1905, in the Esch Papers; *Wisconsin State Journal*, March 22, 27, 1905.

The administration's retreat changed the configurations of the struggle greatly. It did not completely mitigate the fight over regulation, however, for in the minds of many who opposed strict regulation, even the substitute bill contained features which smacked of undue railroad restriction and unsafe commission discretion. And for the administration the battle could not be won by one strategic retreat, for short of completely satisfying the opposition by yielding totally to its objections, La Follette and his colleagues had to rebuild support for this more lenient but still viable kind of regulatory legislation. As the assembly substitute went to the senate, many questions remained to be answered before anyone could assess the kind of regulatory commission Wisconsin would have.

Two questions dominated the minds of the senate railroad committee after it received the assembly substitute and as Chairman Hatten sought to hammer out a final compromise, based on the principle that the railroads would retain initial rate-making powers. They were: what appellate role the courts would have, and how commission members would be selected. On both of these issues La Follette and his opponents differed greatly, and a clearcut victory by either side on either question could do much to determine the role a regulatory commission would have in the state's economy.

Remembering the crippling effect of adverse court rulings upon the Interstate Commerce Commission in the 1890's, both sides were adamant concerning the role the courts should play in relation to the proposed regulatory commission. Hoping to utilize a more friendly court if the commission became too demanding in its regulatory function, the supporters of a mild regulation declared that any commission rate decisions which a railroad chose to appeal should be automatically stayed until the matter was decided by the courts. The initial administration bill, expressive of La Follette's fear of unsympathetic judges, allowed appeal to the judiciary but provided that commission rulings would remain in effect during litigation and until specifically overthrown by the courts. The issue was thus whether or not the commission would have real decision-making power in controversial cases.

Before the question reached the senate committee, the administration had yielded considerably on this point. The assembly substitute allowed an injunction to be issued if upon application by a carrier the court ruled a commission decision to be "clearly illegal."[44] Still unsatisfied, opponents in the senate sought further to encumber the commission. Their efforts during April accomplished two notable changes. No longer was the court required to rule the commission action "clearly illegal" in order to issue an injunction. And stays could be issued on appeals from a circuit court to the Supreme Court, although no automatic stays on appeal were to be issued.

In the sense that the commission retained its identity as a dynamic decision maker unless a concerted effort was made to overthrow the decision, the administration clearly got the best of this compromise. Those who sought to weaken commission power could take consolation in the discretion given the courts to issue injunctions, however, remembering how such power had been so effectively used previously.

More complex and confusing was the question of how the commission should be named. Although La Follette later contended that "all along" he had argued for appointment of all commissioners rather than their election,[45] actually he seems to have come to this position quite late in the fight. In 1903, unsure how to proceed, he had pushed for a commission with one elected member and two which would be appointed by the governor. His conversion to the appointment of all members seems to have come on the advice of such experts as Bacon, Oscar Colquitt of Texas, and Frank Dixon, a noted economist. La Follette relied particularly on the advice of Dixon who, in assessing the Iowa regulation experience, argued that the chief defect in that state's bill was the elective feature. He would quote Dixon's book in his 1905 inaugural as an authoritative opinion in support of the appointment of all members of the commission.[46] Appointment by the chief executive, he and his supporters argued, would keep the commission issue "out of politics" and prevent the commission from falling into the hands of the railroads.

[44] Substitute for No. 444A, Section 4.
[45] La Follette, *Autobiography*, 348.
[46] *Milwaukee Free Press*, January 13, 1905.

Given a neutral set of circumstances, even railroad men would have probably chosen the appointive method. Arguing for appointment of all such commissions, *Railway World* the following year asserted, like La Follette, that the elective method "either influences the commission to cater to the radicals or it brings the railroads into politics in a very objectionable way."[47] Even in Wisconsin the representatives of the railroads seem to have been split over which way was to be preferred in 1905. Determined, however, to deny La Follette the opportunity to pack the commission with men who would seek to skin the carriers, the railroads and other more conservative elements as early as 1903 opted for election of the commissioners. In the 1904 campaign both the stalwarts and the Democrats made the elective principle an integral part of their plan for moderate regulation.

Arguing that no sincere man could support both the direct primary and the appointment of these important new officials, opposition groups throughout the three years of agitation held up this paradox as the prime example of the governor's essential hypocrisy. Voicing La Follettesque declarations of faith in the people and quoting the great Democrat William Jennings Bryan to the effect that even federal judges should be elected,[48] the governor's opponents sought to turn the tables. Although many of them were personally opposed to the direct primary principle, fears that the governor could not be trusted to appoint a commission which would act fairly and objectively drove them to their own brand of hypocrisy.

Cries for the election of all members of the proposed railroad commission also came from a number of sincere supporters of strong regulation who indeed believed in the extension of the direct primary to all top governmental offices, but the Hatten committee finally agreed to support the appointment of all commissioners. For a time, it appears, the committee had yielded to the opposition and decided upon an elective body, but the determined opposition of strong administration men like Frear seems to have tipped the balance.[49] The final bill would call for the appointment of all com-

[47] *Railway World,* 50:91 (January 26, 1906).
[48] *Wisconsin State Journal,* December 2, 1904.
[49] Frear, *Forty Years of Progressive Public Service,* 44.

missioners by the governor "with the advice and consent of the senate." Noted the *State Journal* prophetically, in reference to the antiadministration faction on the senate committee, "These senators reason that confirmation by the senate is a pretty good check, and one that this body would not hesitate to use."[50]

The final irony in this portion of the struggle was some fourteen years in coming when, because of the conservative appointments of Governor Emanuel Philipp, who led the fight for an elective commission in 1905, the Wisconsin progressives sought to make railroad commissioner an elective office, arguing that the commission was "too far from the people."[51]

While those who favored moderate regulation, including such "administration" men as Hatten and Hudnall, labored to complete the compromise during the month of April, forfeiting a bit more of the governor's program, the growing displeasure of the administration became public knowledge.[52] By the same token, members of the senate railroad committee were unhappy that the pro-La Follette leadership in the assembly introduced prematurely, in late March, the compromise plan they had helped conceive.[53] This maneuver seemed aimed at quelling the growing mutiny in the senate which threatened to overturn all administration plans for adequate regulation. The result, however, was a heightening of the dispute which had already shattered La Follette's hold on the upper house. More candid than ever, Hatten in early April declared his preference for a commission that would act as simply a "board of review" able to change "a rate" (his use of the singular was probably intentional), if it found after a full hearing that it was unreasonable.[54] The administration plan for widesweeping changes in the rate structure was repugnant to him, and the views of such staunch supporters of administration policy as James Frear now were seldom sought. E. W. Keyes, on the other hand, found Hatten accessible and receptive.[55] April was the month of final

---

[50] *Wisconsin State Journal,* May 16, 1905.
[51] Maxwell, *Emanuel L. Philipp,* 185.
[52] *Milwaukee Sentinel,* April 8, 1905.
[53] *Ibid.,* April 1, 1905.
[54] *Wisconsin State Journal,* April 8, 1905; *Milwaukee Free Press,* April 5, 1905.
[55] *Milwaukee Sentinel,* April 11, 1905; Keyes to Hughitt, April 19, 1905, in the Keyes Letterbooks.

moderation and compromise. Quipped the *Sentinel,* "If the progress made last week toward the settlement of the railroad rate commission problem continues the governor will find it necessary to interpose a veto message or call out the militia to save his pet issue."[56]

Bemused and uncertain now about the outcome of this his last struggle in the state, the governor began to consider "again going to the people," and enlisted William Jennings Bryan to help convert the four Democratic senators to the administration position. "I think they all want me out of the state," asserted La Follette, "and if they knew that I should stay here and fight if they defeat bill [*sic*], that might make some difference."[57] Meanwhile other key administration personnel sought to shore up the crumbling regulation bill.[58]

On May 5 the senate railroad committee reported out the senate's substitute bill which embodied the important revisions made in the assembly measure a month before by returning initial rate-making power to the railroads and allowing special tariffs. The senate effort further compromised the initial administration position by widening the area of railroad freedom and limiting commission discretion. Concurrence of the more pro-La Follette assembly was no longer demanded for commission appointments, the term "railroad" was defined more narrowly to exclude city transit systems and private logging roads, while certain requirements made upon the carriers were deleted, such as running one passenger train each way daily on all lines. Important, too, was the addition of the provision that the railroads could not raise rates until after January 1, 1906, after which they apparently could do so without commission permission. A single concession to the small shipper was the provision that one carload should be charged the same per load rate as many carloads under special rate structures.

In the following two weeks further modifications were made in the regulation measure as the senate sought a final compromise which would appeal to all of its members. The lone concession to

[56] *Milwaukee Sentinel,* April 17, 1905.
[57] La Follette to W. J. Bryan, April 15, 1905, in the La Follette Letterbooks.
[58] *Milwaukee Free Press,* April 18, 1905; Frear, *Forty Years,* 44–45.

small shippers was deleted and all provisions which required facilities and classifications to be as good for intrastate as interstate traffic were removed. As an apparent sop to the prorailroad forces, the rate schedules which were in force April 1, 1905, rather than December 31, 1904, were declared the maximum rates that could be charged until the end of the year.[59] And in an apparent warning of what was to come, a clause was added which forbade the commission to organize until the senate had formally confirmed the appointment of all members.

On May 18, the final compromise measure was introduced in the senate. The events of that day illustrate the complex changes in support and attitude which had taken place during the long spring of 1905.

Although La Follette employed his usual tactic of sending a special message to the legislature on the eve of the all-important vote, this time charging that the railroads had withheld almost $10,000,000 in taxes, he must have realized that such an effort was no longer crucial, for a compromise had already been forged and it was bound to pass. Still, the day was charged with excitement, for a final resolution of the long-standing fight over regulation was keenly anticipated. The galleries of the senate chamber, special seating on the senate floor, and all available standing room were occupied. The upper house subjected the crowd to a tedious seven-hour debate over various plans for regulation, with many amendments proposed and soundly defeated as the senators clung to the final committee plan proposed two days earlier.

Apparent above all else in the day's activities was the total disunity of the administration forces in the senate, the same group which had so confidently met the preceding December. As if determined to emphasize the complex bifurcation of the pro-La Follette wing, the first business of the day involved a pitched battle between president pro tempore J. J. McGillivray, supposed leader of the senate administration forces and organizer of the December cau-

---

[59] W. D. Connor noted in February that the December 31 date was particularly important to all lumber dealers because lumber rates had been raised again on January 11, 1905. Connor to La Follette, February 27, January 5, 1905, in the La Follette Papers.

cus, and George Hudnall, a leading administration member of the senate railroad committee, over McGillivray's introduction of an amendment calling for the automatic inclusion of present railroad commissioner John M. Thomas as a member of the proposed commission. Hudnall charged that the McGillivray amendment was unconstitutional, and the senate quickly isolated the administration leader by rejecting his amendment; only McGillivray held out for Thomas, who had been so instrumental in developing the governor's case against the carriers.

No sooner had McGillivray been put in his place than E. E. Stevens, another member of the administration caucus, proposed an amendment which would overthrow the appointive principle, for which the governor had held out, and instead provide for the election of all commission members. This too was quickly condemned by other pro-La Follette men and rejected by the senate, although Fred Wilcox, a supporter of the governor, felt called upon to apologize to the throng for voting against the elective principle. It was clear early in the debate that the fragmented La Follette forces posed no threat to the plans of more moderate members.

The stalwart members of the body had their differences also. Senators North and Whitehead in particular worked hard to undermine further the regulation act and achieve the final wishes of the railroads. These efforts were swiftly rejected. Then, in a significant expression of the unity achieved through the efforts of Hatten and others, Hatten, with unanimous consent, withdrew the first committee amendment to the regulation bill. Next, Senator Andrew Kreutzer, author of the substitute which had won wide acclaim from the stalwarts' railroad sources earlier in the session and whom La Follette two years earlier had branded a "corporation hireling,"[60] moved the rules be suspended and the final committee compromise be approved immediately. The senate responded with unanimity, with only the incapacitated Ernst Merton unable to be present to approve the regulation measure.[61]

A bill had finally been passed, but the struggle was not over. Not until the governor wrestled with the political realities would his

[60] *Wisconsin State Journal*, August 4, 1903.
[61] See full account of day's events in *Milwaukee Free Press*, May 19, 1905, and *Wisconsin Senate Journal*, 1905, pp. 1130–1139.

approval come. And not until a list of commissioners was proposed by La Follette would the real cost of the compromise be known.

The bill did not reach the governor's desk for approval until June 9 because of the need to correlate the bills approved by the two houses, a process during which the senate version was meekly accepted by the assembly in all essential details. Acceptance by the pro-La Follette assembly meant that the governor had acquiesced —but not without much soul-searching. In hearing of the passage of the committee compromise by the senate, La Follette had immediately sent copies of the measure to experts whom he had often consulted, asking their opinions on the turn of events. Earlier he had written with hope and confidence, asking how best his goals could be achieved, but now the tone was subdued. "Our senate is very close. Otherwise, the bill would be different," he commented apologetically to S. H. Cowan, the noted Texas expert of rate regulation. "If there are *any defects* which *in operation would cripple* the *work* of a *commission under it,* then it is of the *highest importance* that we *know it now,*" he wrote, underlining all key phrases in the manner of a man deeply troubled by the problem facing him. "Another campaign upon this issue would give us a good working majority in the senate, and enable us to get a bill just as it ought to be."[62] Similar queries went out to E. P. Bacon and O. B. Colquitt.[63]

Cowan's reply, which was particularly critical of the proposed law, emphasized the possibilities for a hostile court to cripple the commission and the crucial lack of commission power to set rates initially. Ignoring the issue of initial rate making, the governor wired the attorney contending that the commission was safe from court intervention because of certain named provisions in the bill and asking the attorney to wire his reply immediately.[64] Cowan, busy in Washington, did not respond and La Follette was left to make the decision on his own.

It had been that way all along, for the astute governor must have

[62] La Follette to S. H. Cowan, May 18, 1905, in the La Follette Letterbooks.
[63] La Follette to Bacon, May 28, 1905, in the La Follette Letterbooks; J. M. Winterbotham to Colquitt, May 18, 1905, Railroad Commissioners' Letterbooks, volume 19, in the Wisconsin Public Service Commission Records.
[64] Cowan to La Follette, May 26, 1905, La Follette to Cowan, May 26, 1905, both in the La Follette Papers.

known where he stood, with a commission not necessarily crippled but without some of the strength which he deemed essential. On June 13 he signed the bill but tacked on a characteristic memorandum, a kind of memo for all purposes, which included all of those elements of tact and ambiguity which made him such an effective politician. After regretting the lack of any provision for the regulation of the sale of stocks and bonds (a strange reference since none of the previous bills had mentioned the subject either), he spun off a remarkable closing paragraph:

> There are other omissions and there are terms of limitation in some of the provisions of the bill which may, in some respects, impair its efficiency. I approve the measure, however, as the best which it is possible to secure at present, and as, in many respects, the most progressive, and, at the same time, the most conservative law yet enacted regulating railway rates and railway services.[65]

Why La Follette signed the bill using this circuitous route through which, in effect, he approved the bill but washed his hands of responsibility for the sins of the legislators is not clear. It is most likely that his pending acceptance of a role as a United States Senator was the most important element in his decision. For months a vigorous fight had been raging in the Congress over regulatory legislation much like that which was discussed in Wisconsin. Since January La Follette, primarily through Bacon and Johnson, had kept in close touch with the fight in hopes that he could get into the fray before it was over. Johnson too was especially eager to see him there and was wont to stress the importance of his coming to Washington as soon as possible for, as he once argued, "nothing will be accomplished before you are in the Senate to aid in securing the desired results."[66] Such blandishments fed the governor's all-consuming ambition to rise as high as he possibly could. (Had not Bacon telegraphed on the occasion of his election as Senator: "White House next.")[67] Apparently convinced

[65] *Wisconsin Senate Journal,* 1905, p. 1665.
[66] G. H. D. Johnson to La Follette, January 28, 1905, in the La Follette Papers.
[67] Bacon to La Follette, January 25, 1905, in the La Follette Papers.

that another fight in Wisconsin to achieve a better bill was not worth the political cost, the governor decided his principles and his ambitions were best served by accepting the compromise and moving on.

In his *Autobiography,* written some six years later, La Follette declared forcefully against all compromise with the forces which sought to interrupt essential reforms. "In legislation," he declared, *"no bread* is often better than *half a loaf."*[68] In spite of this conviction, on this occasion the governor had decided on "half a loaf." Time would reveal whether it was even half.

[68] La Follette, *Autobiography,* 268.

Anatomy of a Compromise

5 Administration leaders would proclaim the passage of a regulation bill a major triumph for reform. The unanimity of the final vote in the relatively conservative senate which insured the bill's passage, the expressions of relief uttered by the railroad journals at the form of the final measure, and the general disorganization of the supporters of the bill, as well as the actual provisions of the statute, however, all highlight the fact that the measure was conspicuously a compromise. The interplay of personalities and interest groups suggested from the beginning that this would be the final resolution of the divisive issue, for each of the sides in the multifaceted struggle claimed significant support but could not claim a decisive consensus for its position.

Central to any understanding of the path to compromise on the railroad regulation question is a clear perception of the strengths and weaknesses of Robert La Follette, the dominant figure in the final stages of the controversy. For years supporters of state regulation had tried in vain to persuade the people of Wisconsin that stricter controls were necessary in order to curb excessive railroad rates. Although they had both data and dedication, they never succeeded in building the popular support needed to mount a viable legislative campaign for the passage of a regulation measure. Unsullied by the reformers' vain efforts, those interests which enjoyed preferences under the existing system simply winked at these attempts and made sure they kept their political fences mended.

In late 1902, La Follette became part of the regulation crusade and the configurations of the struggle changed. Confident of his abilities to appeal to the people, La Follette took the raw data which other reformers had utilized for years and presented it in a more graphic way. In La Follette's orations, rate comparisons were stated in terms of dollars and cents taken from the pockets of families throughout the state. The farmers in Langlade County, for example, were told that they were losing thirty-eight cents per acre because of excessive railroad charges, while the residents of Chippewa County found that the railroad they were paying to transport their produce to market earned $6,000,000 more annually than just profits and dividends warranted.[1] The governor dramatized the struggle as a fight between the greedy, self-serving transportation companies and the common man working to keep house and home together in spite of high consumer prices stemming from excessive freight rates.

Through these means La Follette succeeded in making the noble cause an issue which no one could ignore. The cause which had long languished for lack of a compelling voice to champion it now became a crusade. Legislators who had never given the issue much thought found that they had to deal with the problem of regulation, and more conservative publications which had earlier dismissed it as a chimerical scheme now had to take more moderate stands on the issue. By February of 1905 even the *Milwaukee Sentinel* was forced to admit, "there is a popular demand for the enactment of a statute establishing a railroad rate commission."[2] In the case of regulation in Wisconsin the addition of the voice and personality of La Follette swung the balance toward reform. "Nothing ever would have been accomplished without your campaign of education," wrote a grateful Robert Eliot to the governor after seeing at last the passage of a measure for which he had worked for two decades.[3]

There is, however, a conspicuous difference between generating broad public support for a principle, and mobilizing interested groups to crusade for a specific solution. By failing to do the latter,

[1] *Milwaukee Free Press*, September 9, 3, 1903.
[2] *Milwaukee Sentinel*, February 11, 1905.
[3] Eliot to La Follette, May 24, 1905, in the La Follette Papers.

the governor placed himself in a position where compromise was the only viable solution. Specifically, it was La Follette's failure to mobilize farm support, to galvanize that group which he considered the core of his strength into concerted action on the issue of regulation, which crippled his crusade.

One of the strangest ironies of the period is that La Follette, often dubbed the leader of the agrarian wing of the progressive movement, reached the peak of his state prestige in the same years that farmer organization in Wisconsin reached its nadir. Although the next fifteen years would witness the growth of three strong farmers' organizations in the state, between 1903 and 1905, when La Follette fought the legislature for three major reforms, only the Grange existed as an organization for state farmers interested in participation in national farmers' movements, and it was nearly moribund. In 1904 only ten of the nineteen Granges in the state even bothered to report to the state headquarters with a grand total of 340 members.[4] A. C. Powers, the head of the state organization, attributed the decline in Wisconsin to "an exodus of the better class of farmers from the country to the city" and a lack of interest on the part of many farmers in organization.[5] While specific state organizations like the Wisconsin Cheese Makers' and the Wisconsin Buttermakers' associations retained strength throughout the period, the dearth of vital farm organizations was a severe handicap to reformers who sought to mobilize the farmers in support of regulation.

Oddly enough, the regulation cause had little appeal even to the organizations which did exist. The only organized farmers' group which actively protested existing rail rates and demanded tighter regulation at the outset of the La Follette phase of the crusade was the Wisconsin Cheese Makers. Convinced that inequitable rates to Chicago from various Wisconsin points were pricing them out of that market, the Cheese Makers as early as 1900 had enlisted Graham L. Rice, the powerless Wisconsin state railroad commissioner, to intercede with railroad officials and

---

[4] Walter H. Ebling, "Recent Farmer Movements in Wisconsin" (unpublished master's thesis, University of Wisconsin, 1925), 15.

[5] *Journal of Proceedings of the National Grange of the Patrons of Husbandry,* 1903, p. 75.

try to get a better rate. Rice could only report that the matter involved interstate commerce and he could do nothing.[6] In 1902, after E. P. Bacon addressed the body in support of changes in the Interstate Commerce Act, the association responded with the passage of resolutions supporting such measures and appointed a committee to devise ways and means of reducing their freight rates to Chicago.[7] When the state crusade was undertaken, the Cheese Makers were prepared, and voiced their wholehearted support for that cause also.[8] The influence of the ubiquitous grain merchant from Milwaukee in molding the thinking of the association indicates, however, the degree to which even this group, the first farm organization to take a stand on state regulation, was responding to the initiative of others rather than exercising leadership.

The other major state farm organizations showed far less interest in the struggle. At the annual conventions of the Wisconsin Dairymen's Association in 1903 and 1904 the delegates worried over oleomargarine and milk inspection, passed resolutions thanking the railroads for granting special rates to those who had to travel to attend the convention, and adjourned without mentioning the battle raging about them to free them from railroad oppression.[9] Only in 1905 did the association go on record as "heartily" favoring plans to establish a railroad commission.[10] The Wisconsin Buttermarkers' Association also waited until 1905 before expressing its belated support in a vague resolution "demanding" the passage of a bill organizing a commission, and charging that discriminations by the railroads were "a positive injury to most of the shippers of dairy products in Wisconsin." Ill-equipped to present their own case, the Buttermarkers accepted the offer of T. C. Rich-

[6] *Proceedings of Eighth Annual Meeting of the Wisconsin Cheese Makers' Association*, 1900, pp. 31-33.
[7] *Proceedings of Tenth Annual Meeting of the Wisconsin Cheese Makers' Association*, 1902, pp. 129, 164.
[8] *Proceedings of Eleventh Annual Meeting of the Wisconsin Cheese Makers' Association*, 1903, p. 142.
[9] See *Thirty-First* and *Thirty-Second Annual Reports of the Wisconsin Dairymen's Association*, 1903, 1904.
[10] *Thirty-Third Annual Report of the Wisconsin Dairymen's Association*, 1905, p. 187.

mond, Madison lawyer and leading progressive, to represent them before the legislative committees considering the legislation. Interested but not sanguine on the subject of regulation, the association was willing to co-operate with progressive attempts to bring witnesses from various groups in the state before the legislative commission. Richmond was not a farmer nor a member of the association but, as the resolution noted, "Mr. Richmond has offered to represent this association without remuneration."[11]

Delegates to the Annual State Agricultural Convention showed equal caution. "No state has more or better water, better market facilities, or a better climate," proclaimed C. H. Everett at the convention in Madison in February, 1903, at the time of the launching of the reformers' fight for a railroad commission.[12] Apparently sharing Everett's optimism, the delegates endorsed state regulation only after two years of silence during which most of the important battles for the cause were fought.[13]

The position taken by the Wisconsin State Grange was the strangest of all, for the National Grange had traditionally been in the vanguard of attempts to regulate railroads and improve the bargaining power of the farmer. In the first years of the twentieth century the enthusiasm of the national organization for these causes did not flag. Yearly it recommended strengthening the ICC and increasing state regulation of carriers through state railway commissions empowered to fix maximum rates for freight and passengers on all lines.

In Wisconsin, however, the Grange was curiously silent. The leader of the Wisconsin Grange, A. C. Powers, sought to interest his weakened organization in such matters, but he had little success. The Grange's committee on resolutions studiously ignored the issue of state regulation during the time the crusade reached its climax, and instead submitted to its membership a resolution which had been handed down from the national organization supporting changes in the Interstate Commerce Act.[14]

[11] *Proceedings of Fourth Annual Meeting of the Wisconsin Buttermakers' Association*, 1905, pp. 130, 35.
[12] *Annual Report of the Wisconsin State Board of Agriculture*, 1903, p. 221.
[13] *Annual Report of the Wisconsin State Board of Agriculture*, 1905, pp. 70–71.
[14] *Proceedings of the Thirty-Third Annual Session of the Wisconsin State Grange of the Patrons of Husbandry*, 1904, pp. 9, 10, 20–21.

While farmers' organizations involved relatively few of the state's farmers, there is considerable evidence that the few operating groups well reflected the general state of opinion in agricultural communities. The papers of W. D. Hoard, ex-governor and probably the most influential farm leader in the state, do not contain a single inquiry concerning the rate regulation question. Nor does the correspondence of John J. Esch and Herman Ekern, the congressman and assemblyman respectively for the agricultural area in the vicinity of Trempealeau County include letters from farmers on this subject during the 1904 campaign and the 1905 legislative session.[15] Although the La Follette papers tell a more mixed story, with occasional correspondence from farmers, they reflect no decisive concern about regulation on the part of farmers. (While most farmers generally supported the governor's reform efforts, one refused him his endorsement because of rising taxes, unfulfilled promises, and because "the Rabbits have destroyed 20 Apple trees for me and my neighbors.")[16]

The journals and newspapers with major circulation among the farmers tell the same indecisive story. The *Wisconsin Farmer* printed occasional editorials expressing interest in the problem of regulation and even flirted abstractly with the possibility of public ownership of railroads, but it never became deeply involved in the specific Wisconsin struggle. More hopeful that the strengthening of the ICC would bring results, its comments on the state crusade were limited to measured praise for La Follette and some early endorsements of the regulation program. Early in the campaign the journal remarked that it was "strange that Wisconsin has so long lagged behind her sister states in exercising this function."[17] In May, 1903, the *Farmer* requested its readers to write their representatives supporting a bill to freeze freight rates,[18] but this was the last specific mention of regulatory legislation. It published a damning analysis of railroad thinking in the fall of 1903, charging

---

[15] I am indebted to Stuart Brandes for allowing me to use some of his findings included in "Wisconsin Progressivism Viewed as a Farmers' Movement," an unpublished seminar paper, written in 1965 for Economics 648, University of Wisconsin.

[16] M. Battle to Hoard, April 7, 1904, in the La Follette Papers.

[17] *Wisconsin Farmer*, 22:2 (February 5, 1903).

[18] *Ibid.*, 22:4 (May 14, 1903).

that the carriers were ready "for plucking the feathers, for shearing the sheep, for profit-taking," now that the state's farmers were settled into patterns of agriculture.[19] A few weeks later, however, the *Farmer* strongly praised the Milwaukee road, a target of many attacks by the regulation crusaders, as "a triumph in transportation." "The road," it argued, "is managed purely as a railroad and without reference to Wall Street manipulations, such as affected all lines in the early days and were felt even in the Milwaukee management up to seventeen years ago."[20]

While the *Farmer* showed moderate interest in regulation, the *Wisconsin Agriculturalist*, the other major broad-based rural journal, ignored the matter completely. Although involved in lobbying for better roads, curbs on the production of oleomargarine, and even the raising of the bounty on wolf scalps, during the years of agitation the *Agriculturalist* took no note of the regulation issue. Even when reporting La Follette's inaugural address of 1905, which dwelt on the need for regulation more than any other single issue, the *Agriculturalist* published long excerpts on those matters which it felt pertained to the farmer, but ignored the governor's lengthy attempt to enlist the rural masses in support of his pet measure.[21] "In the proportion that business principles are applied to the business of farming, will profits be returned to the owners of the farms," it remarked in 1903.[22] Self-reliance, not government intervention, was clearly the way to success in farming in the eyes of the *Agriculturalist*.

The same stance was taken in *Hoard's Dairyman*, a journal of broad circulation throughout the Midwest but based in Wisconsin. Convinced that thrift, hard work, and education could guarantee prosperity for the dairy farmer, the *Dairyman* ignored the claims of state reformers that impersonal forces were robbing farmers of their substance.

The local newspaper perhaps more clearly reflected the attitudes of the local farmer than did a journal of broader appeal and

---

[19] *Ibid.*, 22:4 (September 3, 1903).
[20] *Ibid.*, 22:4 (September 29, 1903).
[21] *Wisconsin Agriculturist*, 29:10 (January 26, 1905).
[22] *Ibid.*, 27:2 (April 9, 1903).

circulation. Here too, the regulation issue was underplayed. A recent study of the local newspapers in the rural areas of Rock and Trempealeau counties supports the impression that farmers were more interested in their own private affairs than in state issues. Most of these papers said little about the regulation fight. Those which did discuss the issue showed a remarkable ability to separate their allegiance to the La Follette forces from their stance on rate regulation. Several newspapers supported La Follette but opposed regulation, and one supported regulation while pushing one of La Follette's opponents. Only two supported both regulation and La Follette.[23] Although newspapers do not invariably reflect the opinions of their readers, the positions taken by these papers corroborate both the general lack of farmer concern with regulation and the degree to which the broader regulation issue was a part of everyone's program by 1905.

The difficulty the La Follette forces encountered in reaching the farmer stemmed in part from a curious lack of influence among farm leaders. La Follette apparently did not even know A. C. Powers, the head of the Wisconsin State Grange and a strong supporter of regulation. When Powers wrote La Follette congratulating him on his election to the United States Senate and pledging Grange support for his work in Washington, La Follette addressed an impersonal reply to "A. C. Downs," which was returned unclaimed.[24] The leader of the University of Wisconsin Agricultural Experiment Station, W. A. Henry, a much sought-after speaker for agricultural meetings, expressed interest in the direct primary and railroad taxation during the La Follette governorship, but was never concerned about rate regulation.[25] J. Q. Emery, dairy and food commissioner, remained equally noncommittal during the struggle. Asked in 1906 to sum up the key legislation passed by the state legislature in the last three years which affected the dairy

[23] Brandes, "Wisconsin Progressivism Viewed as a Farmers' Movement."

[24] A. C. Powers to La Follette, January 25, 1905, LaFollette to "A. C. Downs," March 2, 1905, both in the La Follette Papers.

[25] See W. A. Henry to Hoard, January 30, 1903, in the Hoard Papers. Ignoring La Follette's plea for regulatory legislation, Henry remarks, "Now comes primary elections and railroad taxation."

industry, Emery made no mention of the regulation bill.[26] Even
John Luchsinger, president of the Southern Wisconsin Cheesemen's Protective Association, who was deeply involved in the
struggle to achieve lower freight rates for Wisconsin cheese men,
refused to support La Follette for a third term in 1904 in spite of
the promise the governor made to enact strict rate regulation.
"As an executive or as a leader of men," he declared, "he is too
impulsive, too fond of praise, too apt to regard as enemies those
friends who sincerely differ with him, and those who praise and
flatter have their own way no matter how false and treacherous."[27]

Of the major farm leaders, only W. D. Hoard, ex-governor,
prosperous dairy man, publisher of *Hoard's Dairyman*, and the
Jefferson County Union, an influential local newspaper in the Fort
Atkinson area, wholeheartedly supported La Follette and his program for regulation. Although the *Dairyman* remained neutral,
in a 1904 circular letter sent to supporters of the governor throughout the state and widely printed in newspapers, Hoard plumped
for a third term for the "able, honest, fearless champion of just and
equal government" and charged that those who opposed La Follette were dupes of large corporations who feared his attack on
the railroad rate structure. "The 'big shippers' are determined not
to surrender their secret rates, their unlawful money-rebates, and
give the consumers and producers, the laborers and farmers, an
equal chance," Hoard declared.[28]

Even Hoard, however, was late in joining the drive for stronger
regulation. In 1902 he showed strong interest in ballot and tax
reform and no concern for stronger regulation. His praise for the
work of the railroad commissioner during his governorship indicated a strange satisfaction with the weak, custodial role delegated
to a single commissioner by the 1876 Vance Law.[29] A 1903 inci-
dent in which Hoard himself was overcharged on a shipment of
lumber seems to have given him a greater awareness of the need
for stronger regulation, but he took little time to keep up with

---

[26] *Hoard's Dairyman*, 36:1278–1279 (January 19, 1906).
[27] John Luchsinger to Hoard, April 18, 1904, in the Hoard Papers.
[28] Copy of the letter can be found in W. D. Hoard Papers, March 24, 1904.
[29] Hoard to Luchsinger, July 19, 1902, in the Hoard Letterbooks.

developments in this area and was of little use as an adviser on the question when the regulation bills were framed.[30]

Still Hoard's interest in new regulatory statutes set him apart from most farmers. Having campaigned vigorously for La Follette and regulation in 1904, Hoard's paper, the *Jefferson County Union*, remarked on the eve of the election, "The farmers do not seem to realize how much they are interested in this matter."[31] By the time the regulation fight was in full swing in 1905, resignation had turned to cynicism. "It is the old, old story of the people asleep, and doing nothing to make their case good," declared the Fort Atkinson newspaper.[32] In spite of the full co-operation of the governor's staff, which sent him data for use in his numerous speeches to agricultural groups and advised him carefully on possible ways of enlisting farm support for La Follette, Hoard could do little to interest the farmer in the regulation crusade.[33]

In part the strange apathy on the part of Wisconsin farmers seems to have stemmed from the new prosperity they were enjoying. "The hardest part in some places was to get enough to hold a caucus on acct [*sic*] of the farmers being so busy," complained one campaigner in 1903.[34] Expressing the same sentiment more directly, the *Galesville Republican* of rural Trempealeau County declared: "The governor of the state is tearing around the country in an automobile, waving his hands before the farmers whose bins are bursting with a bounteous harvest, whose sleek herds dot their

---

[30] See Hoard to O. H. Johnson, October [mismarked August] 27, 1903, in the Hoard Letterbooks, for a description of his difficulty with a rail shipment. Hoard refused to testify before the Wisconsin senate committee investigating the regulatory legislation in 1905 and had little to offer when consulted concerning specific provisions of the bill. See Hoard to Grant Thomas, March 17, 1905, and Hoard to W. H. Hatten, March 17, 1905, both in the Hoard Letterbooks.

[31] *Jefferson County Union*, November 4, 1904.

[32] *Ibid.*, March 31, 1905.

[33] J. J. Hannan to Hoard, August 29, 1903, and G. E. Bryant to Hoard, September 19, 1904, both in the Hoard Papers, contain advice and information from La Follette advisers for Hoard to use in enlisting the aid of farmers in the regulation fight.

[34] W. H. Cleary to John Thomas, May 6, 1904, correspondence of the Wisconsin Railroad Commissioner, General Correspondence, in the Wisconsin Public Service Commission Records.

broad acres as evidence of prosperity, whose checks are good for thousands at the local bank — shrieking that they are a down-trodden people and little better than serfs."[35]

The prosperity boasted of was primarily a result of the elevation of the dairy farmer to a leadership role in Wisconsin agriculture. By 1900, notes Eric Lampard, dairying had become the "most viable 'type-of-farming' in Wisconsin." By 1910 three-quarters of the gross farm income in the state was derived from livestock and nearly half of that amount stemmed directly from the sale of milk. By that time, also, Wisconsin had become the largest producer of creamery butter in the nation and was producing nearly half of the nation's cheese.[36]

In the midst of a period of dynamic growth in the first decade of this century it is little wonder that the dairyman had little time for politics, especially politics built upon agitation for rate regula-tion. While the farmer who shipped his crop long distances and sold it competitively in the world market was highly dependent upon reasonable transportation costs which would insure him a profitable enterprise, the dairy farmer sold much of his produce locally, and even when cheese or butter were transported by rail, the rate charged represented only a small portion of the value of the produce. No small vacillations in transportation rates could rob the dairyman of the bulk of his profits on his highly valuable products.[37]

Less troubled by problems of commerce, the dairy farmer made fewer demands on government. He sought legislation against but-ter substitutes, encouraged agricultural school expansion and would on occasion seek to prevent carriers from charging rates which discriminated against him and favored another dairy area. For the most part, however, the dairymen were able to go it alone.

---

[35] *Galesville Republican,* September 15, 1904, as quoted in Brandes, "Wis-consin Progressivism Viewed as a Farmers' Movement."

[36] Eric E. Lampard, *The Rise of the Dairy Industry in Wisconsin* (Madison, 1963), 244–245, 267, 295.

[37] Russel B. Nye, *Midwestern Progressive Politics* (East Lansing, 1959), 11–12; Benton A. Wilcox, "A Reconsideration of the Character and Economic Basis of Northwestern Radicalism" (unpublished Ph.D. disser-tation, University of Wisconsin, 1933), 3.

The message of *Hoard's Dairyman* that the wholesome virtues of thrift, hard work, and education guaranteed success in the dairy industry appeared quite literally true in the early years of the twentieth century so the dairy farmer, for the most part, eschewed politics and kept to his chores.[38]

Thus the La Follette attempt to mobilize the farmer in support of regulation foundered. In part the failure was the governor's, for he never enlisted the agricultural leaders in support of his program. More important, however, were the fundamental changes taking place in the state's agriculture, which made the rate question of little relative importance. While the governor clearly appealed to many farmers as a political leader, the specific issue of rate regulation engaged the attentions of only a small minority of the farmers in the state.

The lack of firm public support from the farmers of the state proved a severe handicap to La Follette in his efforts to achieve a legislative victory. His weakness as a legislative leader, however, was the factor which ultimately brought down his program. From his college days a better orator than a debater, the governor proved unable to deal quickly and decisively with the intricate questions that arose in the legislature during the drafting of the regulation statute.[39] Some have accused La Follette of knowing little about complex economic questions.[40] Whether it was this weakness or simply an unwillingness to take the time to study the question in depth, the governor seems never to have fully mastered the regulation question during the years when he championed the cause.

Joining the drive for a regulation bill late, after the ground rules

---

[38] See Lampard, *Rise of the Dairy Industry in Wisconsin*, 334–341, for a highly insightful discussion of the dairyman's attitudes toward government and his profession during this period, which Lampard calls "The Wisconsin Idea of Dairying."

[39] David P. Thelen, *The Early Life of Robert M. La Follette* (Chicago, 1966), 31–33.

[40] In 1919, John Strange, long-time progressive politician and friend of La Follette, remarked that La Follette "has little practical knowledge of business—particularly of manufacture—as possible for any live man to have. . . . La Follette knows nothing whatever about practical manufacture and I am quite sure he has never even seen the inside of a mill of any kind." "Autobiography of John Strange," 40, in the Strange Papers.

for the struggle had been laid down and a group of dedicated reformers had accumulated sufficient information to argue the question persuasively, La Follette was never forced to cope with such
details in his campaigning, for always he could get ready-made
information and analysis by simply contacting the Milwaukee reform group. The result was a conspicuous difference in abilities.
Highly effective on the campaign trail when he could deliver
stirring indictments using the information prepared for him by
others, his lack of personal knowledge concerning key portions of
regulatory legislation handicapped him greatly in the give-and-
take of a legislative session when the exigencies of time demanded
quick and forceful decisions. The result was a breakdown of discipline among administration forces due to a lack of clear guidelines
and forceful leadership.

This is well illustrated in both legislative sessions during which
he spearheaded regulation drives. In 1903, after winning considerable praise for a ringing inaugural, La Follette delayed for weeks
before he brought forth a regulatory measure with his stamp upon
it. Following a poor showing in committee hearings during which
administration spokesmen contradicted each other, La Follette
again shifted his ground, this time standing for the kind of strict
regulation implied by his ideological posture.

The shocking defeat of this La Follette-backed measure in the
assembly, a body generally highly sympathetic to the objectives
of the administration, illustrated most clearly the confusion
spawned by inept legislative leadership, for, lacking clear mandates from the chief executive, many administration assemblymen
had no choice but to succumb to the pressures of business interests in their districts who expressed their priorities forcefully. The
administration never really recovered from this defeat. Perhaps
La Follette did not expect a victory in 1903, but by allowing a
shippers' protest to stampede the branch of the legislature which
was generally loyal to his programs, he created an impression of
overwhelming political power for the opposition. Apparently more
fearful of this rising strength than of the irresolute governor, legislators from this time on never approved any sort of regulatory
measure unless it was first endorsed by conservative forces. By
undertaking the regulation fight and trying to face all directions

without proper attention to the cultivation of popular support or the building of legislative discipline, La Follette suffered an irreparable setback in 1903.

In 1905 La Follette's chances appeared to be a good deal better. Although he had failed in his efforts to build strong grass-roots support for his program, he had transformed the cause into an issue which no one could duck. Unfortunately, the governor had not used this time to master the legislative side of this complex issue. He had neither built a solid coalition united around a concrete measure nor even made inquiry into what sort of legislative enactment would best express his thoughts on the subject. Only in December, 1904, after his election victory, did he begin to send bills about the country asking for criticism and suggestions. Because he had no specific measure about which to consolidate support, he could make few unified demands on the administration senators who caucused during that month. They thus agreed to work for administration causes, then went away voicing different impressions of what they thought would be a good regulation bill.

On February 10, when the administration proposed strong regulation in the legislature, the division was still apparent with two bills being introduced, one by James J. Frear, perhaps the governor's closest friend in the body, and the other by William H. Hatten. The same damaging disunity was exhibited in the committee hearings because the governor neglected the task of finding committed and articulate spokesmen for the administration bill until it was too late. Down to the final day of voting "administration" senators publicly bickered among themselves about the ingredients of a good regulation bill.

In view of this lack of decisive leadership it is quite understandable why even administration assemblymen gave credit to the more conservative senate as well as the governor for the final securing of a regulation measure, stressing not a battle won but harmony achieved. "It is a great victory for the governor and the party and also a great personal victory to the members of the Senate railroad committee, without reference to party or faction," declared the chairman of the assembly committee on railroads.[41]

41 *Wisconsin State Journal,* May 19, 1905.

Albert Hall, away from the halls of the legislature after years of fighting for a commission with initial rate-making powers, declared, "While the bill is not all that the friends of state control would like it's a tremendous stride in the right direction."[42]

This moderate praise, lavished not only on the governor but also on the senate which he had so often condemned, expressed the limits of La Follette's function in the regulation controversy. John M. Whitehead, an archenemy of La Follette's, later glibly asserted that "the foundation for all [La Follette's] legislation was laid during the administration of preceding governors and what came about in the process of development and would have come if he had never been governor."[43] In the case of railroad reform, Whitehead's assertion does not seem to be borne out, for not until the popular La Follette undertook the issue did it have the spark that made it a compelling question of the day. Insofar as Whitehead downgraded La Follette's legislative leadership, however, his insight was worthy of some attention, for the governor was unable to win a final statute which fully reflected his convictions concerning regulation.

Asked about the moderate senate committee measure which had been approved the day before, a progressive assemblyman asserted candidly, "It was the only kind of a bill that could have passed."[44] His remark well summarizes the strength and weakness of La Follette. The governor had been instrumental in promoting the concept of regulation, but he could not marshall sufficient support for his own program and had to settle for a measure which fitted more moderate convictions.

The most influential forces in forging a final settlement were warring groups of businessmen. Certain wealthy merchants in the only large urban center in the state had played the key role in the railroad regulation fight in Wisconsin from the 1880's on. Only when Albert Hall, a well-to-do farmer-businessman, led the drive against the carriers in the 1890's were rural interests highly active

---

[42] Hall to La Follette, May 19, 1905, in the La Follette Papers.
[43] Whitehead to Ralph Gabriel, April 22, 1914, in the John M. Whitehead Papers.
[44] Wisconsin State Journal, May 19, 1905.

in the regulation fight, and even Hall was inducted into the fray by E. P. Bacon, the leader of the Milwaukee Chamber of Commerce-based reform group. When, therefore, La Follette embraced the regulation issue, he too was forced to go to this Milwaukee group for the information and advice he so badly needed to promote the issue. Although he railed against corporations and the wicked city, La Follette took the advice of big-time, urban grain merchants who continued to lead the struggle for a regulation statute in Wisconsin.

No less important in determining the final form which the regulatory act would take, however, were those major business interests who refused to have any part of the La Follette regulation plan. In 1903 many shippers and manufacturers who made heavy use of the railroads descended on Madison twice at strategic times to protest any attempt to pass a regulation plan which might threaten their economic well-being. Their fears, expressed repeatedly, were that strict regulation would inevitably mean an end to special rate concessions upon which they were so highly dependent. In an attempt to placate these important economic groups, late in that legislative session the administration appended a provision to its strong regulation bill which specifically insured the continuance of commodity rates, concentration rates, and all other special rate systems. These large shippers, however, were not turned aside by this belated display of concern. Certain that the commission, in constructing new rate schedules for the state's carriers, would inevitably use distance as the uniform gauge for all rates, they did not accept the assurance that special rates, which specifically violated this concept, would be spared under the new law. Holding firm to their fears, these shippers successfully downed the 1903 rate bill.

In 1905, when a regulation measure was finally passed, the shippers who had been so adamant two years earlier made no public show of opposition at all. Administration supporters later claimed that these shippers did not protest in 1905 because the canny governor held over their heads a list of the names of those who had received rebates from the carriers which the railroad commissioner had compiled during his long investigation of the carriers' financial records. Unwilling to risk exposure of their illegal activities, they argued, the corrupt shippers submitted meekly to La Follette's regulation plan.[45]

Such an analysis omits any consideration of the nature of the final regulation bill. Even in 1903 those large shippers who fought most vigorously to defeat the administration's regulation plan never declared themselves against all forms of regulation. They were, in fact, meticulously careful to attack only the specific features of regulation plans which seemed threatening to them.

During the next two years, these important economic groups joined in a more positive program aimed at the governor and his plans for strict regulation. The platform drafted by the stalwart wing of the Republican party in 1904 expressed their feelings well in supporting a regulatory statute which prohibited "unjust discrimination" if it left the railway companies "free to adopt their rates and regulations to the interests of the sections, cities and industries."[46] By 1905 even the most conservative representative of the large shipping interests, the Wisconsin Manufacturers Association, established specifically to oppose regulation, came out in favor of this limited kind of regulation. While protesting any commission having "full power to make rates on its own initiative," it approved a body "which should look into the matter of alleged discrimination" and would be empowered "to take up and adjust rates only on complaints with the idea of justice to shipper, consumer and carrier alike."[47]

With this new program these important economic interests were not forced to resort to the stopgap tactics of 1903 in order to be influential. Knowing the enormous strength which these interests had when united, the legislature in 1905 did not challenge them. Instead William Hatten, chairman of the senate committee on railroads and himself a wealthy businessman, gave the large shipping interests ample opportunity to express their views and aid in the writing of a more moderate regulation bill. The suggestions of Emanuel L. Philipp, president of a refrigerator car company, who was concerned about the welfare of both railroads and large ship-

[45] Hannan to Philip C. Allen, October 2, 1906, in the La Follette Papers; Barton, *La Follette's Winning of Wisconsin,* 256.
[46] *Blue Book of the State of Wisconsin,* 1905, pp. 1044–1045.
[47] *Milwaukee Free Press,* March 11, 1905.

John Barnes

B. H. Meyer

pers, were sympathetically received, and he apparently played a leading role in the final drafting of the regulation measure.[48] Whether through Philipp or others these shipping interests prevailed upon the senate committee to include specific provisions in the bill which protected their interests. (Asked about the meaning of the words "other special contract rates" in Section 6 of the Wisconsin statute, which insured the continuance of special rate structures, Railroad Commission Chairman John Barnes in 1906 explained: "The clause was inserted in our bill at the suggestion of some shippers, particularly lumbermen.")[49]

In the final measure, therefore, the major fears of these business interests were allayed. Not only did the bill make specific provision for the continuation of special rate structures, but it stripped the commission of the power to initiate an entirely new system of rates for the state. A long-and-short-haul provision, which was advocated by some but which would have robbed the special rate systems of some of their flexibility, was also omitted.

Although La Follette reforms are often construed as antibusiness, opposing business interests in the state were primarily responsible for the final passage of a moderate regulation bill. The *Wisconsin State Journal* in May of 1903 observed that when a regulation measure came "to be considered upon its merits and under conditions that do not arouse the apprehension of conservative legislators, the legislature will create a commission to supervise railroad rates."[50] In the end the fears of both conservative legislators and businessmen were largely eliminated. By the same token, the hopes of certain Milwaukee merchants for some sort of tighter regulation were at last fulfilled.

Only the railroads interpreted the regulation bill as a defeat. There can be little question that the Wisconsin carriers had no desire to be regulated by a state regulatory commission. Even after a moderate commission bill was passed, railroad executives were quite candid in admitting their distaste for the new order of things. "I was opposed to any railroad bill," asserted the general

---

[48] Whitehead to Gabriel, April 22, 1914, in the Whitehead Papers.
[49] Barnes to O. P. Glothin, December 8, 1906, General Correspondence, in the Wisconsin Public Service Commission Records.
[50] *Wisconsin State Journal*, May 12, 1903.

manager of the Green Bay and Western Railroad, while a top official of the Chicago and North Western in a letter to Elisha Keyes referred repeatedly to that "fool law."[51] Numerous other assertions and the actions of the carriers in the first few months of regulation eloquently expressed the anxiety they felt as they faced the problem of assuring their continued prosperity under the new statute.

In spite of these intense fears concerning regulation, the carriers in the final stages of the regulation debate adopted a highly positive attitude toward regulation in Wisconsin. Quite obviously surmising that regulation was coming to the state, especially after the show of unanimity in the 1904 election campaign, railroad lawyers abandoned opposition to all kinds of regulation and argued only against the kind of restrictions which the administration's Texas-like measure seemed to suggest.

Their change in attitude was immediately apparent in 1905. After haranguing the administration measure, Pierce Butler, attorney for the Omaha Road, proclaimed that "no state does its duty that does not plan appropriately how to regulate rates and correct abuses and prevent discrimination." Proper regulation he defined as "the power to hear complaints against a rate and to decide that it is wrong to put it into effect."[52] Burton Hanson of the Milwaukee Road echoed these sentiments. "There is a material and substantial difference between giving a commission power to regulate rates so that there shall be no injustice in transportation charges, and taking substantially all the power of management of the railway properties out of the hands of the companies that own them, and vesting it in the irresponsible hands of a government commission."[53]

Because of the general unity of interest between the influential large shipping groups and the carriers, when these shippers assumed a role in framing the final bill the railroads were also afforded an opportunity to make their views known. Taking ad-

[51] J. A. Jordan to Keyes, July 13, 1905; W. H. Stennett to Keyes, July 24, 1905, both in the Keyes Papers.
[52] Pierce Butler, *Brief in Opposition to Railroad Commission Bill, 1905* (Madison, 1905).
[53] *Milwaukee Sentinel,* March 1, 1905.

vantage of this chance, top railroad men, particularly Burton Hanson of the Milwaukee Road and Thomas Gill, an attorney for the Wisconsin Central, took an active part in forging the final compromise.[54] Emanuel Philipp reported that Hanson "met and labored with the committee to perfect the measure that was to be presented to the senate as the final, finished work of that body" on "each afternoon and evening for weeks," reviewing the bill "section by section" and suggesting "improvements, amendments, additions and eliminations."[55] John M. Whitehead, a leader of the stalwart forces in 1905, later corroborated Philipp's story, naming Hanson, along with Hatten, Hudnall, and Philipp himself, as one of the four principal authors of the measure.[56] The *Milwaukee Free Press*, spokesman for the reformers, confirmed Hanson's key role, complaining bitterly of the deep involvement of the railroad lawyer in the last days when the final measure was being formulated. " 'Conservative' senators will accept no bill, nor agree to any compromise until they refer the subject to Mr. Burton Hanson . . . and take his judgment on it," the Milwaukee paper asserted.[57]

Although the carriers made a contribution toward moderating the final measure, they did not win a clear-cut victory. Their idea of the best possible kind of regulation was expressed in a measure drafted by Hanson and introduced by Senator William C. North which called for an elective commission whose decisions would be automatically suspended pending a court decision if any railroad chose to appeal.[58] These key provisions were not included in the final legislation.

Still most railroad officials were elated at the extent to which the efforts of conservative spokesmen had succeeded in modifying the original administration measure. "If the senate committee's railroad commission bill should pass[,] the railroad companies ought to respond with an appropriate speech of acceptance and thanks," quipped the conservative *Milwaukee Sentinel* in early

---

[54] See *Milwaukee Free Press*, May 4, 1905, for reference to Gill's role.
[55] Philipp, *Political Reform in Wisconsin*, 231, 250.
[56] Whitehead to Gabriel, April 22, 1914, in the Whitehead Papers.
[57] *Milwaukee Free Press*, May 2, 1905.
[58] See Substitute No. 3 for 268S., *Wisconsin Senate Bills, 1905*, and Keyes to Hughitt, May 11, 1905, in the Keyes Letterbooks.

May.[59] Although the carriers were not ready to mount a public platform in praise of more state regulation, they did show appropriate relief when the measure finally passed. "Governor La Follette has not secured anything like so radical a measure as he attempted to inaugurate," declared the *Railroad Gazette*. "Since Wisconsin, under the leadership of Governor La Follette, is bound to abandon the policy towards its railroads under which the state has made such rapid and wonderful progress in the past, the measure must be accepted as being about as good a one as could be devised of the kind."[60] In the same vein, *Railway Age* asserted that the bill was "far from being the measure which Governor La Follette set out to wrest from the legislative branch," although it complained that "the measure abounds in 'shall' and 'shall not,'" and in frequent threats of punishment, so worded as to suggest the assumption that the railways were confirmed and desperate criminals. . . ."[61] Writing privately, W. H. Stennett, the Chicago and North Western official who opposed all such regulation, also took consolation in the fact that the bill was "very very far" from what La Follette had wanted. The administration forces "did not get 1/10 of what they wanted," he declared.[62]

The carriers in Wisconsin did not favor any increased regulation, but they saw the handwriting on the wall and sought a role in drafting a milder bill than the reform governor wanted. Their reward for a rational view of the problem was the satisfaction of undermining the hopes of their archenemy and achieving a kind of regulation less likely to interfere greatly in their normal operations.

The final regulation bill, then, was the result of the efforts of numerous groups, some of them sharply conflicting in their notions about the proper role of government in regulating economic enterprise. While it was quite clearly the power and influence of the popular La Follette that caused the more conservative elements in the state to face up to the issue of state regulation with

---

[59] *Milwaukee Sentinel*, May 8, 1905.
[60] *Railroad Gazette*, 38:716 (June 23, 1905).
[61] *Railway Age*, 39:870 (June 9, 1905).
[62] Stennett to Keyes, May 22, 1905, in the Keyes Papers.

the seriousness the issue deserved, the question remains, why did these interests so quickly give in to the governor's demands for regulation and only fight him on the details of regulation? Certainly the governor did not have such overpowering public support nor so strong a hold on the legislature that such a course was the only one open to them.

Only an understanding of the effects of events beyond the state's borders can adequately explain the tenuous position of La Follette's opposition. Although it is often overlooked by those who study Wisconsin's railroad regulation history, the Wisconsin crusade was simply one of many such campaigns which were waged in states throughout the country during the late nineteenth and early twentieth centuries. It was, in fact, one of the later struggles, coming after thirty state commissions had already been formed and in the midst of a flurry of drives which resulted in the formation of some fifteen more commissions between 1905 and 1907 so that at the end of this period nearly every state in the union had a regulatory commission of some kind.

This widespread acceptance of state railroad regulation made a profound difference in the Wisconsin struggle between 1903 and 1905, for it made it extremely difficult for opponents to debate profitably the legality or even the desirability of state regulation. Realizing the power of this argument, La Follette and his colleagues exploited the tie between railroad abuses in Wisconsin and the lack of regulatory agencies there. They argued repeatedly that Wisconsin shippers suffered because the legislature had failed to make the common carriers accountable for their actions as they were in the neighboring states of Minnesota, Iowa, and Illinois, as well as many other states. This argument underlay all of the incessant comparisons of rates in Iowa and Illinois with those in Wisconsin around which the reform campaign was built. The state was being discriminated against, declared the reformers, because it did not undertake one of the normal functions of government, the regulation of railroads. The kind of telling campaign which the administration carried on using this issue is well illustrated by the *Milwaukee Free Press*'s featuring of an abrasive editorial from the *Duluth* (Minnesota) *News-Tribune* during the closing stages of the 1904 campaign. "Though Wisconsin was ad-

mitted to the union ten years before Minnesota," commented the
Minnesota daily, "she is almost always a decade or more behind
her younger sister in progressive legislation. This is particularly
true in regard to laws meant to check the undue and pernicious
power of the great corporations. For years Minnesota has had a
railroad commission. . . . The mills of reform grind slow the other
side of the St. Louis river, and we Minnesotans may hug ourselves
and rejoice that we are not as other men, and even as those
Badgers."[63]

It was this argument above all others which the more conservative economic groups in the state opposed to regulation found
impossible to counter, and apparently this ordained the form
which the regulation fight took. Unable to argue that regulation
was either evil or unimportant because of its widespread acceptance throughout the country as a proper and effective governmental function, opponents could only argue around the edges.
They began by contending that Wisconsin already had a regulator
in the impotent railroad commissioner. When this argument became too hollow to serve, however, they had no choice but to
advocate the creation of a regulatory commission empowered to
perform more limited functions than La Follette desired.

Ironically, in the state which is often reputed to be at the vanguard of reform, the reformers' most effective argument was that
Wisconsin was woefully behind in its regulatory legislation. By
exploiting this contention they changed the entire emphasis of the
struggle.

The nature of the final statute can be best understood in this
national context. All of the thirty state commissions in operation in
1903 fell into two categories, strong (having the power to make
rates in some form), and weak (possessing only the power to
advise and make recommendations). The strong commissions were
of two types also: those which were empowered to make entirely
new rate schedules for all railroads within their respective states,
and those given power only to investigate particular rates and
make needed alterations. (Several commissions in the latter category also had the power to set maximum rates for carriers oper-

[63] *Milwaukee Free Press*, October 3, 1904.

ating in their states.) The weak form of commission rule was scarcely a viable choice by the end of the nineteenth century. Mostly made up of commissions in eastern states which were holdovers from an earlier day of very mild regulation, only one weak commission had been formed since 1890.

Those states seeking regulatory legislation after 1890 commonly confined their debates to the kind of strong commission which should be formed. Here a clear trend was evident. In 1890 only seven states, including neighboring Illinois, possessed commissions with the power to establish entirely new schedules of rates for state carriers, while two others, Iowa and New Hampshire, could set maximum rates for all intrastate traffic. During the next twelve years, however, six of the eight states which initiated railroad regulation empowered their commissions to enact entirely new schedules. By 1902, of the twenty states which granted their commissions any power to regulate rates, thirteen had the duty of writing new tariff schedules for the state's traffic, while two others set maximums on all intrastate rates. Only five commissions, construed to be more than advisory, were limited to handling complaints and correcting specific rates when hearings proved them to be inequitable.

The other common facet of the regulation debates concerned the means of selecting members of commissions. Whereas in 1890 the overwhelming majority of the commissions were appointed by the chief executives of the states, by 1902, in line with the numerous crusades for more direct public participation in government, the ratio was so altered that but thirteen commissions were chosen by the governor, while fifteen were elected by the people, one other by the legislature, and the other by a special board. The trend here was clearly toward the election of all commission members.[64]

In 1905, two other states, Indiana and Washington, enacted commission laws. Both joined the ever-growing trend toward stronger commissions by empowering their new agencies to rewrite completely the rate schedules for the roads operating within their

---

[64] Information on regulation trends on state level from Interstate Commerce Commission, *Railways in the United States in 1902, State Regulation of Railways*, XVI (1902).

borders. Ignoring the trend toward election of commissioners, however, they both called for the appointment of all commissioners.[65]

In this context the compromise in Wisconsin can be evaluated. And in this perspective the relief of the railroads and the gratification of the large shipping interests can be well understood, for they had scored a signal success. While the Wisconsin statute created a strong commission classification, by empowering the commission to establish new rates only after investigation of specific abuses the legislators left it among a dwindling minority of five strong commissions, which could not set overall standards for intrastate railroad rates. By the same token, contrary to the trend toward election of all commissioners, the Wisconsin lawmakers seemed to exhibit an implicit mistrust of the people by making the office appointive.

La Follette would later call the measure "a very strong regulatory bill . . . more sweeping than any legislation enacted by any state up to that time," while Frederic C. Howe labeled it "probably the most comprehensive measure of its kind yet enacted by any state."[66] When compared to bills passed in other states these boasts seem exaggerated indeed. The Wisconsin measure was better defined by Emanuel Philipp who, speaking from the standpoint of one who was wary of all forms of regulation, called it "a modified, rationalized railroad commission bill."[67] The success of the influence exerted by those who opposed the administration's regulation plans is pointed up by the relative backwardness of Wisconsin's 1905 regulatory legislation.

A number of historians of late have pinned the burden of praise or blame for statutes passed during the progressive era on particular interest groups, the newest stress in the area of regulation being on the role of the railroads as the promoters of their own regulation. In Wisconsin no such monolithic emphasis will serve, for numerous conflicting groups participated in the writing of the final regulation bill, and it seems doubtful that a measure could have

---

[65] Grover G. Huebner, "Five Years of Railroad Regulation," in *The Annals of the American Academy of Political and Social Sciences,* 32:138–156 (July, 1908).

[66] La Follette, *Autobiography,* 342; Frederic Howe, *Wisconsin: An Experiment in Democracy* (New York, 1912), 67.

[67] Philipp, *Political Reform in Wisconsin,* 198.

been passed without such widespread co-operation, given the strengths and weaknesses of the different factions in the struggle.

La Follette, the highly political popular leader, experienced trouble organizing interest groups in favor of the bill and exhibited a pervasive ineptness as a legislative organizer and strategist. He could hardly unite even his closest supporters. At the same time, the large shippers quite clearly would not have worked for regulatory legislation if they had not feared the stronger measure La Follette advocated. And, having shown their prodigious power in 1903 in defeating regulation in La Follette's own bastion, the assembly, had they not agreed to regulation in 1905 it is doubtful whether the legislature would have passed such a measure. Although the railroads were in favor of their own regulation least of all, their rational acquiescence in the final compromise was probably a prerequisite to the acceptance by the highly dependent large shippers.

In the end the flow of events outside Wisconsin ordained passage also, for in the broader perspective the state saw itself not as a bold initiator but as a backward area seeking to catch up with the times. While it caught up in a sense, it still lagged behind the national trends toward stronger regulation. Insofar as the extent of regulation was ordained by the manner in which commissioners chose to administer the act, however, the meaning of the new reform legislation would not be known until the new commissioners had time to establish precedents for regulation by commission in Wisconsin. The dominant questions became who the commissioners would be and how they would approach their new responsibilities.

Naming the First Commission

6 From the outset of the struggle for a railroad regulation bill in Wisconsin, leaders of all sides exhibited an acute awareness that legislation was simply the first step in determining what form of regulation would dominate. Realizing that many key decisions would be made by the commissioners charged with administering any new act, all had contested for a role in deciding who would serve. La Follette, apparently with this in mind, finally chose the appointive form of commission selection so that he could help get regulation started properly. The governor's opponents, intent on depriving him of the chance to pack the commission with appointees who neither understood nor sympathized with the problems of business, worked hard for an elective body. Failing in this struggle, they won veto power for the upper house over all appointments to the commission by the chief executive.

In the early summer of 1905, when at last a piece of compromise legislation emerged from the confused legislature, the problem of appointment seemed even more pressing. With mandates in many areas blurred by the necessities of compromise, commission discretion had been so broadened that no one doubted that the first commission would determine more policy than the legislature had during its many hearings, caucuses, and votes. "All [are] united in the opinion that everything depends on the kind of a Commission that is appointed," commented Robert Eliot.[1] James A. Frear

[1] Robert Eliot to La Follette, May 24, 1905, in the La Follette Papers.

echoed his concern. "In this more than any of the other reforms, the merit of the legislation will largely lie with the manner of its enforcement."[2] On the other side of the fence, the petulant *Milwaukee Sentinel* declared, "A good commission, made up of men chosen because of their peculiar qualifications for the work to be performed and disposed to approach their duties in the right spirit, can produce satisfactory results even with this law."[3]

The task of appointing members to the first commission gave La Follette a new opportunity to effect his kind of regulation and perhaps recoup the losses he had suffered in the legislative infighting of the spring. But it also confronted him with an acute dilemma which many chief executives had been forced to deal with under similar circumstances. While determined to name men he could count on to remedy the widespread abuses in the transportation industry and bring about a better economic climate for consumers and small shippers, La Follette had to comply with the provision in the Wisconsin law which required all members to possess knowledge of railroad affairs and one in particular to be an expert in railroad law. The dilemma was how to find men who knew enough about railroad affairs to qualify for membership on the commission without enthroning commissioners who accepted the thinking of the carriers and thus would be reticent to make new demands on them on behalf of the people of the state.

Even before the passage of the 1905 regulation measure, interested parties had sought to influence the governor in his selection of the first members of the new board. As early as December of 1904 the astute E. P. Bacon, heeding the signs that a commission law would be passed in the next session, began a concerted campaign for the appointment of Frank Barry, a Milwaukee man currently serving in Washington as secretary of the executive committee of the Interstate Commerce Law Convention after stints as secretary of the Millers' National Association of the United States and president of the National Transportation Association.[4] Over the next few months letters poured in from an impressive list of

[2] *Milwaukee Free Press,* May 21, 1905.
[3] *Milwaukee Sentinel,* May 20, 1905.
[4] Bacon to La Follette, December 20, 1904, in the La Follette Papers.

luminaries around the country, including four members of the Interstate Commerce Commission, in support of Barry's candidacy.[5]

Other influential figures also made their bids. Isaac Stephenson, the wealthy lumberman-politician, advised the governor to appoint state Supreme Court Justice Roujet G. Marshall to the new body, while William H. Hatten and friends mounted a drive for Charles McArthur, agent for the Northwestern Land Agency, a subsidiary of Cornell University located in Eau Claire.[6] Captain F. H. Magdeburg, a member of the Milwaukee Chamber of Commerce and a veteran of several decades of campaigning for tighter regulation of carriers, applied personally for an appointment.[7]

La Follette, determined to find that one strong man whom he could count on to lead the commission toward the enactment of a more just system of transportation rates, sought help elsewhere. Such national figures as Henry C. Adams of the University of Michigan, S. H. Cowan, the Texas lawyer who had advised him so often on regulation bills, and Interstate Commerce Commissioner Charles S. Prouty were approached by the governor concerning their interest in heading up the commission.[8]

Even as he weighed his choices, however, the exigencies of politics began to bear down upon him. In the midst of the legislative session, opponents gave notice of their determination to limit La Follette's freedom of choice by summarily rejecting an attempt by a few La Follette supporters to include the present railroad commissioner, John W. Thomas, on the new agency, apparently fearing him because of his key role in uncovering railroad rebate abuses and thus aiding La Follette in his antirailroad, anticorporation campaign.[9] They then succeeded in adding to the final bill pro-

[5] See numerous letters in the La Follette Papers, spring, 1905.
[6] Isaac Stephenson to La Follette, June 13, 1905; O. H. Ingram to La Follette, June 9, 1905; DeAlton Thomas to La Follette, June 10, 1905, all in the La Follette Papers.
[7] See memo on Magdeburg, May 25, 1905, in the La Follette Papers.
[8] John R. Commons to Adams, June 16, 1905, La Follette to Winterbotham, June 7, 1905, in the La Follette Letterbooks; La Follette, *Autobiography,* 349.
[9] See Thomas to Esch, April 22, 1905, in the Esch Papers, and note by Senator Julius Roehr, Secretary of State Records, Elections and Records, Legislative Bills, Senate, 1905, No. 268S, in the State Archives, State Historical Society of Wisconsin.

visions which required senate approval of all appointments to the commission and forbade the body to organize until all such appointments had been ratified. The governor had ample warning of what could be expected if he sought to impose his will too strongly.

In the face of such clear political barriers, the governor abandoned plans to appoint Bacon's candidate, Frank Barry, apparently because his aggressive propensities and long association with hardcore Milwaukee reformers made him clearly unacceptable to those who supported moderate regulation.[10] Others seem to have been eliminated for similar reasons.[11] Never did La Follette flag in his determination to name a strong man to lead the new commission, however, for this was now the key to effective regulation.

One June 16, La Follette finally nominated B. H. Meyer, Halford Erickson, and Nils P. Haugen for membership on the new commission. Haugen's nomination was the key one. Appointed for the eight-year term, it was assumed that he would be the chairman of the commission and its leading member.

To this new task, Haugen brought conspicuous credentials. A dedicated reformer, as railroad commissioner in the 1880's, as a candidate for governor in the 1890's, and presently as a member of the tax commission, Haugen had evinced a clear distrust of the railroads which he never tried to conceal. (In a letter to Roswell P. Miller, then president and now chairman of the board of the Chicago, Milwaukee and St. Paul Railway, in 1893, Haugen asserted, "If I have any prejudices against railway management it grows largely out of the fact that I have had a slight peek behind the curtain.")[12] Sharing La Follette's anticorporation bias and devoted to strong regulation of railroads, the able Norwegian was

[10] Evidence that La Follette wanted to appoint Barry can be found in a long memorandum on him dated May 30, 1905, and in a notation that he had had a personal conference with Bacon concerning Barry, La Follette to Bacon, June 6, 1905, both in the La Follette Papers. See also Bacon to Esch, June 28, 1905, in the Esch Papers.

[11] Emanuel Philipp writes of administration "feelers" which were sent to the legislature concerning several men, whom the senate summarily rejected. Philipp, *Political Reform in Wisconsin*, 234.

[12] Haugen to Roswell Miller, December 22, 1893, in the Haugen Letterbooks, as quoted in Brandes, "Nils P. Haugen and the Progressive Movement," 22.

just the sort of expert the governor had sought to lead the new commission toward a policy of vigorous regulation.

Opponents of the administration immediately sprang into action to stem this attempt by La Follette to revitalize the regulation program which had been watered down in the legislature. Under the leadership of stalwart Senator C. C. Rogers, they set about amassing veto power for the senate vote on the governor's appointments.[13] On the following day these efforts were rewarded. The upper house overwhelmingly approved the appointments of Meyer and Erickson, but Haugen was rejected 16 to 11, in spite of the absence of five stalwart senators. As observers analyzed the final administration setback, the full cost of the compromise which had brought about a piece of moderate regulation legislation in 1905 became clear for the first time.

While eight senators associated with administration causes surprisingly enough voted against the confirmation of Haugen, the most conspicuous dissenting votes were those of William Hatten, George Hudnall, and Herman Wipperman, the key administration men on the senate railroad committee. They had been close to the struggle throughout and their votes seem to indicate a further meaning for the compromise reached in the upper house.

"There is no doubt but that the Railroad Committee entered into an agreement—that is some of them did—that they would not vote for confirmation of anyone to whom railroad apologizers on the committee seriously objected," argued Nils Haugen a week later.[14] Though the evidence is scanty, Haugen's contention seems plausible. Faced with the total breakdown of administration discipline in the upper house, and more conciliatory in their personal views of the regulatory function, these key La Follette supporters apparently conceded conservative interests a veto over commission appointments in exchange for consent to the moderate regulation legislation. The compromise of 1905, which had resulted in a moderation of the regulation bill, now claimed a final victim in ordaining the defeat of the man the governor had groomed to revivify regulation in the state.[15]

---

[13] Keyes to Stennett, June 16, 22, 1905, in the Keyes Letterbooks.
[14] Haugen to Henry Johnson, June 26, 1905, in the Haugen Letterbooks.
[15] The *Milwaukee Free Press*, June 18, 1905, called Haugen the "best quali-

This latest defeat deeply depressed the administration forces, for it seemed the final crushing blow to plans for vigorous regulation. "The House of Lords under the leadership of the Duke of the C. M. & St. P., the Marquis of the C. & N. W. and the Earl of the W. C. felt that its prerogative had been trenched upon, and that the first rights of our American corporation, that to choose the Jury before which it will be tried, had been sorely violated," ejaculated a bitter Haugen after his rejection.[16] Other administration supporters were equally disappointed. "I feel like damning the whole crowd of them," declared John M. Winterbotham, who had worked long and hard in Texas to furnish the governor with information on that strong and effective commission. "There has [sic] been so many things occur that one is not surprized [sic] at anything."[17] After a strategy session with the governor, during which advisors struggled to find a way to secure appointment for some suitable reform representative, Assistant Attorney General Walter D. Corrigan suggested cynically that a motion for the approval of all three commissioners be proposed by "some administration Senator, *if there are any left*."[18]

While some of his supporters despaired, La Follette struggled to find a way out of his newest dilemma. Now time was of the essence for he was scheduled to begin his summer chautauqua tour in Oklahoma City in less than a week. The governor depended upon these appearances as a valuable source of funds, as much as $200 a day, while they also gave him the kind of national exposure he coveted. Important, too, to a man of La Follette's temperament was the exhilaration he gained by thrilling crowds with his oratory. Bound by the intransigence of the state senate, La Follette chafed at the bit. "My first obligation is here and I dare not leave till the session ends," he declared in a letter to his contact in the South.[19]

---

fied man on the list," while Keyes commented, "If [Haugen] had gone upon the Board, he would have been its master spirit, and the railroads would have been knifed at every opportunity." Keyes to Stennett, June 22, 1905, in the Keyes Letterbooks.

[16] Haugen to James A. Stone, June 21, 1905, in the Haugen Letterbooks.
[17] John M. Winterbotham to Haugen, June 19, 1905, in the Haugen Papers.
[18] "Walter" to La Follette, June 19, 1905, in the La Follette Letterbooks.
[19] La Follette to William Busby, June 13, 1905, in the La Follette Letterbooks.

With these other commitments pressing in upon him, the governor first toyed with the idea of stubbornly resubmitting Haugen's name to the senate, then, in desperation, chose to compromise. Earlier he had sounded out John Barnes, a Rhinelander lawyer, concerning his interest in an appointment to the commission, but Barnes had refused to be considered.[20] Now he invited him down to the capital for a conference and wooed him into reconsidering.

On June 21 the senate unanimously confirmed Barnes' nomination. At 12:07 A.M. on June 22 the legislature adjourned *sine die*. Three hours later the tired governor caught a train for Oklahoma City, leaving behind the wreckage of his struggle for strong regulation in Wisconsin.

The senate's veto power had stood the more conservative forces in good stead. They had been able to quell La Follette's attempt to enthrone the antirailroad Haugen as head of the commission. Having achieved this victory, they looked with satisfaction on the new commission.

Appointed for the key eight-year term was the reluctant John Barnes. Esteemed as one of the best businessmen in northern Wisconsin, Barnes was a partner in the Rhinelander Paper Company, owned shares in several Rhinelander banks, and had large land interests in other areas of the country. A competent lawyer as well, Barnes had acted as a legal aide to La Follette from time to time.

Chosen as the legal expert, his training in the area of transportation was rather one-sided. Whereas Haugen had considerable experience in prosecuting the railroads, Barnes had earned his spurs representing the railroads, as Wisconsin attorney for the Minneapolis, St. Paul and Sault Sainte Marie Railroad and as a local attorney for the Chicago and North Western. Slow and measured in his mien and trained in the way of big business and railroads, Barnes seemed unlikely to lead the commission in new paths of regulatory activity.[21] The more conservative factions in the state noted this with great elation. Displeased because the original commission list was bereft of big businessmen and no doubt appre

20 Barnes to La Follette, June 15, 1905, in the La Follette Papers.
21 See *Milwaukee Press*, June 20, 1905, July 17, 1908. The *Milwaukee Sentinel* of July 20, 1907, estimated Barnes' wealth at $300,000.

Aikens and Proctor, Men of Progress, Wisconsin

Halford Erickson

John H. Roemer

ciative of the importance of Barnes' prior railroad connections, the *Milwaukee Sentinel* declared, "By the appointment of John Barnes[,] ... Governor La Follette has, intentionally or not, atoned in a measure for his original blunder."[22]

The appointment of Halford Erickson smacked more of politics for, whereas Barnes was a Democrat, Erickson had served under La Follette as commissioner of labor and industrial statistics and had played an important part in the development of statistical data needed in the governor's regulation crusade. Because of his training and disposition, however, few quarreled with Erickson's appointment. Basically an accountant and statistician, Erickson was not a political man, having labored equally well under three different governors since he had been appointed to head the bureau of labor and industrial statistics in 1895. Moreover, his training prior to that had come primarily through seven years in the employ of the Omaha Railroad, where he had worked his way up to cashier and bookkeeper in the office of the auditor.[23] Hopeful that the new commission would limit itself to the bookkeeping chores Erickson performed so well, and taking careful note of his background as a railroad employee, conservative journals, in and outside the railroad industry, declared him especially well qualified to serve on the new agency.[24]

By far the most dynamic and able man on the new commission was Dr. Balthasar H. Meyer, a professor of political economy at the University of Wisconsin. Although he was appointed for the shortest commission term, he was destined to become the most influential member of the commission.

Born in Mequon, Wisconsin, in 1866 and raised on a farm near there, the intelligent and ambitious young Meyer distinguished himself early in life. At the age of eighteen, he was already a teacher at a district school near his home, by twenty-one he had accepted a job as principal of the school at Fredonia, and at twenty-three he moved to Port Washington to head the school

---

[22] *Milwaukee Sentinel,* June 17, 20, 1905.
[23] *Milwaukee Free Press,* June 17, 21, 1905; *Milwaukee Sentinel,* June 19, 1905.
[24] *Railroad Gazette,* 38:716 (June 23, 1905); *Milwaukee Sentinel,* June 21, 1905.

there. Not satisfied to remain a school teacher and administrator, in 1892 Meyer returned to college at the University of Wisconsin in Madison to finish a course he had begun at Oshkosh State Normal School. After graduating from the university two years later, he immediately entered graduate school at the University of Berlin, where he became interested in the subject of transportation. Within a year he had written a monograph on Prussian railroads, the first of some forty books and articles he published during the next ten years.

Returning to the University of Wisconsin as a teaching fellow in 1895, he rose to the rank of full professor during the next decade, obtaining his Ph.D. along the way in 1897. Because of his quick mind and voracious appetite for hard work, by 1905, at the age of thirty-nine, Meyer had established himself as one of the foremost experts on transportation in the country. Having recently completed several studies of railroad valuation for the federal government, Meyer now divided his time between teaching at the university and acting as director of transportation for the Carnegie Institute.[25]

Although he had supported La Follette consistently, no one could contest Meyer's appointment as political, for the extensive traveling he had done during the last three years had kept him away from Wisconsin for much of the time and, therefore, out of the Wisconsin regulation fight. The carriers, in any case, were not likely to oppose his appointment, for in his many articles and monographs, a number of them published in railroad journals, Meyer had expressed a profound respect and admiration for the railroad men of the country. When called upon to join the commission, Meyer was on a research trip in Germany which had been made possible by a $5,000 gift from his close friend, James J. Hill.[26] "He possesses no spirit of antagonism against the railroads," the *Railroad Gazette* declared in praising his appointment.[27]

Looking back over the perilous week of senate maneuvering,

[25] *Railway Age Gazette*, 49:1200 (December 23, 1910); unpublished autobiography, (box 8), and sketch of Meyer's life, no date or origin, (box 12), both in the B. H. Meyer Papers.
[26] Autobiography, in the Meyer Papers.
[27] *Railroad Gazette*, 38:716 (June 23, 1905).

Elisha Keyes breathed a deep sigh of relief. The defeat of Haugen had "cleared the atmosphere." ("Perhaps the greatest victory of the session," he called it.)[28] Then the completion of the commission with Barnes had made things even more satisfying. Two of the commissioners had worked for the carriers, while the other had written for their journals with sympathy and understanding and was well acquainted with key railroad leaders. Expressing the mood of many who had feared regulation by a commission dominated by the vengeful feelings of La Follette, Keyes declared, "In its personnel the railroads have won a great victory."[29]

Had Nils Haugen's appointment to the railroad commission been confirmed, decision making on the body would have been a lively affair indeed, for the strong-principled Norwegian would not have been likely to defer with impunity to Meyer. The contests between Meyer, the theorist, and Haugen, the experienced, skilled government operative who entertained quite different thoughts concerning railroads and regulation, might have become legendary. With the defeat of Haugen, however, Meyer became clearly the dominant figure on the commission.

Meyer's leadership was, in a sense, inevitable, for neither Barnes nor Erickson were well suited to lead the commission. Barnes, the last-minute replacement for Haugen, had sufficient training as a railroad lawyer to handle the commission's legal affairs, but he had given the problem of government regulation of the carriers little thought. (Asked by La Follette to handle the legal arguments for the administration in the 1905 legislative hearings, Barnes had begged off, declaring he knew little about the issue.)[30] Although the cautious, precedent-dominated orientation of the lawyer which he brought to his new task would have an impact on the pace the commission's work would take, Barnes was not equipped to mold that agency's policy.

Even less disposed to lead the commission was Halford Erickson. Regarded as one of the most able statisticians in the country, Erickson's skills were invaluable in helping the commission wade through

[28] Keyes to Stennett, June 22, 1905, in the Keyes Letterbooks.
[29] Keyes to Stennett, June 21, 1905, in the Keyes Letterbooks.
[30] Barnes to La Follette, February 25, 1905, in the La Follette Papers.

the welter of data which it used in dispatching its duties. His disposition, however, was that of an accountant, not a political or economic theorist. Hence the task of leader reverted to Meyer, a man with the knowledge and the convictions to guide the commission through the difficult early years.

One of the ironies of the "Wisconsin Idea" which brought state government and the state university into close partnership during the early years of this century was the substantial difference in the views entertained by La Follette and those intellectuals who advised him. While both accepted in general the need for reform, often the goals of the university community differed greatly from those of La Follette. The thinking of John R. Commons, for example, predicated on a search for economic harmony through mediation between conflicting interests, differed markedly from the more aggressive, two-fisted, trust-busting thought of the governor. Generally this intellectual contrast was not crucial, however, for university professors were usually content to remain advisors rather than seeking positions of power and influence where they could freely apply their different notions of the political and economic good.[31]

After his appointment to the Railroad Commission of Wisconsin, however, one such university intellectual, B. H. Meyer, possessed the unique opportunity denied to others. Holding a view of the country's economic system which differed markedly from that of La Follette, he had the chance to apply his notions in his work as a leader of the new regulatory body.

Meyer's view of regulation was based upon quite different premises than those which guided the ardent reformers. Having been absent from Wisconsin during much of the agitation for increased regulation, he was not obsessed with the inequities in the Wisconsin rate structure upon which reformers had based their crusade. Speaking of the struggle he and his wife went through in deciding

[31] "I learned," wrote Commons, ". . . that the place of the economist was that of advisor to the leaders, if they wanted him, and not that of propagandist to the masses. The leaders alone had the long experience of success and failure. It was they who took the risks of defeat and deserved the credit of success." John R. Commons, *Myself* (Madison, 1964), 88.

whether to take the post of commissioner, Meyer commented, "We felt handicapped in our consideration because we were so out of touch with things in Wisconsin and we were utterly without concrete information."[32]

More important, however, he entertained quite different views concerning the relative virtues of government and the transportation companies. La Follette and his supporters put great faith in government as the voice of the common man; Meyer was much less trusting. Highly critical of the spirit of public administration in America, he charged that "the misuse of public positions is a matter of daily occurrence."[33] Moreover, he feared the extension of government control at the price of stifling individual initiative. "In those states in which government reaches out into the industrial field and extends the influence of direct state action in the farthest possible limits, the individual is perforce educated into an attitude of dependence upon the state," he declared in 1905.[34]

By the same token, while the ardent Wisconsin reformers evinced a deep and abiding mistrust of the railroads, Meyer venerated the railroad man, elevating him above the government bureaucrat. He pictured the average official for the carriers as "a man of large views and sagacity" who utilized the "principles and facts of science" in making railroad policy. "Such a railway man is a scientist as much as any member of any university faculty," he argued.[35] "No one whose privilege it is to know the railway men of the country will for a moment maintain that they are not, as a body, sincerely desirous of serving the public in the best possible way."[36]

In the light of the differing views of the principals in the regulation controversy, it is not surprising that Meyer advocated a more limited form of government regulation than did the ardent reformers. Condemning any plan for government ownership of the

---

[32] *Autobiography*, in the Meyer Papers.
[33] See transcript of "The Relativity of Economic Institutions," speech delivered January 19, 1905, in the Meyer Papers.
[34] *Ibid.*
[35] "The Federal Government and Business Organization in Relation to University Studies in the Social Sciences," an address before the Wisconsin History and Political Science Association, 1902, in the Meyer Papers.
[36] Balthasar Henry Meyer, *Railway Legislation in the United States* (New York, 1903), 169.

carriers, Meyer declared, "Who is there who is willing to turn over to men of such a type the enormous transportation interests of the United States? The discipline and efficiency which characterize the forces of our great railway companies would, in all human probability, be subverted into mediocrity, if not irresponsibility."[37]

In spite of his relatively conservative views, however, Meyer saw the need for some form of increased government regulation, citing widespread public mistrust of the railroads as the most compelling argument for more government restrictions on the carriers. "That this suspicion is sometimes well founded is beyond controversy," he noted. "And that this same suspicion on the part of the public is often out of all proportion to the cause is equally true." Be that as it may, "the public is much like a boy with a balloon— it wants to know what there is inside."[38] So insistent was the public, he argued, that some sort of government control was inevitable, for "no government can long withstand the clamor of an insistent populace." If the public were not satisfied by effective regulation, "state ownership is inevitable," he predicted.[39]

Augmenting this view of the necessity of placating the public was also a practical understanding that even railway officials required some limited checks upon them. "If . . . we must choose between a rate established by a manager, *practically* unrestricted by law, whose business and duty it is to take the railway point of view, and a rate pronounced reasonable by a body of five capable men whose highest function it is to view impartially the interests of the public *and* the railways, there can be no mistake in accepting the judgment of the latter," he argued, if it were properly restricted by the courts.[40]

Still, ever doubtful of the efficacy of government regulation, Meyer issued a series of caveats concerning the activities of any commission. Convinced that the rate problem was not nearly as serious as staunch reformers claimed, that the rate inequities usually lay in certain fugitive "misfits," rather than in the "basal and fundamental rates" which rested "upon adjustments of long stand-

---

[37] "The Federal Government and Business Organizations . . . ," 1902.
[38] Meyer, *Railway Legislation in the United States,* 47–48.
[39] "The Relativity of Economic Institutions," January 19, 1905.
[40] Meyer, *Railway Legislation in the United States,* 250.

ing," Meyer opposed any initial rate-making function for a commission. The railroads, he argued, were better equipped for this
function and commissions only put themselves on the defensive by
going beyond their depth in this regard.[41]

Even while limiting itself to reviewing the occasional rates which
were clearly inequitable, the commission must be cautious, he
argued. "No one can go far into the problem of rates without feeling
very strongly the utter futility of attempts to reduce all rates to the
basis of a single principle," he declared.[42] Only if a commission
began with a hearty acceptance of the complexity of commercial
conditions which underlay rate schedules could it be just and effective. He also argued that rigid rules, such as the long and short
haul provision of the Interstate Commerce Law, should be avoided
for they were "likely to hinder that free development of traffic
arrangements which the railway business requires."[43] If careful to
limit itself to the remedying of occasional inequities ("when matters
go right there is nothing for the commissioners to do," he declared)
and to avoid all simplistic solutions to the complex railroad questions, such commissions could perform a worthwhile function, he
stated.[44]

In a highly perceptive study of the development of regulatory
commissions in the twentieth century in America, Marver Bernstein
notes:

> We know enough about decision making to recognize that
> the traditional picture of a board or commission determin-
> ing policy in judicial detachment by applying a rule of
> law or public policy to the facts leaves out of considera-
> tion the most influential factors in the process. The values
> which individuals bring to the job, their sense of identifi-
> cation with the purposes for which their agency or office
> stands, the symbols of status and prestige which surround

---

[41] "Government Regulation of Freight Rates," speech delivered to American
   Economics Association, reprinted in *Freight,* 5:60 (February, 1906).
[42] Meyer, *Railway Legislation in the United States,* 210.
[43] "Government Regulation of Freight Rates," in *Freight,* 5:60 (February,
   1906).
[44] Meyer to La Follette, November 21, 1904, in the La Follette Papers. See
   also Meyer to La Follette, March 23, 1906, in the La Follette Papers, and
   Meyer to Thomas Gill, July 19, 1907, in the Meyer Papers.

their position, their estimate of the balance of forces among the conflicting interests in regulation — all have their part to play in the making of decisions.[45]

In 1905 there was a marked contrast in values between those reformers who had spearheaded the drive for regulation and the first commissioners appointed to administer the law. Experienced in railway affairs because they had worked for or with the major carriers, none felt the sense of distrust and alienation from the world of big business which certain of the reformers exhibited. The commission had as its leader, moreover, a resolute man whose notions of what plagued the field of transportation in the United States were far different from those of the proponents of strong regulation. He accepted the need for commissions empowered to remedy rate abuses and exercise tighter review of railroad affairs. In Meyer's mind, however, it was more important to bring together conflicting economic groups and mediate their differences. Such a process would not only remove the misunderstandings between the public and the carriers but ease the destructive tensions existing between the carriers themselves.

In the early years of the commission's work the convictions of the commissioners became as important in determining the path of regulation in Wisconsin as the beliefs of those who had labored long on the hustings and in the legislature for a new order in the state's transportation industry.

[45] Marver Bernstein, *Regulating Business by Independent Commission* (Princeton, 1955), 277.

The Demise of Progressive Hopes

7 While the regulatory statute passed in 1905 included numerous provisions for the supervision of the state's carriers, the real issue had been control of the process of making and changing shipping rates. From the outset reformers had concentrated their attention on the state's rate structure, claiming that the carriers were exacting excessive charges for shippers. The carriers vehemently denied these allegations, arguing that the rates were both relatively and absolutely equitable.

The result of the final legislative fight had been a moderate victory for the carriers in the area of rate making, for the state's representatives, disregarding the claims of more extreme reformers that the railroads were not to be trusted to make fair rates, allowed the roads to retain initial rate-making power. The lack of clarity in the compromise statute, however, meant that the commission would finally determine the relative roles of government and the carriers in making and enforcing rates.

The ambiguity of the mandate facing the new agency was well expressed in the law. Although the commission could not set entirely new rates, it still had the power to revise rates on complaint or on its own motion. And, although the railroads retained the right to make their own rates initially, they were now required to submit all rate changes to the commission at least ten days before these alterations were enacted. Should the commission seize the initiative and use its powers of rate revision to effect radical changes in the state's rate structure, while curbing further rate advances by the carriers, the focus of rate-making power would dramatically shift from the carriers to the representatives of the people, as the reformers had intended. If, however, the commission construed its powers narrowly, limiting itself to a review of specific complaints, then the transportation companies would have little cause to fear the new agency. After years of acrimonious debate, the choice was in the hands of the three new appointees to the regulatory commission.

The most vital question facing the new commission concerned the meaning of the section in the regulation statute which dealt with rate making on the commission's own initiative. The reformers' view of the commission as a body diligently ferreting out and correcting rate abuses was highly dependent upon this provision of the statute. In the wake of the passage of the regulation measure, administration spokesmen had pointed proudly to the new commission's power to initiate investigations of rate inequities in the state as well as handle complaints. This prerogative made the commission a dynamic body, they argued, for it liberated the new agency from the function of simply serving the large shipper and gave it the capacity to help the small man, who was more in need of aid and less able to stand up to the large rail companies.

Enthusiasm faded quickly, however, for when the commission examined the statute under which it had been established, it noted a difference in wording which appeared to make its powers to handle complaints much broader than those of initiating investigations. Whereas the section dealing with complaints stated that the commission could investigate "any rate or rates" which complainants labeled as unreasonable or discriminatory, the provision dealing with commission initiative specified independent investigation of "any rate or charge" which the agency suspected was inequitable.

This kind of semantic distinction might not have been restrictive to a commission determined to effect widespread changes in the rate system of the state. Such an agency perhaps would have simply ignored the difference, or construed the terms "rate" and "charge" to cover broader classifications. But the new Wisconsin railroad commission was not inclined to proceed so boldly. Meyer was skeptical about the ability of railroad commissions to improve on the work of the carriers on a large scale. "No railway commission has ever lived which can prescribe carefully adjusted rates for a state with considerable railway mileage," he proclaimed in 1907.[1] Barnes too seemed reticent, for the cautious lawyer had no intention of allowing the commission to overinterpret its powers and run afoul of the courts. In the first crucial months of the agency's operation, when important precedents were established, the commission refused to take any initiative until an interpretation of its powers to act on its own had been made.

As a result, the matter of the commission's powers was thrown back into the hands of the beleaguered La Follette. While the governor often expressed his satisfaction with the regulation act in the months that followed its enactment, his ambiguous memorandum which accompanied the bill's approval had clearly shown his dissatisfaction with the compromise measure. The unwillingness of the commission to construe broadly its powers of initiative offered him another reason for regret, and strengthened his determination to perfect the regulation bill before he left the state. Instead of abdicating his state post in favor of the position of United States Senator, therefore, La Follette hung on to the state office and called a special session of the legislature for December of 1905.

When the legislators returned to Madison, La Follette presented his new demands. Although he lauded the lawmakers for passing a regulation measure the previous spring, he declared the bill inadequate and enumerated ten amendments necessary to strengthen the hand of the commission.

For the most part, the amendments avoided the central issue, dealing instead with such matters as tighter restrictions on railroad safety and accounting. Conspicuous among them, however, was a provision which granted the commission power to initiate investigations on as broad a scale as it wished. Earlier, when they were more interested in establishing broad mandates under which a commission could freely work to remedy rate irregularities, the governor and his advisers had given little attention to the wording of the sections of the cast which delineated the commission's role

[1] Synopsis of a lecture on the Public Service Laws of Wisconsin before the Milwaukee Chapter of the American Institute of Banking, February 7, 1907, in the Meyer Papers.

as rate maker. Now, however, in an apparent reference to the reticence of the new commissioners to seize the initiative, La Follette declared: "While it might be held by the courts that the commission has this power under the law now in force, the question is not free from doubt. All will agree that any uncertainty in the meaning of this important provision should be removed." Noting that the alteration of single rates would simply result in rank discrimination against contiguous areas, the governor demanded that the section on initiative be "made to harmonize with the provisions of the law relating to procedure upon complaint."[2]

While La Follette sought to treat this distinction between the two sections as an oversight, there can be little doubt that the difference in wording was a purposeful result of the maneuvering which had resulted in a compromise measure. (In early April, William Hatten, in suggesting the sort of bill that might pass, had pointedly referred to the right of a commission to act on its own to correct "any particular rate or charge" it deemed unreasonable or unjust.)[3] Having succeeded in stripping the new agency of the power to initiate an entirely new rate system, opponents of strong regulation apparently had attempted to limit further the commission's initiatory power.

Sensing the importance of La Follette's desperate maneuver, those legislators who had worked to moderate the regulation act wasted no time in amassing their forces once more. Therefore, when the senate railroad committee met to consider the new demands, it steadfastly held to the compromise of the previous spring. It readily accepted the minor changes in the regulation measure but summarily rejected the proposal to enhance the commission's power of initiative. Explaining that this question had been threshed out the previous spring during the drafting of a measure which appealed to all factions, the committee argued it would be "bad faith," as the *Free Press* put it, to make such a change now. Following its lead, the senate voted down the key provision in the governor's last effort to enact more effective regulation.[4]

[2] *Milwaukee Free Press*, December 6, 1905.
[3] *Ibid.*, April 5, 1905.
[4] *Ibid.*, December 12, 1905.

It is not certain that the original commission, highly skeptical of plans to change drastically the state's existing commercial relationships, ever intended to use its powers of initiative broadly. From the outset, rather than volunteering to follow up leads on its own, it informed those who cited abuses that "the law requires the filing of complaints or petitions with the commission, setting forth the grievances complained of."[5] And commission chairman John Barnes, who was asked in September to enumerate the major weaknesses in the regulatory legislation, made no mention of the defect in the initiative clause.[6]

The commissioners' position concerning this important provision was not clearly defined during the early months, however, for on occasion they referred to that day when they might undertake widesweeping rate changes on their own initiative. In early October of 1905, for instance, a discontented Robert Eliot, who had fought for over two decades for a commission which would alter the discriminatory rate structure, wrote the commission suggesting that the new body get at its major task. In reply Barnes alluded to that time after the commission had mastered its task, when it might "act on its own initiative in making [a] general reduction in rates."[7]

Now this opportunity was gone, for by requiring an interpretation of the scope of its prerogatives from the same committee that had written the distinction into the law originally, the commission virtually forfeited its powers to initiate changes. " It is . . . going to be a very slow and tedious process for this Commission to make any adjustment of freight rates if it is obliged to act on its own motion and must take up each and every individual rate in the State one by one and dispose of it," Barnes declared in January of 1906.[8]

Unwilling to embark on such a venture, the commission was forced to redefine its powers. No longer regarding its right to initi-

[5] Commission to C. S. Porter, July 12, 1905, General Correspondence, in the Wisconsin Public Service Commission Records (hereinafter cited as WPSC Records), State Archives, State Historical Society of Wisconsin.

[6] Barnes to La Follette, September 29, 1905, in the La Follette Papers.

[7] Barnes to Eliot, October 6, 1905, General Correspondence, WPSC Records.

[8] Barnes to Eliot, February 7, 1906, General Correspondence, WPSC Records.

ate investigations as broad enough to be helpful, the new agency virtually abandoned efforts to go beyond the complaints it received. In enumerating its powers in 1906, it neglected all mention of its powers of initiative. "The Wisconsin Railroad Commission," it declared, ". . . [is] charged by the state creating it with the duty of hearing complaints, and should it find the rates complained of are inequitable, it may then issue an order correcting the same."[9]

There would be occasions when the commission undertook inquiries "on its own motion." In all cases these actions simply represented a gathering of a series of complaints, which centered about a particular system of rates, into one investigation. In some instances, these actions resulted in extensive alterations of rates, such as the changes made in grain rates from all parts of Wisconsin to Milwaukee, since complaints like the one filed, in this case, by the powerful Milwaukee Chamber of Commerce were quite catholic.[10] The new restriction meant, however, that the commission could not stray from those areas where vocal shipping interests saw fit to state their grievances.

While the commissioners were struggling to learn their new tasks, therefore, the legislature had succeeded in enforcing one final limitation on their powers to affect the state's new rate structure. Ironically, when at last the commission was ready to undertake the intricate task of rate revision, it had lost its prerogative to use its abilities over a broad area. "This Commission . . . now feels it is sufficiently informed as to the general situation to take up

---

[9] Winterbotham to Parlin and Orendorf Company, June 20, 1906, General Correspondence, WPSC Records.

[10] O. G. Kinney vs. Wisconsin Central Railway Company; Walter L. Houser vs. Chicago, St. Paul, Minneapolis and Omaha Railway Company; Investigation on Motion of the Commission of Grain Rates between Stations in Wisconsin and Milwaukee, Wisconsin on the lines of the Chicago, Milwaukee and St. Paul Railway Company, Chicago and North Western Railway Company, Chicago, St. Paul, Minneapolis and Omaha Railway Company, Wisconsin Central Railway Company, July 10–August 8, 1906, in *Opinions and Decisions of the Railroad Commission of the State of Wisconsin* (Madison, 1908), 1:124–129. Erickson, in a letter to George H. D. Johnson, then president of the Milwaukee Chamber of Commerce, notes the commission went ahead with the investigation on its own motion after Johnson became too busy to push the chamber's complaint. July 13, 1906, General Correspondence, WPSC Records.

specific complaints intelligently and dispose of them," announced Barnes in January of 1906.[11]

Having forfeited the right of initial rate making, reformers had hoped that a free-wheeling commission, determined to undertake a radical revision of the state's transportation rates, could reduce rates rapidly and lift the burden from the oppressed consumers and small shippers. The reluctance of the commission to build its own position of power, combined with determined opposition to strong regulation by influential senators, resulted in the limitation of the new agency essentially to the handling of complaints. The victory won by the moderate elements in the spring of 1905 was enhanced by a final triumph the following winter.

Those reformers who had pushed for a commission with broad powers of initiative had been convinced that the processing of complaints alone would result in a highly uneven kind of justice, bestowed only on those groups with the courage and strength to stand up to the transportation companies and demand their rights without fear of reprisals. Determined to democratize the economic system, they argued persistently that regulatory legislation was designed not to serve those who were quite capable of protecting themselves. Rather it was to benefit the common man who possessed neither the knowledge nor the power to confront the railroads. For this reason they had fought to gain for the commission an independence which would allow it to become more than an instrument of articulate shippers.

Having lost the chance to choose its areas of investigation, however, the Railroad Commission of Wisconsin still had one other opportunity to become an instrument of rapid change — through the use of complaints in a creative way. If it chose to construe its prerogative to handle complaints broadly, and investigated the implications of key inquiries which shippers brought before it, then in the hands of the commission this more limited tool might be transformed into a vehicle of change.

The possibility that the commission would take such a course struck fear into the hearts of many a railroad official during the early months of the new agency's activity. Apprehensive that the

[11] Barnes to Eliot, February 1, 1906, General Correspondence, WPSC Records.

correction of a single rate would lead to the alteration of other related rates and so on until the entire rate structure of the state had been changed by the ignition of a single spark, the carriers watched the commission closely for evidence of how it would treat its first complaint cases.[12]

In this highly charged atmosphere, the commission set about calming the fears of the railroad executives. Confident of the carriers' ability to make equitable rates, and fearful that "the violent disturbance of the rates at any point may have a tendency to upset the rate situation as a whole,"[13] the commission handled complaints with the same restraint which caused it to refuse to use its powers of initiative until the statute was clarified. Rather than viewing complaints as pointing the way to broader investigations, it declared that "where there is a complaint . . . on a specific rate or rates[,] . . . the Commission wont [sic] on its own motion on a hearing of that complaint go outside of the scope of it."[14] It consistently followed this course of self-limitation, confining all of its decisions to those rates which were specifically brought into question by the complaint.

The results of this doctrine of regulation in small doses were many. Because they were unwilling to extend complaints to cover related rates, the commissioners sometimes found themselves unable to remedy even the specific abuse at hand, because such an action would result in discrimination on behalf of the complainant, at the expense of other shippers in nearby areas, who were forced to pay the old rates.[15]

---

[12] See, for example, the comments of E. S. Keeley and C. E. Vroman of the Chicago, Milwaukee and St. Paul Railway in Plumb and Nelson Company vs. Wisconsin Central Railway Company, Chicago, Milwaukee and St. St. Paul Railway Company, Minutes of Hearings, (February 28, 1906), 1:20, 24, WPSC Records.

[13] Erickson to Keeley, September 2, 1905, Railroad Informal Cases (D. C. Palmeter Case), WPSC Records.

[14] W. L. Houser vs. Chicago and North Western Railway Company and Chicago, St. Paul, Minneapolis and Omaha Railway Company, Minutes of Hearings, (June 19, 1906), vol. 3, WPSC Records. See also Meyer to John Luchsinger, July 2, 1906, and Meyer to F. P. Eyman, June 28, 1906, Formal Case Papers (Southern Wisconsin Cheesemakers' Association vs. Chicago and North Western Railway Company), WPSC Records.

[15] See Shawano Lumber Company vs. Chicago and North Western Railway

More important, the commission's decision moved it more and more toward an essentially "judicial" construction of its function. This effect could be noted both in its method of procedure and in an important shift which took place in its work as a result of this new posture.

Having resolved that the parties in conflict were the only concerned participants in an investigation, the commissioners evinced an increasing tendency toward passivity in their decision making. While they continued to use some information secured from outside sources, they came to rely more and more on the interested parties to set the limits of the discussion, and hence define the dimensions of the solution. B. H. Meyer, commenting on commission procedures, offered a graphic description of this trend in the work of the agency.

> In advance of the hearings we do comparatively little investigation. We have no direct communications outside the formal notices which are sent to the parties interested, although occasionally, certain information which we deem essential in the hearing of the case is called for in advance. Both sides present their testimony as best they can, and then the work of the Commission begins. We have extensive statistical and other compilations in this office which we naturally use, and in addition, we send men to the various offices to check and test exhibits and other documents introduced in evidence at the hearing.[16]

Soon this drift toward dealing primarily with the wrong done the complainant rather than the implications of the complaint itself was embodied in new legislation.

Reform leaders had consistently contended that complaints should be treated simply as indicators of areas in need of investigation. Rewarding the man who complained was not a sufficient remedy, for the reformers opposed any effort to interpret complaints by shippers as individual matters concerning only the specific parties at odds. In 1905 reformers had defeated conserva-

---

Company, September 8–24, 1908, in *Opinions and Decisions of the Railroad Commission of the State of Wisconsin*, (Madison, 1909), 2:785, 789.
[16] Meyer to E. M. Bassett, January 9, 1909, General Correspondence, WPSC Records.

tive plans to suspend all commission decisions pending review by the courts, with treble damages going to the complaining shipper if the commission's ruling was upheld. Such a plan, they declared, would simply result in remuneration to the large shipper, who often had already passed the higher tariff cost on to the consumer in the form of higher prices, while the small man would gain nothing. In 1906 E. P. Bacon carried this argument to Washington, declaring in letters to several Senators that if the ICC were given the right to grant compensation to those who complained, in at least 75 per cent of the cases where such refunds were ordered, "no part of the refund would reach the actual sufferer."[17]

In Wisconsin, ironically, the commission which Bacon had so valiantly fought for moved in the very direction he argued against as it confined its attention more and more to the shipper who lodged the complaint. In 1907 the lawmakers authorized a final step in that direction. Under strong pressure from the commission (Barnes himself wrote the legislation),[18] the legislature amended the regulation act in order to give the agency the power to authorize refunds to shippers. If, within six months after the delivery of any freight shipment, a shipper wished to complain that the charge exacted from him was excessive, the commission could hold hearings and, upon deciding the cost was indeed exorbitant, authorize the refund of a portion of the charge. If the carrier did not agree to the refund, the shipper could then take the matter to court using the findings of the commission as prima facie evidence of the truth of his allegations. The limitations that the charge must be ruled unreasonable and excessive by the commission and that the commission must specify the exact amount the carrier could refund were safeguards imposed by the legislature, which feared the reintroduction of rebates unless close reins were kept on the new system.[19]

In a sense, the commission's new powers allowed it to remedy

[17] Bacon to La Follette, April 2, 1906, in the La Follette Papers.
[18] See Barnes to Herman L. Ekern, May 17, 1907, and copy of bill in Barnes to Ekern, May 20, 1907, in the Ekern Papers.
[19] In re Observations on the Work of the Railroad Commission, General Correspondence (box 39), WPSC Records.

rate abuses more fully, for shippers who chose to complain were assured of compensation as well as an adjustment of future tariffs. The effect of the measure, however, was to accentuate the tendencies evident in the commission's work from the beginning. Under the new law, the commission, essentially limited to the handling of specific complaints, became more and more a "court of claims," as it phrased it. Hundreds of claims soon flooded its offices and made up a "substantial part of the work of the department." The formal case dockets became jammed with refund cases, some of which involved only a dollar or two. This trend was further accentuated by a 1909 law which allowed refunds for excessive charges exacted during the previous years if complaints were immediately filed and a 1911 statute which permitted shippers to send their receipts to the commission for examination for possible overcharges.[20]

The hope had been for a strong-minded agency which would put the carriers in their place. Not inclined to be an instrument of rapid commercial change, the commission settled back into the less ambitious role of adjudicator of disputes.

The dimensions of regulation in Wisconsin were greatly altered by the manner in which the commission construed its powers to initiate actions and handle complaints. The commission's posture toward rate advances by the railroads completed the transformation.

At the core of the reformers' attempts to bring about a more equitable rate system had been a determination to limit the railroads' right to adjust rates to their own liking. Originally, these men had planned to transfer the entire rate-making function to a commission, with the railroads able to change tariffs set by the commission only if they appealed directly to the agency. A breakdown of legislative discipline, however, doomed this ambitious undertaking and, having lost this fight, the reform leaders took little interest in substituting other safeguards.

Little was said about this question in the final bill. Railroads retained the power to set their own rates and were impelled to file

---

[20] *Ibid.*, and *Sixth Annual Report of the Railroad Commission of Wisconsin, From June 30, 1911, to June 30, 1912* (Madison, 1912), 15.

all rate changes with the commission at least ten days before they went into operation. No indication was given as to how the new agency was to proceed in receiving these new tables, although supporters of the administration program apparently felt that this requirement was sufficient to allow the commission to review all rate changes. By exercising this sort of supervision, the commission could prevent the furtherance of discriminatory practices.

On the heels of its formation, the commission was forced to decide whether this was the intent of the ambiguous provision, for revised rate schedules began immediately to flow into its offices in a stream which grew even larger after December 31, 1905, when the roads regained complete control over initial rate making. The question of how to deal with these numerous requests caused the first major disagreement among the new commissioners.

B. H. Meyer, always willing to trust the judgment of the railroad official, argued that the commission could not and should not bother to review the many rate revisions made by the carriers. Instead, he declared, the carriers should be allowed to make whatever changes they wished, pending complaints by shippers. "Enough of these sheets will come in some days to keep all of us busy," he argued, on behalf of Erickson and himself, in a letter to Barnes. "Unless you think that the law makes it obligatory on our part to require of the companies formal application by letter, we are inclined to feel that it will be expedient for the present to continue on the assumption that the receipt of the schedule is in itself an application [for approval]."[21]

Barnes, more prone toward procedural niceties, disagreed. Proclaiming that it was the convenience of the commission and not the railroads which should be served, he declared: "I think they are assuming a little more than they have a right to assume when they put new schedules into effect without making more application than they have in the past. . . . I do not think we ought to permit any rate to be raised except on a formal application."[22]

It is indicative of Meyer's dominance of the new agency that the

[21] Meyer to Barnes, August 22, 1905, General Correspondence, WPSC Records.
[22] Barnes to Meyer, August 24, 1905, General Correspondence, WPSC Records.

commission chairman lost the argument. In the busy months that followed, the commission interpreted its prerogative narrowly, requiring only that the railroads submit their changes to its office before they were enacted, although it did hold open the possibility of more vigorous review. ("Unless you hear from us with reference to any one or more of the schedules . . . submitted," wrote Meyer to a top official of the Northern Pacific Railway, "you may assume that the [rates] may go into effect on the date indicated without any formal action or additional correspondence.")[23]

In time, even the option of further review was abandoned. As the inertia of this initial decision took hold, both the commission and the carriers came more and more to believe that this area was outside the limits of regulation. In answer to an inquiry concerning the possibility of the commission preventing certain projected increases in rates, commission secretary John M. Winterbotham replied: "We do not believe the commission can take jurisdiction in a matter where the thing complained of is a proposed increase. We believe that the complaint must be filed after the tariff complained of has taken effect."[24]

The railroads became lax even in keeping the commission informed about rate changes. On one occasion Meyer noticed numerous changes in a printed tariff schedule of the Chicago and North Western which that road had never formally submitted to the commission. The co-operative commissioner, therefore, made a list of these alterations and sent it to the office of the carrier with the assurance that these changes were acceptable to the commission![25]

The result of this abdication of responsibility was soon felt by the state's shippers. In the winter of 1908, unencumbered by the commission, the railroads raised their lumber tariffs to levels which, according to one source, "paralyzed" the industry.[26] Apparently

---

[23] Meyer to J. B. Baird, March 7, 1906, General Correspondence, WPSC Records. See also Meyer to F. P. Eyman, August 21, 1906, General Correspondence, WPSC Records.
[24] Winterbotham to R. W. Crary, September 18, 1905, Formal Case Papers, WPSC Records.
[25] Meyer to Barnes, August 18, 1906, General Correspondence, WPSC Records.
[26] *La Follette's Weekly Magazine*, 1:4 (January 9, 1909).

spurred on by this crisis, the Wisconsin legislature sought further to restrict the railroads' right to raise rates at will.

In 1909 the lawmakers pushed through legislation requiring the railroad companies to file all proposed increases in rates with the commission at least thirty days prior to the time they were to go into effect.[27] If the commission had more time to do its work, they apparently reasoned, it could be more restrictive. Dissatisfied with the results of this law, in 1911 the legislature *required* the commission to give explicit approval to all proposed rate changes prior to their enactment.[28]

Deluged with new responsibilities, particularly after 1907 when the commission was put in charge of all public utilities also, and never inclined to hamper the railroads greatly, the commissioners could not be forced to undertake this task with much zeal. Commenting on the 1911 bill, the commission noted that 1,006 requests for permission to change rates, classifications, and rules had come to its offices in the first year of the new law. "Even under the most favorable conditions, . . . with full information at hand as to the effect of proposed changes, why such a change is to be desired, etc., it is not quite clear in all cases just what action should be taken by the Commission," the commissioners complained. Since often even such basic information was not supplied, it is doubtful that the commission's supervision in this area was ever more than perfunctory. The inertia of self-restraint, accentuated by the exigencies of time, could not be overcome by legislative edict.[29]

While this self-willed surrender of power reduced the dimensions of commission power, one effect was simply to increase its task elsewhere. As the carriers, free of commission strictures, raised freight rates at will after 1905, the commission received many complaints designed not to rectify the rates which La Follette and his colleagues had labeled as excessive, but to roll back increases by

[27] *Freight*, 5:191 (June, 1909).

[28] *Sixth Annual Report of the Railroad Commission of Wisconsin*, 15.

[29] *Ibid.* In answer to a request of a shipper that the commission keep him posted on rate changes on lumber and bricks, Commission Secretary John M. Winterbotham asserted pessimistically, "Our tariff force is wholly inadequate to furnish information of this kind." Winterbotham to L. C. Whittet, September 1, 1909, Formal Case Papers, WPSC Records.

the railroads to the level which prevailed when the commission was founded. The new agency was often busy ruling out rate increases which shippers found damaging to their interests, after they were put into effect.

This method of controlling rate changes was simply another manifestation of the change from a commission with the potential for remaking the state's rate structures to a complaint-oriented administrative body, which operated primarily for the benefit of those vocal interests in the state which sought limited rate corrections.

In September, 1905, Halford Erickson, in a letter to the general freight agent of the Milwaukee Road, declared the commission's intention "to avoid propositions that might tend towards a more general rearrangement of rates."[30]

In the early years of commission activity, Erickson's declaration was expressive of the mood of the commission. Convinced that the aims of the reformers were destructive and that their arguments were exaggerated, the new agency refused to take upon itself any rate-making prerogatives which seemed to threaten disruption of the state's economic status quo. Hence the commissioners readily accepted the legislature's limitation of their power to initiate rate changes. They settled back into the role of quasi-judicial adjudicators of complaints. As a result the railroads discovered they could make their own rates in their own way, encumbered only by the power of the commission to redress grievances on complaint.

Such actions by the commission struck the final, fatal blow to the hopes of those reformers who had envisioned the creation of entirely new rate schedules based on a greater regard for the consumer and the small shippers, who could not or would not complain. Having lost a crucial battle in the legislature, these dedicated crusaders saw their dreams finally laid to rest by the new commission which held different aims and purposes. Ironically, however, this crushing defeat simply set the stage for the sort of role which the commission had hoped to perform.

---

[30] Erickson to Keeley, September 2, 1905, Railroad Informal Cases (D. C. Palmeter Case), WPSC Records.

The Quest for Harmony

8 The history of the early years of the Wisconsin railroad commission is the final chapter in the story of a losing battle that ardent reformers fought in Wisconsin for a regulatory commission which would swiftly and decisively change the rate structure of the state and turn the Wisconsin railroads into servants of the people.

In another sense, however, the work of the commission marked a beginning, rather than an end. The ideological leader of the commission, B. H. Meyer, rejected most of the propositions underlying the reform program in Wisconsin, and argued instead that the greatest hope for the betterment of relations with the transportation industry in the country did not lie with government commissions, but in combinations of economic interests achieved outside the framework of government. Convinced that the fundamental public mistrust of the transportation companies was based not on actual abuses, but on a lack of understanding and co-operation between the various segments of society, Meyer preached the need to replace competition with commercial co-operation.

In a sympathetic study of the Northern Securities Company, a combination of major railroads in the upper Midwest which the federal government ordered dissolved in 1902, Meyer asserted "Undiscriminating opposition to all forms of open concerted action on the part of the railways is in my mind the greatest single blunder in our public policy toward railways." The application of the Sherman Antitrust Act to railways he called "one of the gravest errors in our legislative history." If open agreements between rail

152

ways were legalized, the trend toward "progressive anarchy in railway matters" could be stemmed, he declared, to the benefit of both carriers and the public, for such co-operation would end wasteful competition.[1]

Even more important in Meyer's mind than increased co-operation between the railroads was the establishment of concrete ties between the major economic and social groups in the society. To accomplish this co-operation, Meyer proposed the establishment of "advisory councils," a series of state and interstate bodies made up of representatives of many groups. Meyer's plan, derived from a similar system extant in several other countries in the world, notably Prussia, called for the creation of groups made up of persons representing the railways and all of the major economic organizations in an area (farmers, chambers of commerce, retail businessmen, manufacturers, and the like), under one co-ordinated system. If so organized, argued Meyer, these councils would serve as "clearing houses of information through which the railways and the public will learn to know each other's interests better, and through which the material interests of both of these great parties will be built up in accordance with the principles of justice and equity." Although such agencies would only have advisory powers, they would be the "most potent factor in protecting the railways against each other, and in visiting obloquy upon the one weak or unscrupulous manager who persists in defeating the best plans of the one hundred who would adhere to principles of justice without legal compulsion."

Convinced that the railroad problem involved essentially a lack of mutual understanding between railroads themselves, and between the railroads and the public, Meyer declared that these bodies could be a more effective remedy to the current discontent than the strongest of regulatory commissions. "By reflecting accurately the existing conditions, these conferences lead to tolerance, forbearance, and mutual concessions," he argued.[2]

---

[1] Balthasar H. Meyer, *A History of the Northern Securities Case* (Madison, 1906), 305, 307.

[2] See Meyer, *Railway Legislation in the United States*, 36–42, and B. H. Meyer, "Railway Regulation Under Foreign and Domestic Law," in

Meyer did not preach laissez faire. He declared that a commission could fulfill a very important function if it also sought to build greater harmony between groups involved in transportation. The challenge for a railroad commission, he asserted, was to bring dissident elements together. "Cooperation between the traffic man, the producer, the manufacturer, the dealer and the consumer must be real and vital," he declared in 1907, "and to promote this co-operation should be one of the highest aims of the public administrative official and the legislator."[3]

The efforts of the commission in the early years were aimed at building such a co-operative community, based on a harmony of goals and trust in the agent of conciliation, the commission. It is in this context that the lack of zeal for achieving the purpose of the reformers must be understood. The commission, first of all, had little time to seek these ends, for its attention was on a different sort of enterprise. More important, the new agency would have been forced virtually to abandon the goals espoused by its leader in order to embrace vigorous regulation of the sort implied by the ideology of reform. Should the commission choose to undertake a program designed to change rates rapidly, which had oftentimes been in effect for many years, the railroads and other more conservative elements would have immediately looked on the new agency with fear and mistrust. Hence the commission would forfeit the opportunity to act as a harmonizer. The choice, then, was between assuming the role of antagonist to the railroads on behalf of the common man, or seeking to become an agent of reconciliation by establishing amicable relations with all important commercial groups. The commission chose the latter course.

Writing to Robert La Follette in November, 1904, Meyer declared, "Wisconsin has . . . the opportunity to take a step forward which may exert important influences in state and Federal legislation, or, if she fails to seize her opportunity, to retard the growth of rational and effective control throughout the country. The whole

Report of the Industrial Commission on Transportation, (57 Congress, 1 session, House Document no. 178, serial 4339, Washington, 1901), 9:983.
[3] "Commerce As Related to Transportation," speech before the Transportation Club of Milwaukee, May 2, 1907, in the Meyer Papers.

nation may be affected by what Wisconsin does."[4] Now Wisconsin's chance was Meyer's own. Convinced that the railroad problem involved essentially a crisis in public relations and public confidence rather than a basic inequity in the rate structure, Meyer had a blueprint for regulation which was far different from that proposed by the most ardent reformers.

The first step the commission took in establishing new relationships in the transportation industry was the concession of a final opportunity to revolutionize the state's rate structure. During the long struggle over increased regulation in Wisconsin, the railroads and the reform groups shared one assumption: that a regulatory commission would adopt different bases for evaluating rates than those currently used by the carriers. This, more than any other single factor, made the battle over regulation in Wisconsin so heated.

Ingrained in the minds of the railroad men was the notion that regulatory commissions, of necessity, could operate only one way in evaluating rates. A. J. Earling, the president of the Milwaukee Road, on the eve of the passage of the Wisconsin regulation law declared:

> Human nature is so constituted that it is much more easy to solve the question of equality between towns and communities and interests, by giving them all exactly the same rate per mile, than to attempt the difficult task of adjusting rates to the satisfaction of all. The result is that commissions, which have the power to make rates, find themselves constantly drifting toward distance tariffs, in hope of avoiding the criticisms of towns, cities, and regions which are demanding their favor.[5]

Having based their rates on numerous considerations, sometimes the least of these being mileage, the carriers argued that the belated application of a simplistic standard such as distance would inevitably result in the total disruption of commerce in the state. "The rates," declared Frank P. Eyman, an executive for the Chicago and North Western Railway, "do not tell anything unless you

---

[4] Meyer to La Follette, November 21, 1904, in the La Follette Papers.
[5] A. J. Earling, "The Effect of Government Rate-Making upon Internal Commerce," *Harper's Weekly*, 49:720 (May 20, 1905).

know the circumstances and conditions under which the rates are established."[6] Doubtful that a commission would accept that orientation, the carriers fought to reduce a commission's power to make rates as much as possible.

La Follette and the other leaders of the Wisconsin crusade for increased regulation had fanned the flames of these apprehensions by their speeches during the long fight. They had incessantly compared rates for particular distances in Illinois and Iowa with those in Wisconsin, then appealed for a Wisconsin commission which would restore the state to commercial parity with its neighbors. The clear implication was that under such a regulatory commission rates would be made more equitable by applying the standard of distance.

The 1905 legislature had little success in resolving this conflict in values. It proposed a new way of looking at railroad rates by requiring the valuation of all railroad property as the basis for a more scientific sort of rate making than presently prevailed. It did not specify precisely how the commission should apply this new tool. More important, at the height of the regulation controversy, in an attempt to placate important shipping interests, the lawmakers had specifically sanctioned the continuation of the many special rate structures in the state.

Thus the final mandate was extremely ambiguous. The legislature had been forthright in its devotion to valuation; it had not been as singularly dedicated to the underlying concept, that of making each rate fair and equitable in its own right by forcing it to contribute its proper share to the railroads' earnings and dividends. While outlawing "unjust discrimination" and "undue or unreasonable preference or advantage to any particular person firm or corporation," the legislature made no attempt to specify whether distance or some other standard could be be used in rectifying abuses.

As soon as the new regulatory commission had been installed the carriers put its new appointees to their greatest test. In 1874 when the Potter Law was enacted, the Wisconsin roads had taken

---

[6] F. P. Eyman, Minutes of Hearings (October 11, 1906), 4:36, WPSC Records.

a kind of savage pleasure in flaunting the law by proceeding as they had prior to its passage, oblivious of the rate requirements of the new measure. In 1905, however, with the public character of transportation firmly established, the legitimacy of public regulation unquestioned, and a statute which was more acceptable to them, the carriers assumed a different attitude, choosing to abide by the new restrictive legislation in hopes that its effects would not be too harmful.

As the commissioners took office in the summer of 1905, the carriers undertook a series of highly defensive actions designed to illustrate their intention to co-operate with the commission, while guarding against the possibility of severe penalties under the new law and testing the agency's resolve. (La Follette argued that the railroads hoped to discredit the law by illustrating how restrictive it would be, an argument which, while feasible, cannot be proven.)[7]

Every road in the state withdrew all special rates to passengers, thus requiring the payment of regular rates by land companies preparing excursions for those who wished to view lands in the northern part of the state, vacationers who traditionally rode cheaply to chautauqua meetings, and even the state militia preparing to embark for summer drills at Camp Douglas.[8] Individual roads took other steps. The general freight agent for the Omaha road, for example, hurriedly asked permission to label certain rates "concentration rates," thus permitting their continuance in spite of the fact that they were clearly discriminatory. Other tariffs he withdrew, expressing the fear that they were illegal under the new law.[9] The Wisconsin Central, contrary to the law's stipulation which froze all rates at April 1, 1905, altered a portion of its lumber tariffs before sending them to the commission, in order to eliminate

[7] *Milwaukee Free Press,* December 6, 1905. Marvin Hughitt stressed the intention of his railroad to abide strictly by the new law. Hughitt to Keyes, July 5, 1905, in the Keyes Papers.

[8] *Milwaukee Sentinel,* June 21, 27, 29, 1905.

[9] H. M. Pearce to Commission, July 21, 1905, General Correspondence, WPSC Records; In re application of the Chicago, St. Paul, Minneapolis and Omaha Railroad For Leave to Discontinue Tariff on Wood for the Ashland Iron and Steel Co., October 27, 1905, in *Opinions and Decisions of the Railroad Commission of the State of Wisconsin,* 1:16–19.

certain "special contract" rates which it feared were illegal because
they were discriminatory.[10]

In the heat of the summer, therefore, as travelers clamored for a
return of special passenger rates and land companies painted
pictures of a deserted northern Wisconsin unless special conces
sions granted to parties interested in land in that area were
restored, the commission faced its first major choice. Should it
acknowledge the legitimacy of numerous special rate arrangement
and encourage the continuation of the use of multiple criteria in
making rates or aim toward the kind of equality in rates which
reformers had argued for in contending that such concessions
simply benefited special interests at the expense of the public'

To the Meyer-dominated railroad commission the choice was
merely an opportunity. Meyer had never quarreled with the rail
road's use of complex criteria in formulating rates, and he had
repeatedly ridiculed the idea that rigid standards such as distance
could be used as sole criteria for rate making. Nor did he consider
valuation of railroad properties as anything more than a partial
gauge for determining tariff levels. Now he had an opportunity to
express these convictions as a policy maker, while also taking the
first step toward calming the fears of railroad men concerning the
new commission.

The commission enunciated several of its basic principles for
the first time in response to these railroad challenges. Voicing
Meyer's long-standing conviction that regulation must be more
standardized, it declared its intention to apply to those provision
of the Wisconsin statute which were derived from the Interstate
Commerce Law the interpretations handed down by the ICC and
the federal courts. Citing the Interstate Commerce Commission'
ruling that special passenger rates were legitimate, the Wisconsin
agency announced that the carriers could fix as many special rate
as they wished, so long as benefits were made available to everyon
who qualified under their provisions.[11]

---

[10] Testimony of Thomas Gill, Menasha Wooden Ware Company vs. Wisconsin
Central Railway Company, Minutes of Hearings (May 9, 1906), WPSC
Records.
[11] In re application of Wisconsin Immigration and Development Association
to the Railroad Commission of Wisconsin to Place a Construction o

To the satisfaction of the Omaha road officials, the commissioners quickly approved the request for concentration rate classifications for many rates, declaring that "a lesser rate might well be made on a commodity, such as wood or saw logs, where the carrier was to receive a remunerative rate for hauling the manufactured product, than might be made where there was no manufactured product to haul."[12]

In its first two formal decisions, therefore, the commission set a course toward conciliation. By affirming the right of the railroads to establish whatever special categories it wished, the commissioners disavowed any intention of usurping railroad prerogatives or interfering with its commercial planning. More important, its approval of the use of criteria other than distance and valuation in the making of rates calmed fears that it would yield to cries for distance tariff.

In subsequent actions the new agency made even more explicit its intention to safeguard railroad interests in its rate-making activity. "If the state should attempt to establish a system of cast iron rules, the whole subject of transportation charges would be revolutionized," it declared. Unwilling to become the vehicle of such rapid change, the commission shunned the application of reform nolutions like the Iowa distance tariff, which La Follette had extolled, and the principle of long and short haul, which many reformers felt must be the basis of equitable rates. Instead, time and again it declared its desire to avoid any action which "would disturb existing trade relations."[13] "We must deal with conditions as they have grown up and have become established," the commissioners asserted.[14]

Chapter 362 of the Laws of Wisconsin for the Year 1905, July 20, 1905, in *Opinions and Decisions of the Railroad Commission* . . . , 1:1–16.

[2] Commission to Pearce, July 25, 1905, General Correspondence, WPSC Records; In re application of Chicago, St. Paul, Minneapolis and Omaha Railroad For Leave to Discontinue Tariff on Wood for the Ashland Iron and Steel Co., October 27, 1905, in *ibid.,* I:159.

[3] In re Wisconsin Central Railway Company Charge on Construction Material for Manufacturing Plans, October 29, 1906, in *ibid.,* 1:222; Southern Wisconsin Cheesemen's Protective Association vs. Chicago and North Western Railway Co., August 13, 1906, in *ibid.,* 1:159.

[4] A. E. Buell vs. Chicago, Milwaukee and St. Paul Railway Company, February 16, 1907, in *ibid.,* 1:503.

The result of this overarching concern with stability was a almost total reversal in emphasis from that of the reformers. "Generally speaking," declared B. H. Meyer, "the relations of rates i more important than the absolute level of rates. By refusing t establish and maintain just relations among the rates applicabl to different commercial areas it is possible to arbitrarily prescrib the areas within which certain traders may buy and sell."[15]

In line with the conviction that the absolute level of rates wa less important than their relative levels the commission embrace the use of multiple criteria in rate evaluation. While decrying th widespread application of "irrational" standards in making rate and declaring its intention to "fall back upon detailed analyses c earnings and expenses and interpret these in the light of as man of the factors in rate making as we can reduce to a tangible basis the commissioners soon made it abundantly clear that among thos "tangible" features they considered acceptable criteria were mos of the principles that the railroads had used for many years.[16] I their early decisions they cited as proper considerations in rat making "the risk assumed by the carrier," "the value of the com modity," "the volume of the traffic," "competitive conditions," "th need of the community," "the rates in other states under simila conditions," "cost of service," and numerous other categories.[17]

Using these flexible tools, the commission moved to stabiliz relations in the transportation industry through a sensitive handlin of complaints. Sometimes it demanded change when rates wer improperly adjusted, as in the case of a grain dealer unable to ge his produce to market for the same cost as his competitors. ("It of great importance to said petitioner that the rates on these grair should be so adjusted that he is placed in relatively about the sam position in the market, so far as rates on the raw material ar

---

[15] Meyer to La Follette, March 23, 1906, in the La Follette Papers.
[16] Southern Wisconsin Cheesemen's Protective Association vs. Chicag Milwaukee and St. Paul Railway Company, Chicago and Northweste Railway Company, Illinois Central Railway Company, August 13, 1906, *Opinions and Decisions of the Railroad Commission. . . ,* 1:143–166.
[17] *Ibid.* Deposition on Louisiana Case, Halford Erickson questioned concern ing November, 1906 decision of Wisconsin Railroad Commission whic dealt with rates on sugar beets, July 8, 1909, General Correspondenc WPSC Records.

concerned, as his competitors," declared the commission.)[18] At other times it ordered the carriers to rescind rate increases, as in the case of certain lumber rates in the Wausau area. ("It appears to us that freight rates, that have been in effect long enough so that industrial and commercial conditions have become adjusted and established under them, should not be increased except for good reasons.")[19] But often the commission felt compelled to uphold the existing standards. Asked to evaluate certain other rate conditions in the lumber industry, a rate expert for the commission asserted: "The rates complained of do not seem to be out of line. They are about the same as the rates from the nearest competitive point. . . . There seems to be no discrimination of any kind. If any change in the rates complained of is made it would bring about discrepancies in numerous other rates in the same territory."[20]

Always, however, the importance of maintaining commercial equality was stressed, rather than the absolute level of rates. When, for example, a lumber firm complained that the Chicago and North Western Railway was discriminating against it by exacting excessive rates, the commission ordered the railroad to remedy the situation. The carrier immediately raised the rates of all of the competing firms in the area rather than lower those of the complainant. In reply to the lumber company's vehement accusations of bad faith on the part of the carriers, the commission asserted: "Both your complaint and our decision were largely based upon the discrimination in the rates against you. Now this discrimination appears to have been removed. . . . Unless other discriminations can be shown, . . . your case may not be as strong as it was."[21]

Thus, in spite of complaints by some shippers who had hoped for a general reduction in rates, the commission worked toward a

---

[18] F. H. Minch vs. Chicago and North Western Railway Co., Illinois Central Railroad Co., June 18, 1907, in *Opinions and Decisions of the Railroad Commission . . .*, 1:599–607.

[19] The Wisconsin Box Company, Wausau Box and Lumber Company vs. Chicago, Milwaukee and St. Paul Railway Co., Chicago and North Western Railway Co., July 8, 1909, in *ibid.*, 3:617.

[20] "JFH" [Hogan] to Erickson, July 1, 1910, Formal Case Papers (Brown Bros. Lumber Co.), WPSC Records.

[21] Erickson to Shawano Lumber Company, April 22, 1909, Formal Case Papers (Shawano Lumber Co.), WPSC Records.

different goal. Rather than applying principles aimed at restoring any sort of absolute rate equality in the state, it sought instead to bring about greater equality of opportunity among all commercial groups wishing access to certain markets. The establishment of this principle was the commission's first step in seeking to eliminate suspicion and mistrust in the transportation industry.

Although the manner in which the commission pursued its task of rate making was extremely important in its effort to restore confidence among commercial groups and between these groups and the new agency, even more central to the achievement of its goals were the steps it took to allow the principals in a dispute to forge their own agreements.

"Ever since I began to express myself in regard to railway commissions and their functions," B. H. Meyer declared in August, 1905,

> . . . it has been one of my strongest convictions that, irrespective of what technical legal powers might be vested in a railway commission, one of its most important and essential functions should be that of an arbitrator or intermediary. . . . If only the different parties in controversies regarding railway rates or service could be brought together and the entire situation carefully analized [*sic*] and discussed, a clear solution of satisfactory compromise might be reached, and similar difficulties avoided in the future.[22]

Enamored with the possibilities of this plan to create a new spirit of co-operation between commercial antagonists, the commission sought to create the conditions under which railroads and businessmen would willingly come together. Shunning the formal methods of procedure outlined in the statute whenever it could, the commission set about establishing an air of informal privacy more conducive to bringing about economic agreements. Arguing that "formal proceedings may lead to an undue exploitation of the facts, or alleged facts in the case, on the part of the press," while publicity, "even if true, will do no one any good, and may do one or the other or all of the parties in interest some harm," the com-

---

[22] Meyer to Lloyd W. Bowers, August 5, 1905, General Correspondence WPSC Records.

missioners rejected the notion that, as government officials, they should open all of their activities to public scrutiny.[23] Instead, they resolved to carry out their public function in a very private way.

They began by deciding to keep no public record of the many informal sessions they held with railroads and businesses, explaining that "men sitting around a table in informal conferences, discussing the subject at hand with perfect freedom, are much more likely to arrive at some acceptable conclusion than when every word is measured and becomes a part of a record that may figure in the courts."[24] They also established the principle that all railroad agreements and business contracts were private and would not be released for anyone to see. Nor would they allow anyone access to railroad accounts, even if such records were germane to a complaint under consideration.[25]

Having established procedures conducive to private agreement, the commission set about attempting to bring warring groups together. It immediately held a series of informal conferences with the major railroads and several of the leading industrial groups, and explained its intention to be a conciliator. When complaints began to reach the new agency, the commissioners declared, in a letter to one of the leading railroads of the state, that "on general principles, we favor the shipper and the railroads getting together and settling up their difficulties if they can do so."[26] In pursuit of this kind of solution to the problems facing the transportation industry, the commission resolved to defer judgment on all complaints until every path of reconciliation had been tried.

On receiving a complaint, the agency immediately contacted both sides in the struggle and sought to bring them together by mediation through the mail or by arranging a meeting of represen-

---

[23] *Ibid.*
[24] *First Biennial Report of the Railroad Commission from the Organization of the Commission to June 30, 1906* (Madison, 1907), 8.
[25] Burton Hanson to Winterbotham, November 29, 1905; Winterbotham to Hanson, December 5, 1905; S. A. Lynde to Winterbotham, December 4, 1905; Winterbotham to Lynde, December 5, 1905, all in General Correspondence, WPSC Records; Commission to Kreutzer, Bird, Rosenberry and Okoneski, April 1, 1910, Formal Case Papers, WPSC Records.
[26] Barnes to Keeley, January 23, 1906, Formal Case Papers (Southern Wisconsin Cheesemen's Association), WPSC Records.

tatives. More interested in restoring harmony than in exploring the implications of a complaint, if the two sides agreed to settle their difficulties privately, the commission usually dropped the case.[27] If the matter came to a formal hearing before such an agreement was reached, the commission often simply issued a decision formalizing the pact which the shipper and the railroad had forged through commission mediation.

After 1907, this last aspect of commission action became very prominent, as the refund amendment came more and more into use. Because the law stipulated that refunds could only be granted by carriers on orders from the commission, literally hundreds of complaints were filed with the commission involving matters which the railroads and shippers had already informally resolved. Sometimes a railroad even filed complaints against itself in order to gain the right to refund a portion to a shipper. Although the railroad commission persistently phrased its decisions in these cases in such a way as to indicate that cost analysis showed the overcharge to be of a certain amount, very seldom did the amount authorized for refund differ from that agreed to by the two parties prior to the filing of the complaint.

Even when questions were broader than those concerning a single shipper and a railroad, the commission did not flag in its determination to allow the interested parties to forge their own sort of agreement. Often it called the groups affected by a particular question together and asked them to suggest solutions to the problem at hand or sent out questionnaires asking opinions on proposed solutions. For example, a proposal was made by one of the railroads to change the minimum charge on express freight. The secretary for the commission, in explaining how that request was handled, asserted:

> In the matter in question the proposed rule was stated in a letter which we received from Mr. Eyman of the North-

---

[27] "Any settlement that is made of the matters involved in a complaint filed with this commission that is satisfactory to you and the railroad company will be satisfactory to us so far as future rate of charge is involved," wrote Barnes to a shipper in 1906. Barnes to A. H. Krouskop, June 29, 1906, Formal Case Papers, WPSC Records.

western Road. We sent out several hundred copies of this
letter to the shippers of the state, asking for comments,
and receiving a large number of replies. The shippers
almost uniformly approved of the proposed rule. . . .
Consequently this Commission approved the rule.[28]

When a decision could not be deferred to others, the commission
still sought the reinforcement and consent of important interests.
After issuing its important grain rate decision in 1906, which
altered grain tariffs from points all over the state to Milwaukee,
for example, B. H. Meyer personally approached William Rahr,
the president of the Manitowoc Malting Company, and explained
to him the reasons why rates were reduced to Milwaukee from
certain areas which the Manitowoc firm had traditionally considered its area of exploitation. "I do not believe Rahr will object to
anything that has been done," he had explained to Barnes, when
the decision was released. When it turned out that Rahr did, in
fact, mind, the commission immediately called a meeting between
that large Manitowoc manufacturer and the carriers in an attempt
to iron out the difficulty.[29] At the same time, the commission sought
the assurance of George H. D. Johnson of the powerful Milwaukee
Chamber of Commerce that the rates it had set met the approval
of his group.[30]

In every way possible the commission sought to make regulation
a co-operative enterprise by involving the major commercial interests in the process of administrative decision making.

While the commission's efforts to win the assent of shippers to its
regulatory activities was an important part of its quest for greater
harmony, even they were subordinate to the new agency's continuing campaign to involve the carriers in the activity of regulation.

In the eyes of the commissioners the achievement of their major

---

[28] Winterbotham to R. C. Clausen, November 18, 1908, General Correspondence, WPSC Records.
[29] Meyer to Barnes, August 22, 1906, General Correspondence, WPSC
Records; Meyer to William Rahr, August 25, 1906, Formal Case Papers
(In re grain rates), WPSC Records; Rahr to Commission, September 13,
1906, Railroad Informal Case Papers (Manitowoc Malting Co.), WPSC
Records.
[30] Meyer to Johnson, August 17, 1906, Formal Case Papers (In re grain
rates), WPSC Records.

goal of greater economic harmony was predicated on the establishment of close ties with the carriers of the state. "Railways and
commissions can and must co-operate," wrote Meyer, "and by co-
operating year after year, objectionable features can be eliminated
or reduced, a better understanding and feeling between the railways and the public established and maintained."[31] In pursuit of
this goal, the commission kept in constant contact with the carriers,
apprising them of developments and seeking their opinions of
commission activities.

When at all possible the agency turned complaints over to the
carriers themselves, requesting them to apply their own solution
and submit it for commission approval. In a characteristic case, the
commission responded to a complaint by lumbermen concerning
rates on pine clippings by declaring the need for some sort of uniform rate and classification in order to restore equality in the
shipping of this product by all roads. Having thus laid the ground-
work for a decision, it turned the matter over to the carriers themselves, asserting that "should the various railway companies be
unable to come to satisfactory agreement, we shall, after due
hearing, promulgate such uniform classification and rate as may
be just and reasonable."[32] When the railroad officials were unable
to frame a solution on their own, the commission invited them to a
hearing on the question and after a full airing of the issues, during
which the commission guidelines were discussed, Barnes again
turned the matter over to the carriers. "It seems to me," he declared,
"that with the combined wisdom of the gentlemen that have been
getting up the tariffs for the railroad companies for a number of
years, with which they have been pretty successful, you ought to
be able to get up a tariff here that would be fair to all."[33]

More often, of course, the question placed before the commission
could not be solved by simply deferring to the railroads. Still the

[31] "Government Regulation of Railway Rates," address before the Annual
Meeting of the American Economics Association, December 29, 1905, in
the Meyer Papers.
[32] W. J. Campbell vs. Chicago, St. Paul, Minneapolis and Omaha Railway
Co., October 4, 1906, in *Opinions and Decisions of the Railroad Commission . . .*, 1:263.
[33] In re pine clippings, Minutes of Hearings (October 30, 1906), 4:10. WPSC
Records.

agency showed a continual determination to give the carriers a major role whenever possible. In response, for example, to a complaint that certain carload rates on potatoes to Milwaukee were discriminatory, the commission called together the freight agents of all the roads carrying that product in the state. After discussing the question with them, it suggested a common rate for all of the roads. When the carriers balked at the commission proposal, it quickly assented to the carriers' proposal of a higher rate. After receiving new printed tariff schedules from all of the major roads which confirmed the conference agreement, the commission set a date when the new tariffs would go into effect. Not a word was printed in the commission decisions to indicate that any change had been made.[34] This sort of activity, which resolved a troublesome rate question without publicizing the inequities which had existed in the tariffs for a long period of time, symbolized the commission at its best, acting as a harmonizer of economic affairs.

Most of the commission's key decisions in the early years, however, could not be so easily made, for the carriers would not readily give up most of their long-standing rate agreements. It is the manner in which the commission proceeded when no easy answer was available that best illustrates its determination to win railroad support.

In all such cases the commission made the carriers active partners in developing the statistical data to be used in evaluating rates. Hence, they were allowed to help mold the environment in which the final decision was made. After the 1907 legislature overruled a commission decision which lowered passenger rates to two and a half cents per mile and installed a two-cent rate, a railroad publication complained: "In Wisconsin the principal railroads expended many thousands of dollars in efforts to aid the State Commission to arrive at a correct conclusion regarding fares, but all of the labor and money expended went for naught as the recommendations of the Commission were disregarded by the legislature."[35]

---

[34] Meyer to N. E. Pierpont, January 31, 1907; Meyer to W. C. Modisette, January 31, 1907; S. E. Stohr to Winterbotham, February 5, 1907; all in Formal Case Papers, WPSC Records.

[35] *Railway World*, 51:815 (September 27, 1907).

Aware that the application of any radically new rate standard would offend the carriers, the commission kept its decisions within prescribed limits. Often, for example, it selected as the lawful rate the lowest of the rates profitably sustained already by one of the railroads. In two important decisions the commission demanded that all roads apply the special concentration rate schedule which the Illinois Central was using in Wisconsin for shipment of certain dairy products in the southern part of the state, and asked the Milwaukee Road to lower its rates on the shipment of paper in the north to a level which the Wisconsin Central and other roads had put into effect.[36]

If forced to go beyond railroad data and railroad precedents, the commission consulted with the carriers whenever possible. In the case of the important grain rate decision of 1906, for example, after formulating a new rate schedule, the commission submitted it to the railroads for their criticism. When, after a month and a half, all of the carriers had given their assent to the decision and arranged to publish the new rates, the commission finally announced the new tariffs in a formal decision.[37] It is notable that the rate reduction was so moderate that one major railroad saw fit to initiate a schedule below commission guidelines.[38]

By the same token, in the case of the decision lowering rates on a range of dairy products in the southern part of the state, the commission kept impatient dairymen waiting over two months while the carriers mulled over the rate tables they had been sent and finally assured the commission that the new tariffs were satisfactory. The final decision appropriately declared, "We believe that the application of this schedule will not, to any material extent, disturb existing trade relations, and that it will work out with fairness to both railways and the shippers."[39]

---

[36] Southern Wisconsin Cheesemen's Protective Association vs. Chicago and North Western Railway Co., August 13, 1906, in *Opinions and Decisions of the Railway Commission . . .*, 1:156; Keogh Excelsior Manufacturing Co., John W. Keogh vs. Chicago, Milwaukee and St. Paul Railway Company, September 10, 1908, in *ibid.*, 2:717–756.

[37] Meyer to F. P. Eyman, June 26, 1906, and Meyer to Eyman, August 3, 1906, Formal Case Papers (In re grain rates), WPSC Records.

[38] *Milwaukee Free Press*, August 10, 1906.

[39] Meyer to Keeley, June 15, 1906, Formal Case Papers (Southern Wisconsin

In the early years of regulation in Wisconsin the major railroads and the large shippers became the chief participants in the regulatory enterprise which they had so vehemently opposed for such a long period of time. Having surrendered the weapons they could use to punish the carriers, the commission mitigated fears that it would impose rigid standards on the railroad industry by adopting highly flexible standards for rate making. The new agency then sought to build upon this new-found confidence. It brought together shippers and carriers whenever possible and allowed them to forge their own solution to their disputes. When faced with a larger problem, it polled the major interests in the state, courting their suggestions for a resolution of the difficulty. And, most important, it sought to establish close ties with the carriers by allowing them a key role in commission decision making.

B. H. Meyer had been enamored for years with the possibilities of enacting the "advisory council" system in the United States, which would allow a greater participation by the various commercial elements in the enterprise of making rates and stabilizing economic conditions. Under his leadership the Wisconsin railroad commission sought to create this kind of economic community, based on co-operation between major elements. That the small shipper, with little bargaining power, was at a decided disadvantage under such a system is apparent. The success of the commission's attempt to break down the mistrust between the state's railroads and the state government, however, is illustrated by the manner in which the erstwhile opponents of regulation reacted to the new order in Wisconsin.

Cheesemen's Association), WPSC Records; Southern Wisconsin Cheesemen's Association vs. Chicago and North Western Railway Co., August 13, 1906, in *Opinions and Decisions of the Railroad Commission . . .*, 1:159. See also Meyer to S. A. Lynde, January 12, 1907, Formal Case Papers (In re Livestock Rates), WPSC Records.

A Refuge from Reformers

9 One of the crucial problems facing any new regulatory agency is the establishment of viable relations with those industries which it is charged with regulating. Since regulation by government commission is a compromise between laissez faire and public ownership, the nature of the contact between the regulator and the regulated is critical. If an industry refuses to comply with the orders of its regulator, then the attempt at a moderate solution to the economic dilemma of reconciling corporate freedom and public responsibility is doomed to failure. By the same token, if an industry and its would-be regulator become too closely allied, the purpose for which the commission was established is likely to be undermined. Hence the proper balance of harmony and tension must be maintained if a regulatory agency is to retain the flexibility and freedom of action necessary to carry out its legislative mandate.

In Wisconsin the problem of relations between the railroads and the commission seemed especially acute. Although the railroads gave their tacit consent to the final regulatory measure of 1905, they clearly disliked the results of the long struggle for increased regulation in the state. Unwilling to concede that their affairs were in need of review and unable to understand how the creation of another state regulatory commission would aid them in any way, the carriers looked upon the establishment of such an agency as, at best, a grim inevitability.

Still they were determined to abide by the new legal strictures placed upon them. Marvin Hughitt, president of the Chicago and

North Western Railway, in the wake of the passage of the regulation bill, wrote:

> I have no opinion to express regarding the new legislation except to say this most candidly and sincerely, that it is the purpose of the Northwestern Company to work as nearly in harmony with the authorities created under it and in obedience to it as is possible. We have faith in the good sense and fair disposition of the people and are sincere in our determination to work out the problem of development in connection with the transportation interests in a way that will not discriminate against anybody, great or small, and will continue the policy of development in the general interest in the future as in the past.[1]

J. A. Jordan, vice-president of the Green Bay and Western Railroad, commented more cryptically, "I was opposed to any railroad bill, . . . but a bill is here and we propose to obey it to the letter."[2]

As the railroads groped for a position of stability under the new regulatory measure, it became clear that Hughitt's fervent hope that the law would not disrupt commercial affairs masked an almost neurotic fear of what the new commission might attempt. These apprehensions spurred the carriers to revoke all special passenger rates, call in all free passes, and alter certain freight rates and classifications. As the travelers and land salesmen began to clamor for a return to special rates, the *Milwaukee Sentinel,* which had taken the railroad's viewpoint often during the regulation struggle, declared cynically, "Considering the disturbance created by the passenger rates and regulation under the new railway commission law, it is fair to look forward to the coming readjustments of freight rates with anticipation."[3]

Obsessed with the fear that eventually the entire freight rate structure would be undermined by the actions of the new agency, not even the conciliatory measures taken by the commission in its early months could convince many railroad men that a revolution

---

[1] Hughitt to Keyes, July 5, 1905, in the Keyes Papers.
[2] J. A. Jordan to Keyes, July 13, 1905, in the Keyes Papers. See also H. R. McCullough to Barnes, July 18, 1905, General Correspondence, WPSC Records; C. W. Bunn to Keyes, October 5, 1905, in the Keyes Papers.
[3] *Milwaukee Sentinel,* July 3, 1905.

in the state's rates was not imminent. "It is the effect of the new law on the freight rate situation that is most dreaded," declared *Railway World* in October of 1905.

> . . . The railroads are adhering to the laws with a fidelity which is agonizing, and everyone else in the State is walking on tiptoe and speaking in whispers for fear some unfortunate move may start the new law into operation, as a loud word sometimes sets a snow-slide in motion. It is the consensus of opinion that once the rate-tinkering under the new law begins Wisconsin, which is rapidly developing into the great manufacturing State which natural conditions have decreed that it should be, will speedily be reduced to the condition of Iowa, which is actually going backward and losing in population while all the States around it are thriving marvelously. Iowa has had for some years a law to make the railroads behave themselves while in the State.[4]

In the following month, the *Milwaukee Sentinel* branded the regulation bill "bungled legislation," which was workable only because "some of the provisions of this statute are being evaded by the railroad companies apparently with the consent of the railroad commissioners."[5]

Hence the commission, in the early months of its existence, operated in a climate of fear and apprehension. In spite of compromise in the legislature and conservative praise for the appointments made to the new agency, the carriers could not trust the commission until all of the doubts ingrained in their minds by years of acrimonious debate had been dispelled.

Even in the early months when the conservative interests hammered away at the flaws in the new regulation law, however, the efforts of the commission to re-establish a climate of harmony and co-operation did not go unnoticed. As the carriers began to realize that the new agency was not bound to the aims of the reformers, there were scattered expressions of relief.

"The Rate and Commission Law has been in force about a month, and still no railroad manager, under its provisions, has been sent

---

[4] *Railway World*, 49:792 (October 6, 1905).
[5] *Milwaukee Sentinel*, November 11, 1905.

to the penitentiary," quipped Elisha Keyes. ". . . Someone remarked that it must have been [the railroads'] past misdeeds instead of future ones, under the law, that had frightened them so badly."[6]

Lloyd W. Bowers, the general counsel for the Chicago and North Western Railway, expressed surprise and pleasure the following month on hearing of the commission's intention to conduct its affairs in a quiet, informal manner without publicity, in deference to the interests of the railroads and other industries. He responded enthusiastically to B. H. Meyer's letter, in which the commission leader expressed his intention to move in this direction, and asked the railroad executive's advice on the issue. "Your views concerning the special desirableness and effectiveness of quiet amicable consideration of such controversies as from time to time arise in the course of railroad business, as they do in all enterprises, are such as I myself entertain," he replied.

> . . . Usually, the course of the new official tribunals has been . . . to begin with proceedings just the opposite of what you describe, and thereby to precipitate an acrimonious contest which, shortly, the courts were called upon to terminate. . . . I am extremely glad, personally, . . . that the Wisconsin Commission apparently intends to reverse the order of proceedings that I have described as usual, and will seek peaceable adjustments first and induce litigations only in case justice cannot be obtained peaceably. On behalf of this Company too, I know . . . that every effort will be made to meet the Commission in its own spirit.[7]

Officials of the Milwaukee Road, the other major railroad in the state, were also appreciative of the procedural precedents established by the commission. In an apparent reference to its predilection to allow the industry to settle its own disputes, a top executive for the railroad, in the late summer of 1905, commented: "We are agreeably surprised at the way the rate commission act is working so far, since no complaint has as yet come to our notice

---

[6] Keyes to Stennett, July 21, 1905, in the Keyes Letterbooks.
[7] Lloyd W. Bowers to Meyer, August 8, 1905, General Correspondence, WPSC Records.

that has not been settled between the railroad and the shipper. . . .
I am convinced that people who have a grievance will first lay it
before the roads and will call in the commission only when they
can get no redress."[8]

In 1906 the seeds of trust, planted during the early months of
commission activity, grew into a grudging confidence in the new
agency. Although the reasons for the transformation are not entirely clear, some of the factors which motivated the change are
apparent.

La Follette's surrender of the governorship following his abortive
attempt to strengthen the commission in a December special
session removed the ever-present threat that he might use his prodigious political powers to mold commission policy. The railroads
quite clearly feared any government agency operating under his
executive leadership. Then, too, the carriers found that certain
provisions of the new law afforded them a convenient opportunity
to revoke certain special rate privileges they had granted to some
shippers and politicians, which were of little benefit to them now.[9]

Far more important than any of these factors, however, was the
impact which the decisions handed down by the commission during
its first several years had upon the railroads. The railroads entertained intense fears that the rate-making activities of the commission would result in a total disruption of the delicate commercial
relations in the state. Hence they were unwilling to accept the
commission wholeheartedly until clear precedents had been established in this area. When the agency at last began to resolve a
number of important rate questions, the first bridges of co-operation were built.

The railroads were pleased with the commission's first major
decisions, which dealt with rates on grain, livestock, and dairy
products, for several reasons. Not only were they made active
partners in the process of evaluating the current rate schedules
and prescribing revisions, but, more important, the commission,

---

[8] *Milwaukee Sentinel,* August 11, 1905.
[9] Meyer to Frank Warne, October 16, 1905, General Correspondence, testimony of Charles Becker, January 12, 1909. Formal Case Papers, (Wisconsin Coal Co.), WPSC Records.

in apparent deference to their welfare, chose to prescribe only moderate changes in existing rates. In an expression of their appreciation, the carriers quickly approved all changes which the commission ordered. Having already seen the proposed grain rate revisions, Thomas Gill, chief counsel for the Wisconsin Central Railroad, made the first public assertion of confidence in the new agency's ability to alter rates. "I wish to say that we have done the best we can on grain rates and I hope the Commission can do better," he declared in a hearing before the commission in July, 1906. "If you can fix them so they will be more satisfactory to the grain shipping interests of the state we would be glad to have you do it."[10]

Echoing this new confidence, the one-time leader of the anti-regulation element in Wisconsin, the *Milwaukee Sentinel,* in September of that year, began to counsel the public utility companies to welcome the extension of regulation to cover their activities as well. "You can have nothing to fear from regulation and control by a commission organized along the lines of the state railway commission," it declared.[11] Three months later, it amplified this assertion, declaring, "The corporations should welcome the advent of a clean, honest, able and fearless body of men to pass upon disputed matters and settle them on a square business basis and be rid of the political bushwhacker once and for all."[12]

In the first year and a half of its operation, the commission won the acceptance of the railroads. In early 1907, events culminating in a pitched battle over passenger rates between the agency and its originator, the Wisconsin state legislature, resulted in the railroads viewing regulation in an ever more favorable light.

For many years the question of what railroads could equitably charge their passengers had been a matter of dispute throughout the country. By the turn of the century the problem had become a hot political issue. Reformers introduced measures in many state legislatures aimed at forcing the carriers to lower their passenger

---

[10] Testimony of Gill, Minutes of Hearings (July 10, 1906), vol. 3 (O. G. Kinney vs. Wisconsin Central), WPSC Records.
[11] *Milwaukee Sentinel,* September 23, 1906.
[12] *Ibid.,* December 21, 1906.

tariffs, and there was talk in Washington of establishing a two cent maximum charge per mile for all interstate passenger traffic in the country. Responding to growing demands for rate reductions, between the years 1903 and 1908 twenty-two states enacted statutes which fixed a standard rate for all passenger service within their jurisdictions. Half of these states, including several of Wisconsin's neighbors, selected two cents as the proper charge per mile.[13]

In Wisconsin the fervor to reform passenger rates took hold early. Beginning in 1901 legislators introduced bills in every session of the legislature aimed at enacting a two-cent standard for the state.[14] But in the confusion of the fight to create a railroad commission, which would deal with rate questions of all types, these proposals were forced into the background. So strong was the feeling that such a measure should be passed, however, that by 1905 only strong urging that the new commission be given an opportunity to deal with the question prevented the legislature from enacting such a bill.

Even the establishment of the commission did not prevent the issue from becoming a political football. Alert to trends in the popular temperament, many politicians seized upon the demand for a two-cent rate as a tool for winning votes in 1906. Walter Houser, W. D. Connor, and J. J. McGillivray, all office seekers the following year, began as early as October, 1905, to vie publicly for the honor of lodging the first complaint with the commission which demanded a two-cent rate.[15] As Governor James Davidson undertook his campaign for re-election, he, too, took up the cause. "There should be established a passenger rate of not exceeding two cents a mile on first class roads," he asserted. But in deference to the new agency, he counseled the voters that "the commission may be relied upon to make a full investigation and to reach a conclusion just and fair to all interests concerned."[16]

[13] Grover Huebner, "Five Years of Railroad Regulation," in *The Annals of the American Academy of Political and Social Sciences*, 32:146 (July, 1908); *Milwaukee Free Press*, May 24, 1907.
[14] See *Wisconsin Assembly Bills*, 1901, 27A and 32A; 1903, 432A; 1905, 8A.
[15] *Milwaukee Sentinel*, February 27, 1906.
[16] Ekern to La Follette, July 17, 1906, in the La Follette Papers.

Davidson's posture well illustrates the dilemma facing the commission. Reformers, on the one hand, expressed an unquestioning faith in the abilities of the new agency, which had been created largely through their hard work. At the same time, however, these men were convinced that a two-cent passenger rate was not only right, but politically imperative, in the light of the growing public support for the cause.

In the face of these pressures, the self assurance, almost arrogance, with which the commission conducted its investigation of the passenger-rate question is illustrative of how removed the new agency was from the aims and the influence of the reformers who had been instrumental in enacting regulatory legislation. Refusing to allow any reform candidate to take credit for raising a two-cent issue, the commission persuaded a Sun Prairie farmer who asked about passenger charges to file a complaint asking for a two-cent rate.[17] Using this complaint, it then initiated a detailed inquiry on the subject. In answer to a public letter by W. D. Connor requesting swift action on the issue, commission chairman Barnes, who apparently harbored a personal grudge against the ambitious chairman of the Wisconsin State Republican party, peevishly explained that the commission must take many complex steps aimed at ascertaining the financial condition of every railroad prior to any such decision. "There is a right and a wrong way to proceed," he declared. "We think that we should do it regardless of criticism." In a typical expression of the commission's penchant toward passivity, he concluded by asserting that "very few complaints have been lodged with the commission as yet about passenger rates."[18]

After this declaration of independence from reform politics the commission proceeded slowly and cautiously, to the growing consternation of the reformers and the uncontrollable glee of their opponents. "It is evident," declared the *Milwaukee Sentinel* in February, 1906, "that the railway commission is doing its work deliberately and with a determination to reach conclusions that will stand the test of analysis."[19]

[17] *Milwaukee Sentinel,* March 16, 1906.
[18] See letter in *Milwaukee Free Press,* February 18, 1906.
[19] *Milwaukee Sentinel,* February 27, 1906.

Whatever the conclusions were destined to be, the commission refused to allow the reformers to make them a political issue in the 1906 campaign. After holding hearings in May the agency bided its time, apparently consulting with the railroads, in an effort to ascertain exactly what reduction the carriers could sustain without undue losses in revenue, and waiting until the fall election was over before proceeding further.[20]

By February, 1907, assemblymen, unwilling to give the commission more time to resolve the question, began to introduce numerous bills which demanded a two-cent-per-mile rate and warned that some such measure would soon be passed unless the commission immediately ordered the railroads to reduce their tariff to that level.[21] On February 16, resisting such threats and ignoring the recommendation of the retiring, lame duck railroad commissioner John W. Thomas that lines earning over $3,000 a mile could easily sustain a two-cent rate,[22] the commission ordered passenger rates reduced from three cents to two-and-a-half cents per mile. At the same time, it affirmed the legality of the railroads' practice of selling "mileage books" containing five hundred miles worth of coupons and sold at the rate of two cents per mile.

Expressing its irritation with the demands made upon it by reformers, in its formal decision the commission asserted: "We have received not a little advice as to how and when the passenger rate cases should be decided. This solicitude might well have been spared. It is as much the duty of this Commission to protect the rights and the interests of the people of the state. . . . We cannot pervert our judgment at the behest of the popular clamor."

Then, in a striking example of its economic reasoning, the commission set forth the conservative principles which guided it. Refusing to conjecture, as had others, that a lowering of passenger rates would result in increased travel and increased income for the railroads, the commission declared, "We must deal with conditions as they have grown up and have become established." Under this rubric, the agency justified the authorization of special rate classi-

[20] *Ibid.*, October 8, 1906.
[21] *Milwaukee Free Press,* February, February 1, 1907.
[22] *Milwaukee Sentinel,* December 12, 1906.

fications by the carriers. "It was the intent of the legislature to prevent injustice, not to prescribe rules which would hamper the carriers in carrying out the details of their business or prevent them from adopting reasonable methods for increasing it," the commission declared.[23]

On the eve of the commission's decision the *Milwaukee Sentinel,* apparently aware of what the verdict would be, praised the commission in glowing terms. It exalted Erickson and Meyer as "independent and individually assertive," while Barnes received special accolades as a man who "would find pleasure in impaling politicians of the peanut dimension if he did not move upon the axiom that it is a waste of ammunition to load cannon to shoot flies."[24]

After the formal decision was released, the railways joined the *Sentinel* in its praise. Labeling the commission's opinion "one of the fairest and ablest documents ever prepared by a rate regulating body in this country," *Railway Age* declared, "The railroad commission has set an excellent example for the legislatures and railway commissions of other states in handling the passenger fare question." Hopeful that the decision would have broad influence, the railroad journal reprinted long excerpts from the decision.[25] In a letter to the commission, two top executives of the Milwaukee Road expressed similar appreciation, voicing their "profound respect for the consideration" the commission had given the question and for its "obvious desire to arrive at a result which should be at once fair to the people of Wisconsin and just to the railways."[26]

The legislature, which had waited impatiently for the commission to release its decision, was not nearly so enamored with the results of the new agency's efforts to adjust passenger rates. The lawmakers had been under heavy pressure from constituents to reduce Wisconsin's passenger charges to the level prevailing in neighboring states. Growing anger at the insensitive way the

---

[23] A. E. Buell vs. Chicago, Milwaukee and St. Paul Railway Company, February 16, 1907, in *Opinions and Decisions of the Railroad Commission of the State of Wisconsin,* 1:329, 344, 503.

[24] *Milwaukee Sentinel,* February 13, 1907.

[25] *Railway Age,* 43:233, 248–250 (February 22, 1907).

[26] William Ellis to Commission, February 18, 1907, Formal Case Papers (A. E. Buell), WPSC Records.

carriers handled fares on the border between Wisconsin and Illinois, where a two-cent fare was in force, amplified these demands. The railroads charged persons wishing to travel from Beloit to Chicago a half cent per mile more than those leaving from stations a few miles south, and, at the same time, granted interstate rates of two cents per mile between states with two-cent statutes on their books.

In a classic reversal of form, Burton Hanson, a lawyer for the Milwaukee Road, who had been one of the leaders of the fight against increased regulation in Wisconsin, argued eloquently before the legislature that the commission was the best in the country and that its decision should be honored. In support of Hanson, *Railway Age* declared that Wisconsin "is almost the only [state] in which the carriers have received fair treatment at the hands of either commission or legislature since the present anti-railway campaign was begun."[27] Ignoring the pleas that the commission be respected, the legislature struck down the agency's decision in favor of a two-cent fare for all passengers.

In the aftermath of this legislative rebellion against the commission's unwillingness to sanction radical change, the ironic shift in feelings which had taken place among railroad men was even further emphasized. Concerned that the commissioners, whom they had so quickly learned to respect and admire, might resign to protest the legislature's action, Thomas Gill of the Wisconsin Central Railroad, on behalf of the carriers of the state, pleaded with them to remain at their posts. Decrying "the loss to business interests which [resignation] would certainly bring," Gill declared in a letter to Barnes, Erickson, and Meyer:

> I reflect the unanimous opinion of the officers of this company when I say that all of the railroads of this State are most thoroughly satisfied with the manner in which you have administered the rate law of Wisconsin. . . . You have the full confidence and likewise the complete admiration of that large part of the community represented by those engaged in railroad service. Moreover, you have given such close attention and study to the almost unknown

[27] *Milwaukee Sentinel,* June 5, 1907; *Railway Age,* 44:99–100 (July, 1907).

problems of transportation and the delicate relations between the railroads and the people, that it would be little
short of a calamity to wreck all of the permanent founda-
tions for investigations which you have created. . . . Personally I feel like expressing myself more warmly than the
above would indicate, but I want to convey to you in the
fullest way that I believe your duties as citizens absolutely
require you to ignore the nonsense and silliness at the
foundation of recent unpleasantness.[28]

Unmoved by this plea, John Barnes resigned his post in a ringing
protest against legislative interference. Erickson and Meyer, however, chose to continue as commissioners. "The public importance
of the work of an administrative body, like this commission, is far
too momentous to permit petty politics and minor personal interests
to interfere," Meyer declared.[29]

As a result of the conflict over passenger rates, a new congeniality
developed in relations between the railroads and the commission.
Having watched the agency stubbornly fight the attempt to reform
radically the passenger-rate schedule of the state, the carriers put
new faith in the commissioners. Often the carriers took the commission into their confidence, seeking aid on technical matters, and
developing close personal ties with its members.

Sometimes the carriers apparently sought the commission's help
in rate-making matters simply as a means to insure the agency's
approval of their plans before they put them into action. In a surprising number of cases, however, the railroads called upon commission personnel for other sorts of aid. The Chicago and North
Western Railway, for example, asked a commission engineer to
testify before the Nebraska commission on its behalf on a technical
matter concerning land value and right of way.[30] B. H. Meyer, the
leading theoretician on the commission, was consulted numerous
times on questions ranging from the development of a uniform
basis for classification of freight over the entire Midwest, to the
proper correlation of operating expenses and freight classifications.

28 Thomas Gill to "Messrs John Barnes, B. H. Meyer, and Halford Erickson,"
July 18, 1907, in the Meyer Papers.
29 Meyer to E. H. Bottum, July 16, 1907, in the Meyer Papers. See also
Milwaukee Sentinel, July 20, 1907, for Barnes' comments.
30 E. M. Hyzer to L. P. Girard, December 14, 1911, General Correspondence,
WPSC Records.

On at least one occasion railroad men asked his opinion on whether certain applicants for employment with their company should be hired.[31] While acting as a regulator, Meyer also continued to contribute articles to railway journals.

In 1909 the railroads sought to quell a legislative drive to allow shippers having prior claims against them an opportunity to collect on them. In a notable expression of confidence, they turned to the commission for aid since, complained Burton Hanson, "Somehow the bills that we defeat in the committees do not stay defeated." Admitting that "you know better the situation . . . than I do," commissioner John H. Roemer, who succeeded Barnes in 1907, conferred with Hanson on the matter. After agreeing to submit two vital amendments which the railroad man desired, and assuring him that the commission would interpret the new statute in a manner which would not harm the railroads, Roemer advised, "I think it is as well . . . to permit this bill to go through, or a more drastic and less beneficial bill to all concerned might result two years hence." Hanson readily concurred. "It is better to have a measure like this passed than something worse, which would probably be the case if this is not adopted. I am very much obliged to you for arranging matters so satisfactorily."[32]

The air of personal friendship which characterized this exchange between a leading railroad man and a commissioner is indicative of the warmth of feeling which stemmed from a new sense of partnership between the commission and the carriers. Meyer, who greatly respected all top railroad executives, in 1907 called James J. Hill "a great constructive railway statesman." And Hill, equally taken with the man who was charged with regulating a portion of his railroad, donated $2,000 to the University of Wisconsin for the development of a James J. Hill Railway Library, because of his close friendship with the economics professor who had written so sympathetically about the Northern Securities Company. Two years later, courting

[31] Meyer to Hanson, October 1, 1907; Frank P. Eyman to Meyer, September 19, 1907; H. A. Gray to Meyer, April 15, 1908; C. I. Sturgis to Meyer, April 1, 1909, all in the Meyer Papers.
[32] Hanson to Roemer, May 8, 1909; Roemer to Hanson, May 10, 1909; Hanson to Roemer, May 10, 1909; Roemer to Hanson, May 13, 1909; Hanson to Roemer, May 15, 1909, all in General Correspondence, WPSC Records.

Meyer's advice on the growing problem of inadequate terminal facilities, Hill asserted, "I know of no one who from a broad standpoint has more intelligently thought out these questions than yourself."[33] Samuel Lynde and Thomas Gill, top attorneys for the Chicago and North Western and the Wisconsin Central, both were invited by Meyer to address his class on transportation and his Political Economy Club at the university.[34] When railroad men came to Madison, they sometimes wrote ahead to have the commission arrange accommodations for them at the University Club, where the commissioners dined with them.[35] Deep friendships between the would-be antagonists grew and flourished as the railroads learned that a regulatory commission, properly constituted, could act to their benefit.

As relations between the commission and the railroad men became warmer, there was no longer any question about the acceptability of regulation by the state agency in Wisconsin. While the carriers occasionally disputed rulings made by the commission, they never challenged a major commission decision in the courts.[36] Converted by the manner in which the commissioners did their jobs, the chorus of praise for regulation grew with the addition of some rather unexpected voices. Thoroughly won over by the commission, the *Milwaukee Sentinel* now called the idea of regulation itself "a sound principle."[37] Although unwilling to grant such blanket approval to a principle which he had fought against for years, another staunch enemy of reform, Emanuel L. Philipp, was

---

[33] Meyer to Charles Van Hise, October 17, 1907; James J. Hill to Meyer, March 24, 1910, both in the Meyer Papers; *Milwaukee Free Press*, February 23, 1908.

[34] Lynde to Meyer, June 3, 1909; Meyer to Gill, February 4, 1909, both in General Correspondence, WPSC Records.

[35] C. I. Sturgis to Meyer, April 1, 1909, in the Meyer Papers; Samuel A. Lynde to Winterbotham, October 23, 1908, General Correspondence, WPSC Records.

[36] See, for example, Hughitt to Commission, August 19, 1907, Formal Case Papers (In re Livestock Rates), James T. Clark to Commission, August 29, 1907, Formal Case Papers (In re Livestock Rates), Marvin Hughitt, Jr., to Commission, May 3, 1909, Formal Case Papers (In re Milk and Cream Rates), all in WPSC Records.

[37] *Milwaukee Sentinel*, January 24, 1908.

forced to admit that "our own state has a high grade commission."[38]
Vice-President W. A. Gardner of the Chicago and North Western
Railway, a road which had poured much money and time into
defeating attempts to establish a regulatory commission, declared:
"You have a most uncommon railroad commission in Wisconsin.
I sometimes wonder whether the full measure of the ability of this
commission is appreciated. Their integrity of purpose is so marked
that no one can doubt it; their decisions and conclusions are so
broad that they are text books and milestones in this era of feverish
agitation."[39]

Gardner's comment offers a clue to the major reason for the
complete transformation of feeling which took place among the
carriers and certain other conservative business elements. When
B. H. Meyer was appointed to the Interstate Commerce Commission by President William Howard Taft in December, 1910, the
Railway Age Gazette praised the appointment, declaring it would
make the federal agency less "political." Commenting on the work
of the Wisconsin commission under his leadership, it then noted,
"It is a high tribute to those who originally and have since composed it that it has never allowed itself to be used . . . for political
purposes."[40]

Gardner's praise of the "uncommon railroad commission in Wisconsin" in "this era of feverish agitation," the *Gazette's* support of
the agency because it was not "political," and the *Milwaukee Sentinel's* earlier lauding of the commission for getting "rid of the political bushwhacker once and for all" are examples of a unifying theme
evident in all of the accolades received by the commission from its
erstwhile opponents. As such they offer a clue to why the railroads
embraced the commission, and why the transition in feeling was
completed during the controversy over passenger rates.

In those early years of the twentieth century, railroad regulation
was one of the most prominent issues on both the national and state
levels. More regulatory legislation was enacted during this time

[38] *Ibid.*, September 20, 1908.
[39] *Milwaukee Free Press*, December 4, 1908.
[40] *Railway Age Gazette*, 49:1137 (December 16, 1910), 49:1200 (December 23, 1910).

than perhaps any other period in United States history. Threatened by ambitious politicians and sincere reformers, who demanded increased strictures on railroad activities, the carriers sought cases where they would be free from the politics of rapid change. In Wisconsin, quite unexpectedly, they found such a place of rest.

From the outset the railroads had been gratified to learn that the commission did not intend to pursue the more extreme aims of those who advocated strong regulation. This realization, while it led to an acceptance of the agency, was not the occasion for the enthusiasm for the commission which the railroads evinced by the middle of 1907. It simply was a relief to them. When the commission stood up to the political leaders in the legislature and the executive mansion, however, refusing not only to authorize the two-cent rate which most political leaders demanded, but also proclaiming the right of railroads to sell special rate books in the face of a growing sentiment for complete equality of passenger rates, the carriers saw the positive value of the commission. It stood as a bastion against the popular clamor. Having long been subjected to virulent attacks from eloquent reformers, the railroads were quick to recognize the value of this shield against the threat of further intervention in their affairs by legislative reformers.

Hence they gave their devotion unstintingly to the Wisconsin railroad commission. Earlier they had tried to escape regulation by exerting political pressure. Now they won a larger victory by seizing upon regulation as an escape from the threat of politics in an age of reform.

The Betrayal of Reform Ideals

10 In an ironic shift in allegiances, the railroads and the new Wisconsin railroad commission became close allies during the early years of the agency's operation. The railroads found that the commission afforded them relief from reform politics, and the commission welcomed the carriers' support for its attempt to achieve greater commercial harmony in the state.

This strange friendship was only one of several paradoxes facing those who had earlier fought valiantly for strong regulation measures which would insure new commercial priorities in the state. The economic effects of regulation were equally unexpected and heightened the dilemma confronting the long-time reformers. As it became clear that their ideals would not be realized, these men were forced to decide what their obligations to such principles were. The candor and consistency of purpose they exhibited as the configurations of regulation changed, in a large part, determined the degree of public acceptance of the Wisconsin railroad commission as the champion of its rights. It also decided the fate of the noble idea which had spurred men to fight for greater commercial equality for several decades. Because of the peculiar evolution of events, the reformers faced the problem of reacting to a regulatory mechanism which the railroads strongly supported and the large shipping interests widely used.

Prior to the passage of a regulation measure in Wisconsin, the proponents of reform had centered their attacks on the level of freight rates within the state, charging that Wisconsin tariffs were anywhere from 40 to 60 per cent higher than those in the states of Iowa and Illinois. They thus demanded a blanket reduction of their state's rates to the level of those in neighboring areas.

With the available data it is impossible to make an exact assessment of the commission's effect on the rate structure. While its decisions indicate the changes it undertook, for example, they do not show how effective the commission was in enforcing its demands. There is good evidence to indicate that railroads sometimes construed commission decisions as suggestions rather than orders. In 1907, for instance, after the legislature invoked a flat two-cent passenger rate, the carriers advanced the freight rates on cheese from the figure ordered by the commission in 1906, explaining that it was necessary to recoup losses in passenger revenues by raising freight charges.[1] In 1908 certain of the larger railroads disregarded commission orders changing rates on milk and cream and on pulp wood, declaring, in the first instance, that the change in the milk rate amounted to a "very serious reduction . . . and for that reason the rates have not been adopted."[2] The exact effect of commission actions on the rate structure is also impossible to divine because the changes the railroads might have made had they not been under the supervision of such an agency cannot be predicted.

It can be stated with certainty, however, that the commission did not achieve the ends defined by the reformers. In February, 1909, it quite frankly admitted that "this Commission has never made [any] general reduction in freight rates, but has only considered each rate as it came before it upon complaint."[3] A comparison of basic rate tables for Wisconsin traffic on the Chicago and North Western Railway and the Omaha road, two of the state's major carriers, shows this statement to be true for the entire period under consideration. Commission records contain schedules dated January 1, 1904, and December 11, 1911, which list charges

---

[1] *Milwaukee Free Press*, August 16, 1907.

[2] William Ellis to Commission, July 22, 1908, Formal Case Papers (In re Milk and Cream Rates); Ellis to Commission, May 10, 1908, Formal Case Papers (In re Pulpwood Rates), WPSC Records.

[3] Commission to S. G. McLendon, February 8, 1909, General Correspondence, WPSC Records. See also Winterbotham to T. J. Anderson Grocery Company, May 26, 1909, General Correspondence, WPSC Records.

for all distances and classifications, including commodity rates on such goods as lumber, grain, cattle, hogs, cement, and salt. A study of these tables reveals not a single difference between the rates for many items, classifications, or distances in effect the year before regulation began and those which prevailed six and one-half years after the commission began its activity.[4] Since the basic schedules of the larger roads in the state generally coincided, it is reasonable to suppose that few changes were made by the other major roads.

This is not to say, of course, that there were no reductions in specific rates, for all during these years the commission was reducing rates piecemeal. It is notable, however, that never did it order reductions of the magnitude which reformers had promised. Seldom, in fact, did the changes exceed 20 per cent. It is indicative of the commission's unwillingness to force the carriers into excessive reductions that the most conspicuous rate reduction during the first five-and-one-half years, from 20 to 40 per cent on potatoes, was effected voluntarily by the railroads without a formal commission order.[5]

Although they lacked the perspective of time in their evaluation of the commission's work, it did not take long for concerned parties in Wisconsin to recognize that the new agency had no intention of ordering the expected changes in rates. As early as 1907, the *Milwaukee Free Press,* the prime organ of reform in the state, noted that the rate reductions enacted by the commission "have been but a small fraction of what the people had reason to look for." Unwilling to indict the commission during this early stage of its activity, the *Free Press* declared, "The conclusion must follow that the commission is not finding such 'widespread injustice' and such universal unreason in the rates as it may have been expected to find."[6] Burton Hanson, the railroad lawyer who had borne the brunt of attacks on the carriers by La Follette and his colleagues, made a more sinister assessment of the same evidence. Noting that

---

[4] These tariff tables can be found in the unorganized portion of the Wisconsin Public Service Commission Records, in a box marked "Inst Tarf, Box 14—41/3/2–1."

[5] *Milwaukee Sentinel,* June 11, 1907.

[6] *Milwaukee Free Press,* June 28, 1907.

the reformers had implanted in the minds of the voters the idea that the rates were as much as 60 per cent too high, he declared:

> The Commission has . . . selected some . . . classes of rates which it has reduced, but it has not found even in such selection, any single rates, nor have any rates been brought to its attention which, in the exercise of its sound discretion, it felt warranted in reducing any such amount as this or half of any such amount as this. The fact is that the underlying basis upon which the people of Wisconsin voted for the creation of this commission was a basis that the experience of the commission itself has shown was absolutely false. *It was a political issue raised for adventitious purposes.*[7]

In a similar vein, Emanuel L. Philipp argued, "Rates have not been materially lowered since [1905] because the statements made by the governor were untrue in substance and in detail and no sweeping reductions were demanded or justified by conditions." If the reformers' charges had not been spurious, he asked persuasively, why had not commissioner Halford Erickson, who had authored many a rate comparison for La Follette during the campaign for regulation, initiated actions to redress these abuses?[8]

Under commission rule, the promised rate reductions did not occur. In their search for a credible posture concerning regulation in Wisconsin, the advocates of reform were forced to face up to this conspicuous failure.

A corollary of the claim that the railroads were charging exorbitant rates was the contention that they were earning excessive profits on their investment. La Follette had argued repeatedly that a drastic cut in railroad earnings could be effected without depriving the carriers of the profits they deserved. Citing figures concerning the capitalization and earnings of the Milwaukee Road for 1901 and 1902, the governor told a county fair audience in the fall of 1903, that, given its same expenses, "this road . . . could have paid interest and dividends at current rates on its bonds and stock, including water and all, if its earnings had been reduced about

---

[7] *Ibid.*, February 26, 1907. (Emphasis added)
[8] Philipp, *Political Reform in Wisconsin*, 237.

$6,000,000 a year."[9] The major campaign document for the reform cause in 1904 alleged that the Chicago and North Western Railway was earning $3,300,000 to $4,500,000 per year more than was warranted, while the Milwaukee Road took in "about $4,300,000" more than it deserved.[10]

The valuation of the railroads in Wisconsin, a process designed to allow the commission to revise rate schedules on the basis of railroad earnings, was carried on under the direction of a man who strongly opposed any sort of strict rate regulation, and who became a top railroad official immediately after valuation was completed. In an article in the *Review of Reviews* of July, 1905, W. D. Taylor, a professor of engineering at the University of Wisconsin, who supervised this work, charged that the public was badly deluded in complaining about railroad rates in the country. Arguing that the "present rates are reasonable" and that "the unrivaled prosperity and progress of the country is due primarily to cheap transportion," Taylor warned, "In any authority given a political commission over railway rates the utmost care is necessary lest there be endangered that elasticity in rate-making which has been the first essential in the plan upon which our transportation system has developed."[11]

It is not surprising that a team of experts under Taylor's leadership valued railroad properties within 2 per cent of the figures which the railroads had published.[12] Refusing to use even this moderate gauge as the sole basis for rate making, the commission did little to curb rising railroad earnings.

During the first five-and-one-half years of the agency's work, the roads of Wisconsin increased their earnings at a rapid rate. Their net earnings over the entire state shot up $2,700,000, or more than 13 per cent, while their net earnings per mile showed an increase of over $4,000 per mile, or over 16 per cent. These figures compare favorably with the net earnings of these railroads over their entire

[9] *Milwaukee Free Press*, September 3, 1903.
[10] *Lower Freight Rates Demanded For Wisconsin* (Milwaukee, 1904), particularly 37, 40.
[11] W. D. Taylor, "The Freight Rates that Were Made By the Railroads," in *Review of Reviews*, 32:70 (July, 1905).
[12] Haugen, *Pioneer and Political Reminiscences*, 134.

lines, which rose about 10.5 per cent, but fell about 7 per cent in terms of net earnings per mile.[13]

Without further analysis, such figures must be used quite cautiously, for they do not reveal such things as possible shifts in the kinds of goods transported, nor, in fact, do they indicate any causal relationship between the existence of the commission and the continued well-being of the roads. It is conceivable that the roads thrived in spite of regulation rather than because of it. Still, such data aptly illustrate another failure of the commission to achieve the aims outlined by the reformers, and deepen the dilemma which these men faced. Having based much of their campaign for a commission on the charge that drastic reductions in railroad earnings were necessary if the consumer were to receive fair rates from the carriers, they now saw the commission allow railroad earnings to increase rapidly during these early years. Declared John M. Whitehead, an archenemy of reform, "I think the railroads have been dealt with by the commission very leniently."[14]

During the campaign for regulation, La Follette and other reform leaders had consistently argued that the regulatory mechanism was designed primarily to benefit the small shipper who could not protect himself. Expecting little aid from such a regulatory commission and fearing the disruption of their relations with the railroads, most of the large shipping interests in the state had fought against the plans to increase regulation. Under the commission's rule, however, an interesting reversal of opinion took place within the shipping community.

From the outset the commission took special pains to pacify large shipping interests, assuring them that it did not intend to "'disturb' the business situation."[15] As the commission's actions began to bear out its assertions, these groups took a much more cordial attitude toward the new agency. In an expression of this

[13] Data compiled from *First Biennial Report of the Railroad Commission from the Organization of the Commission to June 30, 1906*, 562, 576, 600, and *Fifth Annual Report of the Railroad Commission of Wisconsin from June 30, 1910, to June 30, 1911*, 22–23, 40.
[14] Whitehead to Gabriel, April 22, 1914, in the Whitehead Papers.
[15] Meyer to A. L. Osborn, September 11, 1905, General Correspondence, WPSC Records.

new faith in the commission, in 1907 many former opponents of regulation supported legislation to extend controls to cover all public utilities.[16] This measure was passed with little of the acrimony which had attended the earlier fight for railroad regulation. In its 1909 report the influential Merchants and Manufacturers Association of Milwaukee asserted: "We have always found the Railroad Commission very fair and ever ready to listen to the important commercial interests of Milwaukee. We have every assurance that there will be no radical changes of rates which will affect our interests disadvantageously."[17] Exhibiting this confidence, that same year a number of the large shipping interests pushed hard for legislation to increase the commission's power to grant refunds to shippers.[18]

Many erstwhile opponents of regulation, however, did not stop with assertions of new faith in the commission. Rather, they used the agency's facilities to good advantage. During the first five-and-one-half years of the commission's existence, companies which had earlier actively opposed La Follette's drive for increased regulation filed over thirty formal complaints with the commission requesting relief from railroad abuses. Several of these actions, interestingly enough, were brought by companies which, according to the investigation made by the railroad commissioner between 1903 and 1906, were regular recipients of rebates from the roads. (John Barnes, after his resignation from the commission, represented one of these firms in an action it brought before the commission.)[19]

The most notable reversal of opinion among the large shipping

[16] Notes John R. Commons in relation to the extension of commission power to cover the utilities: "The existing commission . . . had the confidence of all parties and interests on account of the ability and moderation of its members." John R. Commons, "The Wisconsin Public Utility Law," in *Review of Reviews*, 36:221–224 (August, 1907).

[17] *The Bulletin of the Merchants and Manufacturers Association of Milwaukee* (February, 1909), 11.

[18] Roemer to Hanson, May 10, 1909, General Correspondence, WPSC Records; *Milwaukee Sentinel*, May 13, 1904.

[19] Jefferson Ice Company vs. Chicago and North Western Railway Company, May 15–June 3, 1908, in *Opinions and Decisions of the Railroad Commission of the State of Wisconsin*, 2:439; rebate list (box 80), and J. W. Thomas to La Follette, September 1, 1904, both in the La Follette Papers.

interests took place within the ranks of the lumbermen. Perhaps no other single group had been so strongly opposed to regulation during the years when reformers fought to achieve the establishment of a regulatory commission. When the large shippers signed petitions, then marched on Madison in 1903 to fight against La Follette's plans, a large number of lumbermen were conspicuous in the front ranks of the protesters. Almost totally dependent on the railroads to get their product to market, they feared any measure which threatened to cripple the carriers or disrupt the normal flow of traffic.

Soon after the formation of the new agency, however, they changed their minds. During the first five and one-half years of the commission's operation, lumbermen filed over eighty formal claims against the carriers and made innumerable other informal inquiries of the agency. In 1909 Neal Brown, who had earlier spearheaded the drive against regulation as a representative of the large lumber interests in the Wausau area, advised the Northwestern Electrical Association to look upon regulatory commissions as their protectors.[20]

This shift in the feeling of lumbermen toward regulation has received attention from the eminent legal scholar, James Willard Hurst. His theory of why this group changed its mind about regulation can be applied to many other large shipping interests as well. Tied to the railroads by a highly conservative ideology which was expressed by membership in the most conservative wing of the Republican party and by dependence upon the carriers for their livelihood, the lumbermen could not support regulation during the time of agitation for a legislative measure, he argues. "On the other hand, when public policy had taken a definite new direction, manifest in the creation of specialized administrative agencies to police the railroads, there was less overt challenge to ideology or party loyalty in testing out the benefits which the new agency might give. Moreover, in the context of specific controversies focused in particular administrative records there might seem less daunting

[20] *Milwaukee Sentinel,* January 22, 1909.

challenge to the total power of railroads than in meeting them in
legislative battle."[21]

As the railroads themselves came to accept the commission as
an appropriate arbiter, much of the element of challenge which
Hurst refers to was even eliminated. With remarkable swiftness
regulation became an asset to those large interests which had so
recently feared the new agency.

When B. H. Meyer left the Wisconsin commission in December,
1910, to join the Interstate Commerce Commission, his successor
was David Harlowe, traffic manager of the large Allis-Chalmers
Company in Milwaukee, who had worked his entire life as a freight
agent for the Milwaukee Road and that large manufacturing firm.
The replacement of the commission's economic theorist with a
practical big businessman was a fine expression of the change in
attitude of that segment of the commercial community which
earlier had been so skeptical of the regulatory enterprise.

While the large shipping interests found the work of the commission a pleasant surprise, there is scattered evidence which indicates that the small shipper was far less satisfied with the agency
which ostensibly was established to serve him. The commission's
persistent unwillingness to use its powers to force radical changes
in railroad policy which would benefit small shippers exasperated
some merchants. A Milwaukee retail lumber dealer complained
"If you simply have the power to request the railroad to do that
which they should do, we cannot expect that you will accomplish
much."[22]

More important, the commission's refusal to examine existing
rate schedules without specific complaints deprived the timid of
needed aid. In September, 1905, an administration assemblyman
wrote Governor La Follette that, although faced with a rise in
freight rates on crushed stone, quarry owners were "frightened"
and would not appeal to the commission.[23] Advised the following

[21] James Willard Hurst, *Law and Economic Growth: The Legal History of
the Lumber Industry in Wisconsin, 1836–1915* (Cambridge, Massachusetts, 1964), 561–562.
[22] Fay L. Cusick to Commission, August 5, 1905, Railroad Informal Case
Papers, WPSC Records.
[23] R. Ainsworth to La Follette, September 1, 1905, in the La Follette Papers.

spring that it must file a complaint if it wished relief from an unfair
rate situation, a shipper replied, "We think it would be against our
interest to make the complaint, as we are situated in a good many
places on their road and use lands belonging to them, and it might
make us a good deal of trouble if we should sign the complaint. . . .
We do not like to pull the chestnuts out of the fire and get our
fingers burned to accommodate the rest of the shippers."[24]

Many other shippers, after appealing to the commission for aid
and receiving instructions that a formal complaint was necessary,
pushed their grievances no further. No doubt a number of them
entertained the same fear of recriminations. How many shippers,
like those stone quarry owners, were unwilling even to contact the
commission initially is impossible to estimate. It is clear, however,
that the commission's procedures and inclinations made it more
able to aid the strong shipping interests, who desired limited reme-
dies, than those who wanted more radical changes but had to be
more guarded in their relations with the carriers. The cause of the
small man, therefore, was seldom served by the new agency.

To many who had struggled to subdue the railroads by legislation
which would change the focus of commercial power in the state,
the manner in which the commission proceeded during its early
years was a source of dismay. Highly optimistic in 1905, even after
the lack of legislative unity had compromised some portions of the
regulatory measure, they watched with growing perplexity as the
new agency, working in close co-operation with the railroads, made
only minor changes in rates, encouraged higher railroad earnings,
and served primarily the large shipping interests of the state.

To some, the course pursued by the new commission represented
a clear betrayal of the principles for which they had fought for
many years. Robert Eliot, who had devoted much of his life to an
effort to perfect governmental machinery which would curb railroad inequities, was the first to complain of the commission's unwillingness to fulfill its functions, as the reformers saw them. As
early as the fall of 1905 he began to protest to the new agency about
its activities. Noting that the Illinois commission had recently

---

[24] Wilber Lumber Company to Commission, May 24, 1906, Railroad Informal
Case Papers, WPSC Records.

ordered a general reduction in freight charges designed to save the shippers of that state at least $8,000,000 annually, Eliot chided the Wisconsin commission for its slowness to act, asserting that this ruling simply widened the discrepancy in tariffs between the two states. "As we understand it the law of the last winter makes it the duty of the Commission to take this matter up without complaint," he argued. "Nobody likes to make a complaint and make himself disliked by the great corporations."[25] Failing to arouse the commissioners to appropriate action, the Milwaukee merchant made more forceful demands in the early months of 1906. "Nothing seems to have been done yet with regard to Wisconsin rates," he complained in late January.[26] A month later, he was more biting. Reiterating that the commission was shirking its responsibilities by failing to take up rate questions on its own, he declared, "We think that is what the State Commission is for and that it ought to get busy."[27] When, at last, John Barnes informed Eliot that the commission could not initiate investigations because of the adverse ruling of the special session of the legislature, Eliot, apparently in despair, no longer bothered the commission.[28]

There were others, however, who continued to prod the agency. Eliot's close ally, George H. D. Johnson, for instance, while appreciative of the commission's effort to lower grain rates, complained of the new levels set by the agency. "The new Wisconsin rates are still considerably in excess of the Illinois rates for corresponding distances," he declared in a letter to the agency in late 1906.[29] W. H. H. Macloon, another long-time supporter of the reform, also noted the continued inequities in Wisconsin rates and demanded action. "By a comparison of classifications and rates thereunder in

[25] Eliot to Commission, October 5, 1905, General Correspondence, WPSC Records.
[26] Eliot to Winterbotham, January 30, 1906, General Correspondence, WPSC Records.
[27] Eliot to Winterbotham, February 6, 1906, General Correspondence, WPSC Records.
[28] Barnes to Eliot, February 7, 1906, General Correspondence, WPSC Records.
[29] G. H. D. Johnson to Commission, September 3, 1906, Formal Case Papers (In re grain rates), WPSC Records.

the states of Illinois and Iowa with those at present in effect in this state I think that it will show in a general way that the internal commerce of this state is taxed a much larger percent by the railways for its transportation than the commerce of those states," he complained in a letter to the commission that same year. He implored the agency to undertake a radical revision of the state's entire schedule of rates and classifications.[30]

In 1907 the scattered complaints by devout reformers spilled over into a wider protest against commission activities. Just as the commission's ruling on passenger rates pleased the railroads greatly, it deeply disillusioned numerous ardent supporters of regulation.

Many were troubled by the agency's failure to order a two-cent-per-mile rate. In explaining why the legislative measure which overruled the commission decision was passed, Oliver Munson, Governor James Davidson's secretary, asserted, "Wisconsin would simply have been laughed out of court if her citizens had been compelled to continue under the conditions which would have surely developed, when all of the surrounding people in the neighboring states were enjoying the two cent fare."[31]

Even more criticism, however, was directed at that aspect of the commission's decision which allowed the sale of special rate books at a lower price to frequent travelers, for it violated all of the principles for which reformers had struggled. A year prior to this decision, the *Milwaukee Free Press* had expressed the general feeling of many who sought greater equality in rates. "On a public thoroughfare," it declared, "the man who travels 2,000 miles . . . is not entitled to do it for less money than the other man who rides 1,000 or 100 miles. . . . There is no real difference, from the viewpoint of justice, between rebating freight charges and rebating passenger charges."[32] In the wake of the commission's action, an indignant citizen echoed this contention. "If a 2 ¢ a mile [*sic*] is confiscation of Rail Road property for short distances of 200 or 300

---

[30] W. H. H. Macloon to Commission, September 20, 1906, Railroad Informal Case Papers, WPSC Records.
[31] Oliver Munson to Captain M. T. Park, July 25, 1907, in the James O. Davidson Papers.
[32] *Milwaukee Free Press*, February 16, 1906.

miles, why did the state commission request the Railroads to let persons go 500 miles, at that rate?"[33]

When John Barnes, who resigned from the commission in protest to the legislature's enactment of a two-cent rate on the heels of the commission decision, sought a seat on the state supreme court in 1908, the frustration engendered by that commission action became a political issue, and public cries of "pro-railroad" were heard for the first time in reference to the commission. Commenting on the possibility that the roads might still take the legislature's two-cent bill to the high court to test its constitutionality, one anti-Barnes man asked: "Do you not suppose that if such a man gets to the Bench the railroads will be only too anxious to get their case before the Court? Will you elect a man to the Supreme Bench who has already publicly expressed himself as against equal railroad fares for all people?"[34] W. D. Hoard, leader of the dairymen of the state and longtime supporter of La Follette and regulation, declared, "Surely there is a deep scheme behind Barnes' candidacy."[35] While the *Free Press* publicly condemned such charges against Barnes, its editor, H. P. Myrick, was suspicious also. "Mr. Barnes stood for the very discrimination against which the public has been contending—a lower rate of fare for the man who had ten dollars to buy mileage books and a higher rate for the man who could not afford to buy his mileage at wholesale. I always considered this a very serious injustice."[36]

The interesting reversal of positions concerning the commission was pointed up here by the conservative *Milwaukee Sentinel's* wholehearted support for Barnes' successful candidacy. Responding to charges that Barnes was "a tool of the railroads and other corporations," it declared these indictments "so unworthy as to be beneath attention. . . . Good public policy for many manifest reasons urges the election of Mr. Barnes."[37]

Many who had entertained fond hopes that their efforts to secure

[33] A. K. James to Davidson, July 17, 1907, in the Davidson Papers.
[34] See E. Kennedy to A. D. Stevens, enclosed in Barnes to Haugen, March 23, 1908, in the Haugen Papers.
[35] Hoard to Keyes, March 16, 1908, in the Keyes Papers.
[36] H. P. Myrick to Hoard, March 19, 1908, in the Keyes Papers.
[37] *Milwaukee Sentinel,* April 4, 1908.

regulatory legislation would result in greater commercial benefits for the small man and a new sense of public responsibility on the part of the carriers were sorely disappointed by the work of the commission. Throughout the early years of its activity, therefore, there was a murmur of discontent with the agency.

Conspicuously missing from the ranks of the critics of the commission, however, were the top political leaders who had earlier fought so hard for the principle of regulation. No doubt for many of them, including La Follette, the first years of regulation in Wisconsin were chastening, for their expectations were by no means realized. Having built their political careers on championing reforms, however, it was extremely difficult for these men to affirm the failure of one of their pet projects. For a man like La Follette to become a critic of the regulatory agency, he would have had to admit at least implicitly that he had been naive in his optimistic predictions, ineffective in his leadership in framing a statute, and undiscerning in his appointments to the new agency. Having earlier seized upon the regulation issue as a vehicle for the promotion of their careers, many ambitious reformers now decided that the necessities of politics dictated equivocation. The very men who possessed the power to expose the agency's failures and perhaps change its procedures chose to accept the commission on its own terms. They made the most of the accomplishments of the new body while ignoring its failures.

Earlier these men had argued that Wisconsin rates were 40 to 60 per cent too high, and that the railroads were earning millions of dollars more per year than they deserved. Now, apparently well aware that the regulatory agency had made only limited changes in these conditions, in speaking of the work of the commission many erstwhile advocates of strong regulation changed their focus and devoted their attention to the concrete gains for specific groups achieved through various commission decisions. On the hustings men like La Follette, Frear, and Davidson recited various estimates of how much the commission had saved the shippers of the state. Their estimates ran between $2,000,000 to $5,000,000 per year, depending apparently upon the relative candor of the speaker, and whether the commission was credited with the savings which the legislature's passage of the two-cent measure in 1907 had effected

for many travelers.[38] They skirted the basic questions of whether
the commission had made general rate reductions and lowered
railroad earnings.

It was more difficult for these men to explain away the implications of the close ties between the railroads and the agency which
was designed to regulate them. With unerring political instinct,
however, they fitted the answer to the occasion. La Follette was a
master at this ploy. Sometimes he sought conservative support by
emphasizing how happy the roads were with the new law. A frustrated John M. Whitehead, leader of the conservative opposition
to the Wisconsin progressives, complained:

> It is a singular outcome, of the campaigns that were
> conducted that we should now justify the railroad rate
> commission on the grounds that it was not hurting the
> railroads but rather was helping them. La Follette's cam-
> paigns were so largely based upon his charges of legis-
> lative corruption brought about by the railroads and
> general debauchery of business men due to the same
> malign influence, and the railroad rate commission was
> held up as the panacea of tremendous wrongs, as the cure
> for dreadful evils, in fact, as the salvation of the state.
> *Now Mr. La Follette reads letters on chautauqua plat-
> forms in other states, to prove that he is not radical in his
> views on railroad rate regulation, written by railroad
> people in which they find no fault with our state railroad
> rate commission.*[39]

On other occasions La Follette pressed the aggressive side of
regulation, charging that the railroads had no choice but to support
the agency because of its consummate efficiency. "Why have the
railroads accepted the decisions of the Wisconsin Commission?"
he asked rhetorically in 1908. "Because we have the value of the
railroad property of that state, and our commission is in a position
to make orders based upon exact knowledge and the carriers know
that any appeal would avail them nothing."[40] Later, in his *Auto-*

---

[38] *Milwaukee Free Press*, October 7, 1908, for campaign speech by Frear,
and October 19, 1908, for Davidson campaign speech. See La Follette,
Autobiography, 353.

[39] Whitehead to Gabriel, April 22, 1914, in the Whitehead Papers. (Emphasis
added).

[40] *Milwaukee Free Press*, July 24, 1908.

biography, he altered this stand a bit, contending that the railroad commission was so scientific in its rate making that the railroads were afraid to appeal its decisions because such action might spread its influence. "While the railroad companies do not enjoy having their rates cut down," he declared, "they are not overeager to advertise the Wisconsin system of rate-making."[41]

The tactics used by La Follette and other political reformers varied. Always, however, their emphasis was on the accomplishments of the agency. Failure would have made a poor political issue.

The overwhelming approval given the commission by such former advocates of change was extremely important, for these political leaders were highly instrumental in molding popular attitudes toward the new agency. To a large degree, they could decide what the public reaction to the commission would be. Earlier such men had attempted to spark a revolt; now they spurred consensus.

In May of 1905 the perceptive Amos Wilder, editor of the *Wisconsin State Journal,* predicted the future significance of the commission which was to take office two months later. "The commission once in operation, its chief value will be in abating discontent," he declared. "It is doubtful if the rank and file of us will know, by any marked reduction in prices of commodities, that anything has happened. But the distrust and suspicion born of secrecy and unqualified power will be relieved for there is appeal to the commission."[42] Because of the posture taken by the leaders of reform, Wilder's prediction bore fruit in the next five and one-half years.

By administering the act in a highly conservative way, heeding all of the complex commercial arrangements which existed within the state and asking only a modicum of change, the commission won over the railroads and their industrial allies, who had earlier fought so vigorously against the establishment of a regulatory agency. Hence, few complaints about commission action were heard from conservative quarters.

By adding their support to that of these more moderate elements, the leaders of reform insured the overwhelming acceptance of

---

[41] La Follette, *Autobiography,* 353–354, 360.
[42] *Wisconsin State Journal,* May 31, 1905.

the commission and its manner of administration by those who had supported plans to increase regulation in the state. Hearing praise and adulation for the agency from those who had set themselves up as guardians of the people, the public apparently resolved that the commission was fulfilling its appropriate function under the new law. The people fell into line with the railroads and the large shipping interests and put their faith in the commission.

In the final analysis, then, the balance sheet of regulation was rather one-sided. The railroads continued to receive the benefits of spiraling earnings and high rates, enhanced by a greater insulation from the threat that the politics of reform would disrupt their operations. The public, on the other hand, gained a new sense of participation in the state's commercial decision making through the establishment of a government agency charged with safeguarding its welfare. It did not, however, earn the conspicuous economic benefits which it had been promised.

Regulation then became not a principle but a palliative. In 1908, the *Milwaukee Free Press* declared:

> The public wants good service and reasonable rates, and reasonable rates do not necessarily mean lower rates. . . . But the public wants to be shown. It wants the opinion of a competent, disinterested commission, after an investigation of all of the facts.
> This is the Wisconsin idea, embodied in the best law as yet written dealing with the problem of public supervision and control of the great public service corporations, and administered by a commission whose ability, integrity and thoroughness have commanded the respect of the people for its judgment.[43]

The old notion that regulation should result in direct economic benefits to the consumer, the small man, even at the expense of the growing wealth of the railroads, had been replaced with a new, less ambitious idea, that commission rule was good in and of itself. Legislative bungling and the orientation of the first members of the new commission prevented the achievement of the primary aims of the long fight for increased regulation. The lack of per-

[43] *Milwaukee Free Press,* July 22, 1908.

sistence and candor on the part of the leaders of political reform in Wisconsin insured the enthronement of this more limited notion. These reformers rendered the death blow to the cause of strict regulation by their docile acceptance of the procedures of the commission. This was the crowning irony of Wisconsin's attempt to regulate railroads during the progressive era.

An Essay on the Sources

Primary Sources

The Fight for Legislation

In any historical study manuscript collections are highly important for they yield private insights needed to understand fully the
flow of public events. The papers of the Milwaukee Chamber of
Commerce, at the Milwaukee County Historical Society, contain
some valuable information concerning relations between the chamber and the railroads prior to 1900 but are disappointing for the first
decade of this century. For this period other collections, at the
State Historical Society of Wisconsin in Madison, are of far more
value. The primary source of information concerning the reform
struggle is the voluminous Robert M. La Follette Papers. They
give a remarkably full picture of the "progressive" politics of the
period. The correspondence between the governor and the Milwaukee reform group to be found in these manuscripts is particularly useful, for it illustrates the differing roles these men played
in pushing for stricter regulation.

Other collections supplement the La Follette Papers. The Albert
R. Hall manuscripts contain some revealing letters concerning the
background of railroad reform. The Nils P. Haugen Papers are also
useful in studying the origins of the reform movement and contain
occasional letters which pertain to the last stages of the regulation
fight. Albert O. Barton's papers contain several useful exchanges
between Barton and La Follette's widow in 1930 concerning the
regulation fight. The John J. Esch manuscripts focus on national
politics primarily. The correspondence between Esch and Eliot and
Bacon, however, shows the ubiquity of the Milwaukee reform
group. The sparseness of the John R. Commons Papers is dis-

appointing, for there are indications that Commons was highly influential behind the scenes in the regulation fight. The W. D. Hoard Papers, the James A. Stone Papers, and the Herman L. Ekern Papers deal primarily with partisan politics of the period and say little about regulation. In the case of the Hoard Papers this is significant, however, for it indicates how little concern a major farm leader had for this "popular" crusade.

In studying the opposition to regulatory legislation, the Elisha W. Keyes Papers are invaluable. They contain numerous valuable letters from railroad men which reveal their feelings toward events in Wisconsin, plus the incisive sarcasm of Keyes, which sometimes is highly insightful. The Emanuel L. Philipp Papers are less helpful, although they contain a few letters pertaining to the regulation fight. The long letter of John M. Whitehead to Ralph Gabriel of April 22, 1914, in the Whitehead Papers, is an interesting commentary on La Follette's *Autobiography* from the point of view of his archenemy. Some of his remarks concerning regulation are extremely interesting.

In fitting the Wisconsin fight into the broader national context, "Letters Commenting on Bill 623A, A Bill to Create a Board of Railroad Commissioners in Wisconsin," a collection in the Legislative Reference Library in the Wisconsin State Capitol in Madison, is helpful. It contains correspondence from such noted national regulation experts as Emory J. Johnson, Frederic C. Howe, Frank P. Dixon, Henry C. Adams, Harrison S. Smalley, Jesse Macy, Edward A. Moseley, and B. H. Meyer.

Supplementing these manuscript collections is much partisan literature from the period, mostly in pamphlet form, which can be found in the State Historical Society of Wisconsin. It is helpful in defining the positions taken by the various elements in the state during the regulation struggle. *Granger Legislation and State Control of Railway Rates*, a reprint of a speech delivered by La Follette at Milton Junction, January 29, 1904, expresses well the continuity of the regulation fight from the 1870's through the early years of the twentieth century. *Lower Freight Rates Demanded for Wisconsin* (Milwaukee, 1904) is the major campaign document for the La Follette forces in 1904. *Railway Legislation, State and Interstate* (Chicago, 1905), a collection of articles by Robert La Follette originally published in the *Saturday Evening Post* in February of 1905, indicates the governor's posture on the eve of the final regulation fight.

The Truth About Freight Rates (Milwaukee, 1904) by Emanuel L. Philipp and *A Criticism of the Plan for Maintaining Industrial Freight Rates Contained in the Governor's Message* (Racine, 1905) by Thomas M. Kearney, a leader of the Wisconsin Manufacturers Association, state well the position of the opponents of the administration.

Unfair Railway Agitation (Chicago, 1905) and *A Reply to Those Portions of Governor La Follette's Message of 1905 Which Relate to Railways* (Chicago, 1905) by Burton Hanson and *Brief in Opposition to Railroad Commission Bill* (1905) by Pierce Butler indicate the railroads' stand prior to the final fight over a regulation act.

There are numerous firsthand accounts of Wisconsin politics during the progressive era, some of which are helpful in studying railroad regulation reform. The most informative of these are Robert M. La Follette, *Autobiography* (Madison, 1911), and Emanuel L. Philipp, *Political Reform in Wisconsin* (Milwaukee, 1910). While La Follette's *Autobiography* is by far the better known of the two works, in piecing together the story of regulation in the state and assessing the results of the crusade, Philipp's account is more valuable, for it calls attention to the positive role of conservative elements in that reform movement. Both sources, however, must be read critically for each distorts facts in order to make a politically inspired point.

Other such accounts are less helpful. Nils P. Haugen, *Pioneer and Political Reminiscences* (Evansville, Wisconsin, 1929) contains a few insightful comments on the regulation fight, although there is no evidence to support his contention that he wrote the 1905 regulation bill. James A. Frear, *Forty Years of Progressive Public Service* (Washington, D.C., 1937) is disappointing, for Frear probably could have told the story of the administration's loss of control over the legislature in 1905 better than anyone other than the governor himself. Instead he simply mentions his participation in the fight as a member of the senate railroad committee. *Myself* (Madison, 1964), John R. Commons' thoroughly entertaining autobiography, is of little help. Commons' solution to the problem of economic tensions in the country, however, is remarkably like that pursued by the commission. The "Autobiography of John Strange," an unpublished manuscript in the Strange Papers, contains some pithy comments about La Follette and Hatten from the point of view of one who was in the progressive inner circle.

Legislative sources aided my study also. Testimony by Bacon and Eliot to be found in *Report of Senate Select Committee on Interstate Commerce* (49 Congress, 1 session, Senate Report no. 46, pt. 2, serial 2357, Washington, 1886), 692–713, and by Bacon in hearings before the Committee on Interstate Commerce, Senate of the United States, *Regulation of Railway Rates* (58 Congress, 3 session, Washington, 1904–1905), indicates the persistence of these

Milwaukee reformers and points up their major concerns. The latter hearings also contain testimony by a number of influential Wisconsin businessmen who opposed extension of regulatory controls. In following the path of various regulation bills, the *Senate* and *Assembly Journals of the Wisconsin Legislature* are useful. Even more valuable, however, are the bound volumes of *Senate* and *Assembly Bills* which contain all bills and amendments proposed in the Wisconsin legislature and can be found in the State Historical Society of Wisconsin. Through a careful reading of these original proposals the path of compromise can be followed.

The actual copies of these measures can be found in the State Archives section of the Historical Society. Notations on these bills sometimes indicate what provisions of these measures are at issue. The archives also contain the records of the Wisconsin Public Service Commission. The railroad commissioner's letterbooks for the early years of the century, a part of this collection, reveal the contribution the last railroad commissioner, John O. Thomas, made to the fight for legislation which would strengthen controls on the carriers.

Key newspapers in the state proved the best source for comprehensive coverage of all phases of the regulation fight as well as a sampling of public attitudes toward that reform. The *Milwaukee Free Press* fought consistently for strong regulation. Although it always supported the administration, its views were probably more representative of those held by the Milwaukee reform group than those of La Follette. The *Milwaukee Sentinel* opposed the administration throughout the struggle. Its changing attitude toward regulation points up the dilemma which the conservative factions faced in fighting La Follette's regulation plans. The *Wisconsin State Journal* (Madison), edited by the astute Amos Wilder, is an excellent representative of the middle position in politics in the state. It supported regulation throughout but frequently opposed La Follette. Because of its ambivalent position, it is often extremely helpful in assessing the status of the fight at particular points. The *Vernon County Censor* (Viroqua), edited by Oliver G. Munson, a leading progressive senator, and the *Jefferson County Union* (Fort Atkinson), owned by the progressive Hoard family, are helpful at times in covering the regulation fight because their editors were personal friends of La Follette and close to affairs in the legislature.

The conspicuous lack of farmer concern for the regulation issue is evident in these newspapers, but is even more striking in those journals tailored specifically for an agrarian audience. The *Wisconsin Agriculturist*, *Wisconsin Farmer*, and *Hoard's Dairyman* all offer persuasive evidence that the farmer in Wisconsin had other more pressing concerns. This conclusion is buttressed by a study of the proceedings of the annual meetings of the Wisconsin State Grange, the Wisconsin Cheese Makers' Association, the Wisconsin Buttermakers' Association, the Wisconsin Dairymen's Association, and the annual reports of the Wisconsin State Board of Agriculture. Only the Cheese Makers show any early concern for the regulation issue. The *Journals of Proceedings of the National Grange of the Patrons of Husbandry* for the first years of the century indicate the strong interest of the national farmers' organization in stricter regulation and thus dramatizes the contrast between Wisconsin farm groups and those in other areas.

The most fertile sources of opinion concerning the carriers' attitudes were the national railroad journals, *Railway World, The Railway and Engineering Review, Railway Gazette,* and *Railway Age.* These remarkably candid periodicals are especially helpful in divining the carriers' reactions to the final regulation measure.

John R. Commons, "The La Follette Railroad Law in Wisconsin," in *Review of Reviews,* 32:76–79 (July, 1905), is the best short description of the nature of the compromise reached in 1905 on the regulation issue. E. P. Bacon, "The Inadequate Powers of the Interstate Commerce Commission," in *North American Review,* 174:46–58 (January, 1902), is a concise statement of the principles of the leader of the Milwaukee reformers.

The *Annual Reports of the Trade and Commerce of Milwaukee,* issued by the Milwaukee Chamber of Commerce, show that organization's continuing interest in securing stronger regulation of Wisconsin railroads from the mid-1880's.

Regulation By Commission

One of the major problems confronting commissions is the lack of public interest and support for the regulatory enterprise once a statute is enacted. Tired after the long, acrimonious fights which normally precede such measures, the public and the press quickly turn their attention elsewhere. Hence news concerning the work of these new agencies is difficult to find. In the case of the Wisconsin railroad commission this lack of coverage was exacerbated by the agency's avowed intention to maintain an atmosphere of privacy. The problems of divining what the commission was thinking and doing, as well as the public reaction to its work, therefore were compounded.

Fortunately the Wisconsin Public Service Commission Records in the archives of the State Historical Society of Wisconsin are

voluminous and complete. The General Correspondence section
includes all letters dealing with the general activities of the new
agency, arranged chronologically. The Formal Case Papers contain all correspondence dealing with any of the formal decisions
which the commission made, arranged by case. The Informal Case
Papers, in chronological order, include more routine and minor
inquiries. They are helpful mainly because they contain some comments by small shippers on the work of the commission. Twenty-
two volumes of Minutes of Hearings contain all testimony taken
by the commission on formal complaints to mid-1908. After that
time such transcripts are to be found in the Formal Case Papers.
The Official Minutes of the commission are completely routine and
of little help.

Few manuscript collections are of much help, unfortunately, in
carrying the political side of the regulation story beyond the
passage of the bill in 1905. The Keyes Papers, the James O. Davidson Papers, and the B. H. Meyer Papers are the only manuscripts
which yield any comments on the manner in which the commission
administered the regulation act. The Keyes Papers contain the
reactions of a few railroad men to the new measure plus Keyes'
own incisive comments. The Davidson Papers are helpful in un-
raveling the story of the two-cent passenger rate controversy in
1907. The Meyer Papers, however, are the most valuable. They
contain most of Meyer's important writings and speeches on regulation, an unpublished autobiography, and some interesting correspondence between Meyer and railroad men, including Thomas
Gill's remarkable plea in July of 1907 that the commissioners remain at their posts in the wake of the legislature's snubbing of the
agency's passenger-rate decision.

In studying the implementation of the regulation law, several
railroad commission publications are helpful. The *Annual Reports
of the Railroad Commission of Wisconsin* contain valuable statistical data and suggest by their general comments some of the difficulties plaguing the agency. The initial six volumes of *Opinions
and Decisions of the Railroad Commission of the State of Wisconsin* include all the formal decisions of the agency for its first
five and one-half years. If read critically they are a fertile source of
information concerning the manner in which the commissioners
construed their task, and they also reveal who benefited most from
the work of the agency.

The thinking of B. H. Meyer, the leading member of the commission, concerning the regulatory enterprise can be sampled in
"Railway Regulation under Foreign and Domestic Laws," a study
included in the *Report of the United States Industrial Commission*

on Transportation (57 Congress, 1 session, House Document No. 178, serial 4339, Washington, 1901).

Other published sources are also helpful in understanding Meyer's point of view. *Railway Legislation in the United States* (New York, 1903) contains an excellent summary of his feelings about the proper role of government in regulating transportation companies, while his *History of the Northern Securities Case* (Madison, 1906) reveals his sympathy with the prevailing methods of railroad operations.

In their reminiscences some political figures give their partisan evaluations of the results of regulation. La Follette's *Autobiography* makes a number of extravagant claims for the commission which are questionable, while mentioning none of the weaknesses in his pet project. Philipp, in *Political Reform in Wisconsin,* eloquently expresses the changed attitude of state conservatives. While he still condemns the idea of regulation, he praises the commission, largely for not doing those things which reformers intended it to do.

Research concerning public reaction to the commission is made extremely difficult by the paucity of commentary on the agency's work in public journals. Only during the two-cent rate controversy is there much discussion of the commission's procedures in the state's press. The similarity of opinion concerning that agency's work expressed sporadically by the arch-antagonists, the *Milwaukee Free Press* and the *Milwaukee Sentinel,* is an interesting commentary, however, on the difference between regulation as a political issue and an administrative reality.

La Follette's Weekly Magazine, after its creation in 1909, praises the commission highly while noting the continuance of certain excessive rates in the state. *Freight,* a national forum for shippers' opinion, contains occasional comments on the work of the agency. The national railroad journals, *Railway World, The Railway and Engineering Review, Railway Gazette, Railway Age,* and *Railway Age Gazette* (the latter a product of the merger of *Railway Age* and *Railway Gazette* in June of 1908), continue to be fruitful sources of railroad opinion concerning regulation in Wisconsin. Their gradual shift in attitude is indicative of the ironic change which took place in opinion during the initial years of commission activity.

The *Proceeding of the Seventeenth Annual Convention* of the National Association of Railway Commissioners for 1906 contains John Barnes' assessment of the contributions the commission had made to date. The 1910 *Proceedings* includes a report by Halford Erickson on rate making which overemphasizes the commission's preoccupation with making all rates on the basis of "cost of service."

The *Bulletins of the Milwaukee Merchants and Manufacturers Association* indicate the salutary attitude of that important group toward the new agency. The June, 1907, *Bulletin* contains a speech made to that organization by Barnes which reveals the essential values of the commission.

Secondary Sources

The Fight for Legislation

There is no adequate study of the fight for a railroad regulation measure in Wisconsin. Robert S. Maxwell, *La Follette and the Rise of the Progressives in Wisconsin* (Madison, 1956) is the best analysis of La Follette's governorship, but it rather uncritically accepts the progressives' story of the evolution of this struggle. Maxwell's study, *Emanuel L. Philipp: Wisconsin Stalwart* (Madison, 1959) does not deal with the conservative businessman's important role in the regulation fight at any length.

An older study, Albert O. Barton's *La Follette's Winning of Wisconsin* (Des Moines, 1922) contains some interesting anecdotes concerning the politics of the regulation fight, but it too suffers from a pronounced pro-La Follette bias. Frederic C. Howe's *Wisconsin: An Experiment in Democracy* (New York, 1912) is even less discerning in dealing with the origins and results of regulation. The two-volume biography, *Robert M. La Follette* (New York, 1953), written by his widow, Belle Case La Follette, and his daughter, Fola La Follette, contains some valuable details which cannot be garnered elsewhere but, understandably, accepts the account of events related in La Follette's *Autobiography* as a true description.

The general histories of Wisconsin such as William Francis Raney, *Wisconsin, A Story of Progress* (Appleton, Wisconsin, 1963) are too general to be helpful in this sort of study.

The most insightful study of La Follette is David P. Thelen, *The Early Life of Robert M. La Follette* (Chicago, 1966). Although it does not deal with this period in La Follette's life, its analysis of the governor's essentially political personality is astute and offers helpful clues toward understanding his role in the regulation fight.

William F. Raney, "The Building of Wisconsin Railroads," in the *Wisconsin Magazine of History*, 19:387–403 (June, 1936), and James P. Kayser, *The Railroads of Wisconsin* (Boston, 1937) are useful in studying the early growth of railroads in the state. Robert S. Hunt's insightful *Law and Locomotives: The Impact of the Railroad on Wisconsin Law in the Nineteenth Century* (Madison, 1958)

is the best analysis of the impact of carriers on politics and law
prior to 1900, while Richard N. Current's *Pine Logs and Politics:
A Life of Philetus Sawyer, 1816–1900* (Madison, 1950) traces well
the growth of a coalition between conservative Republican politicians and the major industrial interests in the state, the railroads
and the lumbermen.

The initial attempt at regulation of Wisconsin roads in the 1870's
has been studied numerous times with varying conclusions. While
Hunt's *Law and Locomotives* is valuable on this subject, three
more specific studies are available also: Robert Daland, "Enactment of the Potter Law," in the *Wisconsin Magazine of History*,
33:45–54 (September, 1949); William Burton, "The First Wisconsin Railroad Commission: Reform or Political Expediency" (unpublished master's thesis, University of Wisconsin, 1952); and
Dale Treleven, "Commissions, Corners, and Conveyance: The Origins of Anti-Monopolism in Milwaukee" (unpublished master's
thesis, University of Wisconsin, 1968). Treleven's study deals most
insightfully with the question of opposition and support for that
measure.

Two studies by Stuart Brandes were of value in understanding
the nature of the regulation fight. "Nils P. Haugen and the Wisconsin Progressive Movement" (unpublished master's thesis, University of Wisconsin, 1965) emphasizes the antirailroad bias of
Haugen and provides good reasons why the carriers might object
to his leadership of the first commission, although the author does
not deal with Haugen's rejection in June of 1905. A seminar paper,
written in 1965 for Economics 648 at the University of Wisconsin,
entitled "Wisconsin Progressivism Viewed as a Farmers' Movement" offers valuable evidence indicating that the state's farmers
cared little about the regulation issue and seem to have supported
La Follette, when they did, for other reasons. Walter H. Ebling,
"Recent Farmer Movements in Wisconsin" (unpublished master's
thesis, University of Wisconsin, 1925) offers a clue to the strange
lack of farmers' zeal for regulation in his discussion of the paucity
and weakness of farmers' groups during the first decade of the
twentieth century. Eric E. Lampard, *The Rise of the Dairy Industry in Wisconsin* (Madison, 1963) is even more helpful. In his discussion of "The Wisconsin Idea of Dairying," Lampard argues
persuasively that the values of the dairymen, centered about thrift
and hard work, largely discouraged the resort to government regulation for aid except to prevent such blatant abuses as the sale of
butter substitutes.

While farmers showed less interest in regulation than might be
expected, the grain merchants exhibited continual concern about

alleged excessive railroad rates. William E. Derby, "A History of the Port of Milwaukee" (unpublished Ph.D. dissertation, University of Wisconsin, 1963) is helpful in explaining the key role the Milwaukee merchants took in the regulation fight.

Two studies which deal more directly with La Follette's governorship are disappointing. Carroll Lahmann, "Robert Marion La Follette as Public Speaker and Political Leader, 1885–1915" (unpublished Ph.D. dissertation, University of Wisconsin, 1939) is an encyclopedic account which relates many interesting incidents but attempts little analysis. Antoinette J. Merrill, "Wisconsin Newspapers and Railroad Regulation, 1903–1905" (unpublished master's thesis, University of Wisconsin, 1940) is an unrewarding study of an interesting topic.

Useful tools for comparing the Wisconsin regulation law with other statutes drafted during that period are the special study by the Interstate Commerce Commission, *Railways in the United States in 1902, State Regulation of Railways* (58 Congress, 2 session, House Document no. 253, serial 4699, Washington, 1904), and Grover Huebner, "Five Years of Railroad Regulation," in *The Annals of the American Academy of Political and Social Sciences,* 32:138–156 (July, 1908).

In studying regulation in the progressive era, Robert E. Wiebe, *Businessmen and Reform* (Cambridge, Massachusetts, 1962) and two books by Gabriel Kolko, *The Triumph of Conservatism* (New York, 1963) and *Railroads and Regulation* (Princeton, 1965) are extremely helpful. While Kolko's point seems overstated, these studies are an important corrective to the antibusiness image of the progressive image and blaze the trail for a more balanced view.

Regulation By Commission

Although there are few case studies of regulatory agencies, several works dealing with general trends in regulation are helpful. Robert E. Cushman, *The Independent Regulatory Commission* (New York, 1941) is the result of a New Deal inquiry into the proper place of administrative agencies in the American governmental structure. Kenneth Culp Davis, *Administrative Law* (St. Paul, 1951) deals with the legal problems facing administrative agencies.

More informative than these rather formal studies, however, are three recent works concerning administrative bodies. Marver Bernstein, *Regulating Business By Independent Commission* (Princeton, 1955) is the best general study of the concept of regulation.

It emphasizes the weaknesses in the idea of government by commission. Peter Woll, *American Bureaucracy* (New York, 1963) emphasizes the independent strength which the "administrative branch" of government possesses. William W. Boyer, *Bureaucracy on Trial* (Indianapolis, 1964) is the first real attempt to construct a model of administrative policy making.

There have been no previous critical inquiries into the results of regulation in Wisconsin. Robert S. Maxwell's *La Follette and the Rise of the Progressives in Wisconsin,* Frederic C. Howe's *Wisconsin: An Experiment in Democracy* and LaFayette G. Harter, Jr., *John R. Commons: His Assault on Laissez-Faire* (Corvallis, 1962) all make extravagant claims for the Wisconsin railroad commission without any hard evidence to support their conclusions. Maxwell, for instance, declares that regulation worked so well that even the conservatives liked it. In view of the profound difference in orientation between reformers and those who opposed regulation, one must question whether the progressives can have their cake and eat it to that extent.

Fred L. Holmes, *Regulation of Railroads and Public Utilities* (New York, 1915) is the only study which specifically deals with the work of the Wisconsin commission. Like the above works, it is written from a pronounced pro-La Follette viewpoint and stresses the accomplishments of the agency without relating them to reform aims. Still it is useful in gaining the positive side of regulation.

James Willard Hurst, *Law and Economic Growth: The Legal History of the Lumber Industry in Wisconsin* (Cambridge, Massachusetts, 1964) contains some insightful comments about regulation, although the author does not deal with the subject at length.

Herbert F. Margulies, "Issues and Politics of Wisconsin Progressivism, 1906–1920" (Ph.D. dissertation, University of Wisconsin, 1955) is a balanced study of the years following La Follette's governorship. It is indicative of the general acceptance of the railroad commission that regulation is little mentioned in Margulies' discussion of the prominent issues of that period.

In this bibliographical essay I have dealt with those sources of substantial value in my study. The footnotes indicate other works which were incidentally helpful.

Index

222 THE MYTH OF A PROGRESSIVE REFORM

lation, 132–135, 138–139, 148,
152, 153–154, 155, 162, 166,
169; on Wisconsin commission,
145, 154–155, 173, 181; on
Northern Securities Company,
152; on Sherman Antitrust Act,
152; on rate making, 158, 160;
and grain rate decision, 165;
Milwaukee Sentinel on, 179; and
Gill, 180, 183; and Lynde, 183.
See also Railroad Commission of
Wisconsin
Michigan, 82
Michigan Southern and Northern
Indiana Railroad, 13
Miller, Roswell, 52, 60, 125. *See
also* Chicago, Milwaukee and
St. Paul Railway; Railroads
Millers' National Association, 16,
123
Milwaukee and Mississippi Railroad Company, 4, 13
Milwaukee and St. Paul Railroad,
9
Milwaukee Chamber of Com-
merce: and Potter Law, 7, 14;
and Eliot, 14; and Bacon, 14;
role of, in early agitation for
regulation, 14, 17–18, 23, 111;
and railroads, 15, 15n; and Interstate Commerce Commission,
15–16, 18; and Hepburn Act,
17; and Albert Hall, 18; and La
Follette, 19–20, 27, 111; and
Milwaukee Free Press, 20; and
Erickson, 25; and 1903 regulation fight, 28, 29; seeks popular
support for regulation, 56; and
1905 regulation fight, 80, 81;
and Barry, 125; and grain rate
decision, 165; mentioned, 124.
See also Bacon; Eliot; Johnson;
Reformers
Milwaukee Free Press: and Milwaukee Chamber of Commerce,
20; launches regulation campaign, 22–23, 30; on 1903 regulation fight, 46, 50; seeks popular support for regulation, 56,
61, 63, 117–118; on 1904 elec-

tion, 68; and 1905 regulation
fight, 70, 74, 115; on commission, 188, 197, 202; on Barnes'
candidacy for supreme court,
198; mentioned, 140. *See also*
Reformers
Milwaukee grain market, 14. *See
also* Grain rates
Milwaukee Road. *See* Chicago,
Milwaukee and St. Paul Railway
Milwaukee Sentinel: on Potter
Law, 10, 34; on 1903 regulation
fight, 34, 38, 44, 50–51, 52, 53;
on Albert Hall, 34, 38; on Bacon, 34, 38; on Richmond, 38;
on Gilman, 38; on Frear, 38; on
1905 regulation fight, 77, 79,
90, 97, 115–116; on commission
appointments, 123, 129; on commission, 171, 172, 177, 179, 183,
184; on Quarles-Cooper bill, 77;
on regulation of public utilities,
175; on Meyer, 179; on Erickson, 179; on Barnes, 179, 198.
See also Conservatives
Milwaukee YMCA, 13
Minneapolis, St. Paul and Sault
Sainte Marie Railway, 5, 128.
See also Railroads
Minneapolis grain market, 14–15
Minnesota, 43–44, 56, 82, 117–
118
Mitchell, Alexander, 8
Monroe Sentinel, 33
Munson, Oliver G., 54, 197
Myrick, H. P., 198

N. O. Whitney club, 59
National Association of Manufac-
turers, 16
National Board of Trade, 16
National Transportation Associa-
tion, 123
Nebraska, 181
New Hampshire, 119
New York and Erie Railroad, 13
New York Central Railway, 16
North, William C., 92, 115
Northern Pacific Railway, 149

226

THE MYTH OF A PROGRESSIVE REFORM
Railroad Regulation in Wisconsin, 1903-1910

*Awarded the D. C. Everest Prize
in Wisconsin Economic History*

Born in Huron, South Dakota, in 1940, Stanley P. Caine was raised in the Dakotas, Minnesota, and Illinois. He received his B. A. from Macalester College in 1962, then went to the University of Wisconsin where he completed his M.S. in 1964 and his Ph.D. in 1967. He is currently an assistant professor of history at Lindenwood College in St. Charles, Missouri, where he lives with his wife Karen and their two children. Besides teaching and writing, the author spends an inordinate amount of time playing tennis.